LIBRARY OF NEW TESTAMENT STUDIES

385

formerly the Journal for the Study of the New Testament Supplement Series

Editor
Mark Goodacre

THE GENTILE MISSION IN OLD TESTAMENT CITATIONS IN ACTS

Text, Hermeneutic and Purpose

James A. Meek

t&t clark

British Library Cataloging-in-Publication Data
A catalogue record for this book is available from the British Library.

ISBN-10:   HB: 0-567-03380-5
ISBN-13:   HB: 978-0-567-03380-2

Typeset by ISB Typesetting, Sheffield
Printed by the MPG Books Group in the UK

CONTENTS

PREFACE

Questions about the relationship between the OT and the NT are as old as the ministry of Jesus. My own preoccupation with these issues has lasted well over thirty years. I recall one morning in college calling my pastor to ask how the NT writers found Christ in the OT. He referred me to Hengstenberg's classic study of the *Christology of the Old Testament*, and so my first serious exploration of the topic began with a Lutheran, recommended by a dispensationalist. Subsequently I was exposed to a biblical and covenantal theology that emphasized the organic and progressively unfolding character of biblical redemption and revelation.

I continue to wrestle with a related group of questions: How does the OT speak about Jesus? How do the OT and NT fit together? How does the OT function as canon for the church of the new covenant? Is the NT interpretation of the OT responsible? Should the church seek to reproduce it in our own exegesis, i.e. does the NT function as canon (norm) not only in content, but also in its interpretation of the OT? These questions led to a Th.M. thesis on typology as one way to explore the relationship between the testaments. The present study, initially undertaken as a doctoral dissertation, is another.

Many have helped me along the way. I am grateful to the faculty of Concordia Seminary in St Louis, for their warm welcome of a Presbyterian into their community. I am indebted to Drs Jack Preus and James Voelz, who allowed me to develop facets of this study in work for their courses, as well as to Drs Paul Raabe and Leo Sanchez, who, as readers, offered valuable counsel. I am especially grateful to my *Doktorvater* and fellow Rice Owl, Dr Jeff Gibbs, who provided needed focus, guidance and lots of encouragement. I am also grateful to Covenant Theological Seminary, where it was my pleasure to serve for thirteen years, to President Bryan Chapell, who encouraged me to undertake doctoral studies and extended financial support, and to former colleagues on the faculty for periodic counsel and frequent encouragement. And I remain indebted to Dr Ed Blum, my college pastor, for indulging my questions about the relationship between the testaments (and many other things) so very long ago.

I benefited greatly from the resources of the Buswell Library at Covenant Theological Seminary (especially the inestimable Director Jim Pakala and the patient Associate Librarian Denise Pakala), Concordia Seminary Library, Duke Divinity School Library, the Barbour Library at Pittsburgh Theological Seminary, the Library of Trinity Episcopal School for Ministry (especially its gracious Director, John Doncevic), and the Stevenson Library at Lock Haven University.

Most of all, I am indebted to Esther, Starr, Stacey and Stephanie, who so often suffered from my distraction and preoccupation with this project. I appreciate your sacrifice more than I can say. I hope that seeing the work in this form is some reward.

As the Preacher says, 'of making many books there is no end'. Several important works appeared or came to my attention too late to receive the consideration here that they deserved: Max Turner's *Power from on High: The Spirit in Israel's Restoration and Witness in Luke–Acts*, Chris Wright's *The Mission of God: Unlocking the Bible's Grand Narrative* and Terence Donaldson's *Judaism and the Gentiles: Jewish Patterns of Universalism (to 135 CE)*.

Unless otherwise noted, citations of the Hebrew Bible/Old Testament are from *BHS*, of the Septuagint from Rahlfs' edition, of the Greek New Testament from NA[27], of the Vulgate from *Biblia Sacra Iuxta Vulgatam Versionem*[1] and of the English Bible from the RSV. Chapter and verse references are from the English; the occasionally divergent numbering of the MT and the LXX are noted when relevant. Citations from the apocrypha and pseudepigrapha are from Charlesworth, *OTP*. Abbreviations of standard scholarly works follow the *SBL Handbook*.[2]

---

1. Bonifatio Fischer et al., eds. (4th edn. Stuttgart: Deutsche Bibelgesellschaft, 1994).
2. Patrick H. Alexander et al., *The SBL Handbook of Style: For Ancient Near Eastern, Biblical, and Early Christian Studies* (Peabody, Mass.: Hendrickson, 1999).

THE OLD TESTAMENT IN LUKE–ACTS

1.1 *The Old Testament and Gentile Mission*

The importance of the OT in Luke–Acts has long been recognized. In an influential 1953 essay, Paul Schubert argued that 'proof-from-prophecy theology is Luke's central theological idea throughout the two-volume work',[1] specifically the proof 'that Jesus is the Christ'.[2] Although Schubert's thesis was not new (he acknowledged his debt to Henry Cadbury's *The Making of Luke–Acts*[3]), his article has become the point of departure for a considerable discussion of the purpose and hermeneutic involved in Luke's use of the OT.[4]

The most substantial contributions have focused on the Christological use of the OT in Luke–Acts.[5] While Darrell Bock has correctly observed that Christology is 'the key area of Luke's OT usage as acknowledged by all',[6] it is not the only area in which Luke employs the OT. Consider, for example, the important summary of OT application in Luke 24.46-49a.

> And he said to them, 'Thus it is written, that the Christ should suffer and on the third day rise from the dead, and that repentance and forgiveness of sins should be preached in his name to all nations, beginning from Jerusalem. You are witnesses of these things. And behold, I send the promise of my Father upon you.'

Schubert notes that in this text,

> The kerygma includes the proclamation ... of repentance and the forgiveness of sins in his name ... which is to go to all the nations ... that the 'apostles' are to be witnesses of these things ... and the coming of the Holy Spirit.[7]

---

1. Paul Schubert, 'The Structure and Significance of Luke 24', in *Neutestamentlichen Studien für Rudolf Bultmann* (ed. Walther Eltester; BZNW 21; Berlin: Alfred Töpelmann, 1954), 176, cf. 178.
2. Schubert, 'Structure and Significance', 173.
3. Henry J. Cadbury, *The Making of Luke–Acts* (2nd edn.; London: SPCK, 1958).
4. See the literature cited in Darrell L. Bock, *Proclamation from Prophecy and Pattern: Lucan Old Testament Christology* (JSNTSup 12; Sheffield: Sheffield Academic Press, 1987), 13–26; Gert J. Steyn, *Septuagint Quotations in the Context of the Petrine and Pauline Speeches of the Acta Apostolorum* (CBET 12; Kampen: Kok Pharos, 1995), 1–21.
5. The two most substantial studies are Bock, *Proclamation*; Martin Rese, *Alttestamentliche Motive in der Christologie des Lukas* (SNT 1; Gütersloh: Gerd Mohn, 1969).
6. Bock, *Proclamation*, 47.
7. Schubert, 'Structure and Significance', 177. Yet Schubert himself seems to understand 'proof from prophecy' primarily in terms of demonstration 'that Jesus is the Christ' (173).

This OT-based kerygma includes more than Christology proper (i.e. Christ's suffering, death and resurrection). It includes the resulting proclamation of repentance and forgiveness to the nations, the appointment of the apostolic witnesses to Christ and his work, and the empowering gift of the promised Spirit.[8] While these are all dependent on Christology, they are not identical to it. Similarly, Jack T. Sanders has observed that 'there are two other things that Luke thinks the Scripture has prophesied, and they go together. These two things are the rejection of the gospel by many Jews and its acceptance by the Gentiles.'[9] Luke's use of the OT with reference to the Gentiles has been largely omitted from studies of the OT in Luke–Acts.[10]

Jacob Jervell found the 'center of Scripture' for Luke in 'the suffering and death of Messiah' and 'the exaltation of this very suffering Messiah' and relegated the Gentile mission to 'other phenomena in the gospel and even in the history of the church',[11] surprising in light of his interest in the people of God in Luke–Acts. In his important study of *The Gentiles and the Gentile Mission in Luke–Acts*, Stephen G. Wilson focused attention on the Gentile mission and the fact that Luke used the OT to 'prophesy, explain and justify' it, but he did not explore how.[12] In an article promisingly entitled 'The Gentile Mission and the Authority of Scripture in Luke–Acts', Joseph Tyson recognized the centrality of the mission, but his focus on Jervell's view that 'Luke treats scripture as authoritative' did not lend itself to consideration of how the authoritative OT was used to legitimate the Gentile mission.[13]

A few scholars have noted the importance of the 'missiological' or 'ecclesiological' role of the OT in Luke–Acts in relation to Christology. Nils Dahl spoke of

---

8.   For the view that 24.48-49 may be included in what 'is written', see ch. 2.

9.   Jack T. Sanders, 'The Prophetic Use of the Scriptures in Luke–Acts', in *Early Jewish and Christian Exegesis: Studies in Memory of William Brownlee* (ed. Craig A. Evans and William F. Stinespring; Atlanta: Scholars Press, 1987), 194.

10.   This in spite of the fact that 'the central concern of much of Acts is the mission to the Gentiles'. John T. Squires, *The Plan of God in Luke–Acts* (SNTSMS 76; Cambridge: Cambridge University Press, 1993), 188. The status of the Gentiles is 'un des grandes thèmes du livre'. Justin Taylor, *Commentaire Historique*, vols 4-6 of *Les actes des deux apôtres*, Marie-Emile Boismard and Arnaud Lamouille (*EBib*; 2/12–14, 23, 30, 41; Paris: J. Gabalda, 1994), 4.197.

11.   Jacob Jervell, 'The Center of Scripture in Luke', in *The Unknown Paul: Essays on Luke–Acts and Early Christian History* (trans. Roy A. Harrisville; Minneapolis: Augsburg, 1984), 135–36. The same argument, with some identical language, is also found in Jacob Jervell, *The Theology of the Acts of the Apostles* (New Testament Theology; Cambridge: Cambridge University Press, 1996), 61–82.

12.   'The proof-from-prophecy theme is one of the most widespread phenomena in Luke's version of the Gentile mission. Throughout the Gospel and Acts quotations from (Lk. 3:6; Acts 2:17, 3:25, 13:47, 15:17) and allusions to (Lk. 2:32, 4:25-27, 24:46; Acts 1:8, 2:39, 10:34, 15:14, 26:17, 28:26f) the OT are used to prophesy, explain and justify the proclamation to the Gentiles'. Stephen G. Wilson, *The Gentiles and the Gentile Mission in Luke–Acts* (SNTSMS 23; Cambridge: Cambridge University Press, 1973), 243. Wilson's list of texts follows that advanced previously by Nils A. Dahl, 'The Story of Abraham in Luke–Acts', in *Studies in Luke–Acts* (ed. Leander E. Keck and J. Louis Martyn; Nashville: Abingdon, 1966; repr., Mifflintown, Pa.: Siglar Press, 1999), 157, n. 50.

13.   Joseph B. Tyson, 'The Gentile Mission and the Authority of Scripture in Luke–Acts', *NTS* 33 (1987): 619, 621.

a 'double function' in the use of prophecy in Luke–Acts: 'to prove the legitimacy of Gentile mission and Gentile churches, and to prove that Jesus is the Anointed One of whom the prophets spoke'.[14] J. Dupont, while holding to the priority of the Christological application of the OT in Luke–Acts, conceded the presence of 'a secondary theme … that the salvation the Messiah brings was intended for all peoples'.[15]

> The Gentile mission is willed by God, and it realizes the prophetic promises that the Messiah would bring salvation to the pagan nations; thus it is part and parcel of the program assigned to the Christ by the Scriptures. That is the reason why Luke decided to add the story of the apostolic missions to his narrative about Jesus, for without those missions the work of salvation described in the messianic prophecies would not be complete.[16]

John T. Carroll has put the case even more strongly.

> A 'christological' function of scripture is foundational in Acts …. Yet this is only Luke's starting point, the basis for an 'ecclesiological' use of scripture which proves to be the overriding interest in Acts. In Jesus, God's Messiah, Israel receives the salvation promised in scripture, and that salvation encompasses gentiles as well. That is, Acts appeals to scripture in order to legitimate the gentile mission.

For Carroll, the Christological use of scripture in Acts 'stands in service of an even more crucial theological concern within the narrative … Who are the people of God?'[17] Kenneth Litwak has recently argued that Luke's use of the OT for Christology 'functions in the service of ecclesiology', i.e. 'to legitimate the followers of the Way',[18] although he pays little attention to the specific question of the Gentiles. Bock writes that 'a major portion of Luke's purpose for his work is related to a christological justification of the Gentile mission'.[19] 'Christology is not unrelated to mission. Jesus is Lord of all, so the message can go to all (Acts 10:36-43). Mission has two expected elements: Gentile inclusion and Israelite hardening and rejection.'[20] Reviewing influential studies by Cadbury, Schubert, Rese, Bock and others, David Pao concluded:

14. Dahl, 'Abraham', 151. 'Salvation of the Gentiles was from the beginning envisaged by God and included as part of his promises to Israel.'

15. Jacques Dupont, 'Apologetic Use of the Old Testament in the Speeches of Acts', in *The Salvation of the Gentiles: Essays on the Acts of the Apostles* (trans. John R. Keating; New York: Paulist, 1979), 156.

16. Jacques Dupont, 'The Salvation of the Gentiles and the Theological Significance of the Book of Acts', in *The Salvation of the Gentiles: Essays on the Acts of the Apostles* (trans. John R. Keating; New York: Paulist, 1979), 13.

17. John T. Carroll, 'The Uses of Scripture in Luke–Acts', in *Society of Biblical Literature Seminar Papers, 1990* (ed. David J. Lull; *SBLSP*; Atlanta: Scholars Press, 1990), 513–14. Carroll devotes almost one-third of his article to the Gentile mission, but since the article is brief, he provides only five pages on this topic.

18. Kenneth D. Litwak, *Echoes of Scripture in Luke–Acts: Telling the History of God's People Intertextually* (JSNTSup 282; London: T&T Clark, 2005), 202.

19. Bock, *Proclamation*, 238.

20. Darrell L. Bock, 'The Use of the Old Testament in Luke–Acts: Christology and Mission', in *Society of Biblical Literature Seminar Papers, 1990* (ed. Edward J. Lull; *SBLSP*; Atlanta: Scholars

> Their strong emphasis on Christological uses of scriptural citations tends to overshadow concerns for the ecclesiological function of the 'evocation' of scriptural traditions in the Lukan writings. ... *A study focusing on the ecclesiological function of scriptural citations in the Lukan writings still needs to be written.*[21]

Pao himself attempts to partially remedy this concern, but his focus on *Acts and the Isaianic New Exodus* prevents a full consideration of ecclesiological and missiological citations.[22] There remains no substantial study of how the OT is used to legitimate the Gentile mission in Luke–Acts.

1.2 *The Use of the Old Testament in Luke–Acts*

The discussion of the use of the OT in Luke–Acts has focused on three main areas: text, hermeneutic and purpose.[23]

1.2.1 *Text*
Are OT citations in Luke–Acts based on a Hebrew or Greek original? If from Hebrew, does the text conform to the MT or reflect another Hebrew textual tradition? If from Greek, is there evidence of a Hebrew textual tradition that may explain the Greek form of the text? If the citation appears to come from a Greek original, is the use of the citation dependent on distinctive features of the Greek text, or would a translation from the Hebrew have served as well?

It is generally agreed that Luke most often cites the OT from the LXX, and from the A text in particular, except when he quotes from memory or takes his OT text from another source.[24] Dupont claims that not only the text but 'the whole

---

Press, 1990), 509–10. Bock had hoped to explore this connection further, but wrote that 'enough material has been brought forward ... to open a possible fruitful field for further research. It is the relationship between Luke's use of the OT for christology and Luke's use of the OT for Gentile mission.' Bock, *Proclamation*, 278.

21. David W. Pao, *Acts and the Isaianic New Exodus* (WUNT 2/130; Tübingen: Mohr, 2000; repr., Grand Rapids: Baker, 2002), 7–8. Emphasis added.

22. Sabine van den Eynde speaks of 'a christological and ecclesiological aim. The main point of Luke's use of the Old Testament is the proclamation of Jesus. The hope of Israel and the messianic expectations have now come to fruition and climax in the life, suffering, death, and resurrection of Jesus, who is portrayed as "the prophet like Moses", the Servant, the Davidic Messiah, the Lord. The ecclesiological aim can be discovered in two essential items: the Gentile mission and the rejection by Israel.' Sabine van den Eynde, 'Children of the Promise: On the *ΔΙΑΘΗΚΗ*-Promise to Abraham in Lk 1,72 and Acts 3,25', in *The Unity of Luke–Acts* (ed. J. Verheyden; BETL 142; Leuven: Leuven University Press, 1999), 479.

23. E.g. Bock, *Proclamation*, 47–53; Charles A. Kimball, *Jesus' Exposition of the Old Testament in Luke's Gospel* (JSNTSup 94; Sheffield: Sheffield Academic Press, 1994).

24. William Kemp Lowther Clarke, 'The Use of the Septuagint in Acts', in *The Beginnings of Christianity, Part I: The Acts of the Apostles* (ed. Frederick J. Foakes Jackson and Kirsopp Lake; 5 vols.; London: Macmillan, 1920–33; repr., Grand Rapids: Baker, 1979), 2.66–105; Traugott Holtz, *Untersuchungen über die alttestamentlichen Zitate bei Lukas* (TUGAL 104; Berlin: Akademie Verlag, 1968). For the view that Luke's sources included traditions besides the LXX, see Max Wilcox, 'The Old Testament in Acts 1–15', *ABR* 4 (1956): 1–41.

argumentation of the speeches in Acts is based on the Septuagint text',[25] i.e. there are 'passages in which the whole weight of the argument depends on readings proper to the Greek version, and in which the Hebrew text would offer no support to the argument at all'.[26] Bock has sought to distinguish between the form of the citation and its use or 'conceptual form'; he contends that the conceptual form of the text in the speeches of Acts in no case depends on distinctive LXX readings.[27]

1.2.2 Hermeneutic
How has Luke used (interpreted and applied) the OT text? Is this use congruent with the meaning of the text in its OT context? Is the text's significance changed or expanded in order to function in its NT context? How does the argument develop from the text? Is the hermeneutic controlled by assumptions that interpreters today cannot embrace, or may the NT's use of the OT play a positive role in guiding exegetes today?

Many scholars view the use of the OT by NT authors as essentially similar to that of first-century Judaism. In both rabbinic and sectarian interpretation, context seems of little importance, meanings can be found in wordplay or linguistic ambiguities, and texts may be linked merely on the basis of catchwords. Early Christian interpreters are said to show equally little interest in the original context or meaning.[28] Dupont claims that 'the scriptural interpretation practiced in the speeches [of Acts] betrays no interest in the original meaning of the Hebrew text' and, in at least one case, 'distorts the original meaning'.[29] Jervell asserts, 'obviously, one cannot expect too much logic in the use of Old Testament quotations in New Testament writings'.[30]

Such negative estimates deny Luke's OT hermeneutic any relevance for our interpretation of the OT[31] and deny any canonical role for the NT in guiding theological and exegetical method. These assessments, however, are premature. The supposed absence of hermeneutical logic has been asserted, but not established,

---

25. Dupont, 'Apologetic', 139.

26. Dupont, 'Apologetic', 153.

27. Bock, *Proclamation*, 270.

28. Important works include Jan W. Doeve, *Jewish Hermeneutics in the Synoptic Gospels and Acts* (Assen: Van Gorcum, 1953); Edward Earle Ellis, 'Biblical Interpretation in the New Testament Church', in *Mikra: Text, Translation, Reading and Interpretation of the Hebrew Bible in Ancient Judaism and Early Christianity* (ed. Martin Jan Mulder; CRINT 2.1; Assen: Van Gorcum, 1988), 691–725; Michael Fishbane, 'Use, Authority and Interpretation of Mikra at Qumran', in *Mikra: Text, Translation, Reading and Interpretation of the Hebrew Bible in Ancient Judaism and Early Christianity* (ed. Martin Jan Mulder; CRINT 2.1; Assen: Van Gorcum, 1988), 339–77; Richard N. Longenecker, *Biblical Exegesis in the Apostolic Period* (2nd edn.; Grand Rapids: Eerdmans, 1999).

29. Dupont, 'Apologetic', 154, 133. 'Playing upon the various possible meanings of an ambiguous term was a popular and legitimate procedure in early Christian interpretation' (144).

30. Jacob Jervell, 'The Divided People of God: The Restoration of Israel and the Salvation of the Gentiles', in *Luke and the People of God: A New Look at Luke–Acts* (Minneapolis: Augsburg, 1972), 52.

31. For such a judgement on the use of the OT in the NT as a whole, see Longenecker, *Biblical Exegesis*, 219–20.

and its frequent assertion discourages investigation that might find such logic. We will never know for certain whether there is a logic if we do not look.

1.2.3 *Purpose*

How does the citation function rhetorically in its NT *context? What is Luke's purpose in citing the* OT*? What does he hope to achieve? How is this purpose realized in the work? Reversing the question, what do the citations tell us about the purpose of the work?*

The starting point remains Schubert's assertion that 'Luke's proof-from-prophecy theology' is the 'central theological idea throughout the two-volume work'.[32] Schubert focuses on Luke 24, but also finds evidence in the first half of the gospel and the conclusion to Acts. Others have advanced similar views.[33] Cadbury had earlier proposed a similar understanding of prophecy and fulfilment in Luke–Acts, although he spoke of an 'apologetic motive' in Luke's use of scripture rather than 'proof from prophecy'.[34] Conzelmann, whose *Die Mitte der Zeit* appeared the same year as Schubert's article, speaks of 'evidence of promise and fulfillment' and 'proof from Scripture' that 'points to Christ'.[35] Dahl, in the Schubert festschrift, speaks both of 'prophecy and fulfillment' and 'proof-from-prophecy'.[36] More recently, Luke Timothy Johnson has written that ' "proof from prophecy" is an important weapon in Luke's apologetic armory' that 'Luke extends and refines ... by including not only the life, death and resurrection of the Messiah, but the development of the messianic community as well'.[37]

Others have been less enthusiastic about 'proof from prophecy'. Charles Talbert has noted that not all OT citations or allusions can be seen as promise and fulfil-ment, not all prophecies in Luke–Acts come from the OT (e.g. some come from Jesus, angels, contemporary prophets), and the purpose of promise-fulfilment must be understood in light of Luke's cultural context.[38] Talbert concedes, how-ever, that 'the theme of prophecy-fulfilment is a major one in Luke–Acts'.[39] Martin Rese has argued that few quotations and allusions display the 'linear' tem-poral relation that 'proof from prophecy' requires and believes this casts doubt on Cadbury's 'apologetic motive' and the prominence of Schubert's 'proof from

---

32. Schubert, 'Structure and Significance', 176, cf. 178.

33. See the survey in Bock, *Proclamation*, 27–37.

34. Cadbury, *Making of Luke–Acts*, 304.

35. Hans Conzelmann, *Theology of St. Luke* (trans. Geoffrey Buswell; New York: Harper & Row, 1961), 157.

36. Dahl, 'Abraham', 147, 150, 151.

37. Luke Timothy Johnson, *Septuagintal Midrash in the Speeches of Acts* (Milwaukee: Marquette University Press, 2002), 11–12.

38. Charles H. Talbert, 'Promise and Fulfillment in Lucan Theology', in *Luke–Acts: New Per-spectives from the Society of Biblical Literature Seminar* (ed. Charles H. Talbert; New York: Cross-road, 1984), 93–101. Schubert did not claim that all OT citations and allusions were prophetic, and had already called attention to the presence of prophecies by characters in the NT narrative, which were a part of his understanding of 'proof from prophecy'.

39. Talbert, 'Promise and Fulfillment', 101.

prophecy'.[40] Robert F. O'Toole believes that 'proof from prophecy' and 'promise-fulfilment' call too much attention to the use of scripture compared to other 'ways of portraying God's saving action among his people'. He believes that these wrongly suggest an historical 'break' between ancient Israel and the Christian movement, when in fact 'Christianity just continues the Old Testament'.[41] Litwak has similarly argued that 'promise-fulfilment' accounts for only a small portion of the demonstrable OT quotations, allusions and echoes, which all serve to highlight the continuity of the people of God.[42] Bock has argued that 'Luke's use of the OT for Christology is not primarily ... a defensive apologetic', but 'the direct proclamation of Jesus', and that 'Luke sees the Scripture fulfilled in Jesus in terms of the fulfillment of OT prophecy and in terms of the reintroduction and fulfillment of the OT patterns that point to the presence of God's saving work'[43] – hence his characterization, *Proclamation from Prophecy and Pattern*. But Bock also demonstrates that the promise-and-fulfilment motif plays a prominent role in the development of Luke's Christology.[44] While some of these may be more quibbles than objections, they require a reevaluation of Schubert's claim that 'proof from prophecy' is at the heart of Luke's use of the OT.

The question of 'proof from prophecy' has dominated the discussion of Luke's purpose in using the OT, but the citations raise other important questions about the author's purpose. An appeal to scripture is an appeal to authority, a rhetorical strategy designed to persuade the readers about matters of some importance to the author. Considered along with other rhetorical strategies, citations may then offer insight into the overall purpose of the work.

1.3 *The Rhetorical Use of Old Testament Quotations*

In a series of articles and a recent book,[45] Christopher D. Stanley has argued for rhetorical study of biblical quotations in the NT, since 'the decision to introduce a direct quotation into a piece of discourse is a rhetorical act'.[46] Stanley's work

---

40. Rese, *Alttestamentliche Motive*, 210. For an interaction with Rese's views, see Bock, *Proclamation*.

41. Robert F. O'Toole, *The Unity of Luke's Theology: An Analysis of Luke–Acts* (GNS 9; Wilmington, Del.: Michael Glazier, 1984), 17.

42. Litwak, *Echoes*.

43. Bock, *Proclamation*, 274. 'Proof' can refer to a positive demonstration as well as a defensive response. Bock may wrongly assume that Schubert thought primarily in terms of defence. The two are not as far apart as Bock suggests and his discomfort with 'proof' is unnecessary.

44. Bock, *Proclamation*, 275–77.

45. Christopher D. Stanley, 'Biblical Quotations as Rhetorical Devices in Paul's Letter to the Galatians', in *Society of Biblical Literature Seminar Papers, 1998 Part Two* (SBLSP; Atlanta: Scholars Press, 1998), 700–30; '"Pearls Before Swine": Did Paul's Audiences Understand His Biblical Quotations?', *NovT* 41 (1999): 124–44; 'The Rhetoric of Quotations: An Essay on Method', in *Early Christian Interpretation of the Scriptures of Israel* (ed. Craig A. Evans and James A. Sanders; JSNTSup 148; Sheffield: Sheffield Academic Press, 1997), 44–58. I am indebted to Professor Stanley for sharing with me portions of the pre-publication manuscript of *Arguing with Scripture: The Rhetoric of Scripture in the Letters of Paul* (Edinburgh: T&T Clark, 2004).

46. Stanley, 'Rhetoric', 57.

differs from much of the scholarly discussion of the OT in the NT,[47] because it focuses on 'how quotations "work" within the surface structure of [Paul's] letters, not how Paul himself read and understood the biblical text ... on the way the quotations advance (or fail to advance) Paul's rhetorical aims in a given passage'.[48] Although Stanley focuses on biblical quotations in Paul, he raises important issues for the study of quotations throughout the NT.

First, Stanley argues that we must distinguish the way in which the OT shapes the author's thought from the way in which the author uses the OT to instruct and persuade his audience. A rhetorical analysis calls attention to the way in which the OT is actually used, and particularly to quotations that the author's intended audience would have recognized (most often because these are clearly marked as quotations in the text). [49]

Second, quotations are a rhetorical strategy by which an author seeks to persuade the audience.[50] A quotation is usually an 'argument from authority ... used to anticipate and/or close off debate'; its effectiveness 'will depend in large part on the audience's perception of the authority and/or credibility of the original source'.[51] For the early Christian community, an appeal to scripture would be the highest appeal possible.[52] Surprisingly, even though an appeal to scripture would seem sufficient to clinch Paul's argument, Stanley notes that Paul seldom relies on quotations alone.[53] In fact, 'the use of multiple lines of argumentation is a standard recommendation of rhetoricians as far back as Aristotle'.[54] The use of quotations, with other rhetorical strategies, provides insight into the author's rhetorical purposes.[55]

Third, Stanley warns that limited access to biblical scrolls[56] and low rates of literacy[57] mean that few in the audience would have been able to identify and

47. 'While there is much to be gained from studying early Jewish and Christian hermeneutical techniques, this should not be confused with an investigation of how the Bible was actually *used* in early Jewish and Christian literature.' Stanley, 'Rhetoric', 58.

48. Stanley, 'Quotations', 702–03.

49. Stanley, 'Pearls', 131–32. Of course, some texts would have been recognizable without explicit textual markers, just as 'let there be light', 'God is love' and 'do not judge' may be recognized as biblical today, even by those with limited biblical knowledge. Many others would have needed to be marked in order to be recognized.

50. Stanley, 'Quotations', 707.

51. Stanley, 'Quotations', 703.

52. 'From Paul's quotations we can see that he, like other Jews, believed that quoting the words of Scripture should close off all debate on a subject.' Stanley, 'Quotations', 714.

53. Stanley, 'Quotations', 714–15.

54. Stanley, 'Pearls', 140, n. 35.

55. Stanley, 'Quotations', 724.

56. Stanley argues that private ownership of biblical scrolls would have been rare and that, once tensions developed with official Judaism, Christians would have had limited access to synagogue scrolls. Stanley, 'Quotations', 717–19; 'Pearls', 127.

57. Stanley cites data indicating literacy rates of perhaps 10–20 per cent. Stanley, 'Quotations', 719; 'Pearls', 129. *OCD*, s.v. 'literacy', estimates rates of at most 20–30 per cent, but notes that this varied over time, location, gender and social class. Slaves were generally less literate, but 'much reading and writing was done by slaves, especially in Rome'. Where much of the church was drawn from the lower classes (e.g. 1 Cor. 1.26-29; 2 Cor. 8.2; Gal. 2.10), literacy in the church may have been

examine the background or original contexts of biblical quotations.[58] Fewer still would have possessed sufficient biblical knowledge to recognize more subtle scriptural allusions or 'echoes'.[59] Still, in Paul at least, usually 'the rhetorical point is clear enough',[60] although the audience's understanding of the quoted text would be shaped as much 'by the broader rhetorical context in which the quotation was embedded' as by the original context.[61]

1.4 *Goals, Methodology and Assumptions*

The present study seeks to contribute to the understanding of the OT in Luke–Acts (and in the NT generally) by focusing attention on the neglected use of the OT to legitimate the Gentile mission in Luke–Acts. By doing so, we expect to shed fresh light on the text of the OT cited by Luke, his OT hermeneutic and his purpose in citing the OT. The hermeneutical issues are of particular importance: if, as C. H. Dodd has argued, the source of the NT's distinctive approach to the OT is Jesus himself,[62] its hermeneutic is of more than mere literary or historical interest for those who regard him as 'teacher and lord' (John 13.13). In addition, the study will contribute generally to the ongoing discussion about the purpose of Luke–Acts and will have implications for wider questions about the relationship between the testaments, the doctrine of the church and its mission, and the relation of Israel and the church.

This study will focus on explicit OT citations. The OT has influenced the NT in a variety of ways: linguistic influence (or imitation), explicit quotation, and implicit influence (e.g. allusion, reference, motifs).[63] Recent studies have increasingly focused on scriptural allusions and intertextual 'echoes'.[64] Such studies can

quite low, but 'the ancient habit of reading aloud meant that written texts could often be shared the more easily by others'. Stanley's overall point is unaffected by differing estimates.

58. Stanley, 'Pearls', 133–36, 138.

59. Stanley, 'Pearls', 131–33, 139. This is not to say that the audience was completely biblically illiterate. 'The Christian gospel was accompanied by biblical prooftexts from its earliest days', including the ten commandments, 'stories about important biblical figures', 'texts that could assist the members in defending their faith before a hostile world'. 'But this is a far cry from the kind of biblical knowledge that would be required to grasp the significance of the many quotations that Paul offers, for example, in Romans 9–11, especially when the letter was being read aloud before a gathered congregation.' Stanley, 'Quotations', 721.

60. Stanley, 'Pearls', 139.

61. Stanley, 'Quotations', 720. See also Stanley, 'Rhetoric', 53.

62. Charles H. Dodd, *According to the Scriptures* (London: Fontana Books, 1952), 110. See also Bock, *Proclamation*, 274.

63. Steyn, *Septuagint Quotations*, 2. Larkin divides the latter category into allusions and use of OT ideas. William J. Larkin, 'Toward a Holistic Description of Luke's Use of the Old Testament: A Method Described and Illustrated from Luke 23:33-38, 44-49', in *Evangelical Theological Society Papers* (Portland, Ore.: Theological Research Exchange Network, 1987), 1.

64. Richard B. Hays, *Echoes of Scripture in the Letters of Paul* (New Haven: Yale University Press, 1989). For Luke–Acts, see Rebecca Denova, *The Things Accomplished Among Us: Prophetic Tradition and the Structural Pattern of Luke–Acts* (JSNTSup 141; Sheffield: Sheffield Academic Press, 1997); Litwak, *Echoes*; David P. Moessner, *Lord of the Banquet: The Literary and Theological*

legitimately provide insight into the ways scripture may have shaped the author's thought and presentation, but questions of identification and resulting disagreements will always leave a degree of uncertainty. As Stanley has observed, only clearly identifiable quotations (and allusions) are likely to be part of the author's intentional rhetorical strategy. However, by focusing on explicit quotations, we may develop a framework by which to evaluate more objectively other proposed allusions or intertextual references.

Recent contributions to the study of the OT in Luke–Acts have focused on the role of the OT in the development of Luke's Christology. As a result, they address 'the problem [of the OT in Luke–Acts] from the perspective of only one aspect of the Lukan theology'.[65] To understand the role of appeal to the OT in Luke–Acts, other OT citations must be brought into the discussion. Because of the central place occupied by the Gentile mission in the ecclesiology of Luke–Acts, an examination of related OT citations will constitute a major step toward meeting this need.

This study will examine four explicit OT citations in the book of Acts that are related to the Gentile mission. These will identified by an analysis offered in chapter 2.[66]

Table 1.1

NT Reference	Reference to Gentiles	OT Citation
Acts 2.16-21	All flesh … everyone who calls on the name of the Lord	Joel 3.1-5 MT
Acts 3.25	All the families of the earth will be blessed	Genesis 22.18
Acts 13.47	A light to the nations	Isaiah 49.6
Acts 15.16-18	All the Gentiles called by my name	Amos 9.11-12

Each of these is plainly marked as an explicit citation by the use of an introductory formula. Two, Acts 13.47 and Acts 15.16-18, explicitly function in the narrative to legitimate the Gentile mission. In the other two, Acts 2.16-21 and Acts 3.25, the Gentile mission has not yet begun or become an issue in the life of the church, but it is nevertheless anticipated by these citations.

These four texts come from four OT books, evoke four major prophetic themes, and occur in speeches by three of the most important characters in Acts.[67]

Significance of the Lukan Travel Narrative (Minneapolis: Fortress, 1989); Pao, *Acts*. For the use of allusions in Jewish interpretation, see Martin Hengel and Daniel P. Bailey, 'The Effective History of Isaiah 53 in the Pre-Christian Period', in *The Suffering Servant: Isaiah 53 in Jewish and Christian Sources* (ed. Bernd Janowski and Peter Stuhlmacher; trans. Daniel P. Bailey; Grand Rapids: Eerdmans, 2004), 80.

65. Steyn, *Septuagint Quotations*, 3.

66. A fifth text, Luke 3.6 (Isa. 40.5), also may be related to the Gentile mission, but limiting the present work to the four citations in Acts makes for a more focused and coherent study. Luke 3.6 will receive brief attention in the discussion of Acts 2.16-21. The same five texts have also been identified by Dahl, 'Abraham', 157, n. 50; Wilson, *Gentile Mission*, 243.

67. Three of these speeches 'are strongly Davidic-Messianic' and they are given by 'three of the most *theologically* important characters in Acts' (emphasis in original). Mark L. Strauss, *The Davidic Messiah in Luke–Acts: The Promise and Its Fulfillment in Lukan Eschatology* (JSNTSup 110; Sheffield: Sheffield Academic Press, 1995), 192.

Table 1.2

NT Reference	OT Citation	OT Theme	Speaker	Reference to Gentiles
Acts 2.16-21	Joel 3.1-5 MT	Spirit	Peter	All flesh ... everyone who calls
Acts 3.25	Genesis 22.18	Abraham's seed	Peter	All the families of the earth
Acts 13.47	Isaiah 49.6	Isaianic servant	Paul	A light to the nations
Acts 15.16-18	Amos 9.11-12	Davidic kingdom	James	All the Gentiles called by my name

Tannehill has argued that two of these (Acts 2.17-21; 13.47) occur in texts with broad significance for the rest of the narrative.[68] The centrality of the themes and speakers underscores the importance of the issues.[69]

Once these OT citations have been identified, each text will be studied in detail.

- Examination of text-critical issues related to the citation in the MT, the LXX, and the NT.
- Examination of the OT text, with particular attention to its meaning in its original context.
- Examination of the NT citation, including its context, interpretation in this context, and apparent purpose, i.e. the way in which it contributes to its NT context.

Two texts, Acts 13.47 and Acts 15.16-18, will be examined in greater detail because of their role in explicitly legitimating the Gentile mission, because of complex issues involved in their interpretation, and because they have received less attention in recent studies of the OT in Luke–Acts.[70] The citations in Acts 2.16-21 and 3.25 will be examined more briefly, with a focus on the way in which they legitimate the Gentile mission.

A number of assumptions and limitations are necessary. This study focuses on the extant book of Acts and the way in which selected OT citations function within it. The complexities posed for an 'extant text' of Acts by distinctive readings of the Western text will not be a significant factor in studying these four texts.[71] We

---

68. Tannehill finds important parallels in the way that the missions of John, Jesus, Peter and Paul are introduced in Luke 3.4-6 (Isa. 40.3-5); 4.18-19 (Isa. 61.1-2); Acts 2.17-21 (Joel 3.1-5); 13.47 (Isa. 49.6). 'There is a sermon by each of these figures near the beginning of the story segment that will concentrate on his work, and the sermon either includes or is accompanied by a scriptural quotation which reveals the divine purpose behind the mission that is beginning. These scriptural quotations have a significance beyond the scenes in which they appear.' Robert C. Tannehill, *The Narrative Unity of Luke–Acts: A Literary Interpretation* (2 vols.; Philadelphia: Fortress, 1986–90), 1.52.

69. All four of these themes are introduced early in the third gospel: the Spirit (1.15, 35, 41, 67; 2.25-26), the promise to Abraham (1.54-55, 72-73), the Lord's servant (1.69) and the Davidic kingdom (1.32-33, 69; 2.4, 11). Three appear in the song of Zechariah (servant, David, Abraham) as he is filled with the Spirit. All four of these citations and associated themes play a prominent role in Max Turner's interpretation of Luke–Acts, which I discovered too late to give the attention that it deserves. Max Turner, *Power from on High: The Spirit in Israel's Restoration and Witness in Luke–Acts* (Sheffield: Sheffield Academic Press, 1996).

70. Because they focus on Christology, neither Bock, *Proclamation*, nor Rese, *Alttestamentliche Motive*, treats these texts.

71. Distinctive Western readings occur around and within these four texts, but none present

will not attempt to identify sources or traditional material lying behind the text, nor to examine the way in which the author may have used such material. The present form of the work is worthy of study, particularly by those who view it as part of the authoritative canon of the church.

This study assumes the unity and common authorship of Luke–Acts, both of which are widely accepted.[72] For convenience, the author of the two-volume work will be referred to as 'Luke'.[73]

The study focuses on the narrative sequence and world as presented in the work. Questions concerning the historicity of the account are beyond the scope of the present study.[74] The speeches will be treated as, within the narrative world of the work, 'at least faithful epitomes, giving the gist of the arguments used'.[75]

---

significant obstacles to their interpretation. For a concise and current summary of the textual issues, see Bruce M. Metzger, *A Textual Commentary on the Greek New Testament* (2nd edn.; Stuttgart: Deutsche Bibelgesellschaft, 2002), 222–36.

72. See e.g. Frederick F. Bruce, *The Book of the Acts* (rev. edn.; NICNT; Grand Rapids: Eerdmans, 1988); Joseph A. Fitzmyer, *The Gospel according to Luke* (2 vols.; AB 28–28A; Garden City, NY: Doubleday, 1981–85); Donald Guthrie, *New Testament Introduction* (3rd rev. edn.; Downers Grove, Ill.: Inter-Varsity, 1970); Werner Georg Kummel, *Introduction to the New Testament* (trans. Howard Clark Kee; Nashville: Abingdon, 1975); Ben Witherington III, *The Acts of the Apostles: A Socio-Rhetorical Commentary* (Grand Rapids: Eerdmans, 1998). For a recent response to some arguments offered against the unity of Luke–Acts, see Litwak, *Echoes*, 35–47.

73. The present study does not depend on the identification of the author, although a strong case can be made for the traditional identification of the author of the third gospel and Acts, as by, e.g. Fitzmyer, *Luke*, 1.35–39. The proposal that the Alexandrian text represents a substantial post-Lucan redaction would, if established, complicate references to the 'author' of the work; see Marie Emile Boismard and Arnaud Lamouille, *Le texte occidental des actes des apôtres: reconstitution et réhabilitation* (2 vols.; Synthèse 17; Paris: Editions Recherche sur les civilisations, 1984); *Les actes des deux apôtres* (6 vols.; *EBib* 2/12–14, 23, 30, 41; Paris: J. Gabalda, 1990–). Their position, however, has not met with wide acceptance (see e.g. Charles K. Barrett, *A Critical and Exegetical Commentary on the Acts of the Apostles* (2 vols.; ICC; Edinburgh: T&T Clark, 1994–98), 2.xix–xxii; Joseph A. Fitzmyer, *The Acts of the Apostles* (AB 31; New York: Doubleday, 1998), 84–85).

74. Nonetheless, there are indications that the narrative is at least a reliable account of the events it records. See e.g. the defence of Luke as historian in Ian Howard Marshall, *Luke: Historian and Theologian* (3rd edn.; Downers Grove, Ill.: InterVarsity, 1988).

75. Frederick F. Bruce, *The Speeches in the Acts of the Apostles* (London: Tyndale Press, 1942), 27. See also Conrad Gempf, 'Public Speaking and Published Accounts', in *The Book of Acts in Its Ancient Literary Context* (ed. Bruce W. Winter and Andrew D. Clarke; vol. 1 of *The Book of Acts in Its First Century Setting*, ed. Bruce W. Winter; Grand Rapids: Eerdmans, 1993), 259–303; W. Ward Gasque, 'The Speeches of Acts: Dibelius Reconsidered', in *New Dimensions in New Testament Study* (ed. Richard N. Longenecker and Merrill C. Tenney; Grand Rapids: Zondervan, 1974). By contrast, many view the speeches as mostly or entirely compositions by Luke. Cadbury found them 'devoid of historical basis in genuine tradition'. Henry J. Cadbury, 'The Speeches in Acts', in *The Beginnings of Christianity, Part I: The Acts of the Apostles* (ed. Frederick J. Foakes Jackson and Kirsopp Lake; 5 vols.; London: Macmillan, 1920–33; repr., Grand Rapids: Baker, 1979), 5.426. So also Cadbury, *Making of Luke–Acts*, 184–93. Similarly, Dibelius believed that 'all of the preaching ... has Luke as its author. ... The author did not feel himself obliged to be loyal to what he had heard or the text that had come into his possession.' Martin Dibelius, *Studies in the Acts of the Apostles* (New York: Charles Scribner's Sons, 1956), 183–84. E. Schweizer believed that 'the speeches are basically *compositions by the author of Acts*' (emphasis his). Eduard Schweizer, 'Concerning the Speeches in Acts', in *Studies in Luke–Acts* (ed. Leander E. Keck and James Louis Martyn; Nashville: Abingdon, 1966; repr., Mifflintown, Pa.: Siglar Press, 1999), 208.

This study will not explore in detail the theme of the rejection of the gospel by many Jews, although this has been related to the Gentile mission both historically and theologically.[76] Haenchen, for example, has argued that 'for Luke, the Jews are "written off"' and 'the Jewish people … has forfeited salvation' and, as a result, the effort to reach the Jews has ended and 'now the mission goes only to the Gentiles'.[77] This view has come under increased attack, as 'a growing chorus of scholars … are protesting the notion that Luke depicts the triumph of gentile Christianity at the expense of Jews'.[78] In Acts, not all Jews reject the gospel; in every text in which 'the Jews' oppose the gospel, there are also Jews who believe.[79] Thus 'the schema that sees the rejection of the gospel by the Jews as providing the impetus for the Gentile mission is not supported by a reading of Luke–Acts as a whole'.[80] Rather 'the salvation of the Gentiles and Israel are inseparable'.[81] This is an important and sensitive area. Jewish scholars are understandably troubled by the idea of the 'replacement' or 'supersession' of Israel by a Gentile church as the true heir of the scriptures and 'heritage of Israel'.[82] Christian scholars are eager to claim the OT as part of the heritage of the church. These questions are as old as the book of Acts, and their sensitivity has not been diminished by the long history of anti-Semitism that has sometimes been based on readings of this work. The present study, however, can only hint at how such questions might be addressed.

76. See e.g. Acts 13.36; 18.6; 28.28. Sanders believes Acts 4.11 also connects the rejection of the gospel by Jews with the Gentile mission, arguing that the establishment of the cornerstone ensures that the building goes on, but with other builders (compare Luke 20.16-17). Sanders, 'Prophetic Use', 195–97.

77. Ernst Haenchen, *The Acts of the Apostles: A Commentary* (trans. R. McL. Williams; Philadelphia: Westminster, 1971), 128, 129. In a similar vein, Jack T. Sanders can speak of Christ as 'the cornerstone [the reference is to Ps. 118.22] not of a "renewed Israel", of "the redeemed within Israel", but of the church, which is Gentile'. Or, more bluntly: 'The Jews are out and the Gentiles are in.' Sanders, 'Prophetic Use', 196, 197.

78. Robert L. Brawley, *Luke–Acts and the Jews* (SBLMS 33; Atlanta: Scholars Press, 1987), 3. See also Jervell, 'Divided People', 53, 44–49.

79. While many Jews (and official Judaism) rejected the message about Jesus, many did not. The expression 'the Jews' will appear in quotation marks, both to signify that this is language Luke uses to characterize Jewish adversaries and as a reminder that 'the Jews' does not mean all Jews.

80. Earl Richard, 'The Divine Purpose: The Jews and the Gentile Mission (Acts 15)', in *Luke–Acts: New Perspectives from the Society of Biblical Literature Seminar* (ed. Charles H. Talbert; New York: Crossroad, 1984), 197. 'The partial rejection on the part of the Jews does not provide the basis for preaching to Gentiles because preaching to Gentiles was already contained in the missionary command of God.' Jervell, 'Divided People', 61. (The argument is based on the citation of Isa. 49.6 in Acts 13.47. See below, ch. 3.) Similarly, 'salvation of Gentiles was from the beginning envisaged by God and included as part of his promises to Israel. Luke does not claim that the church has replaced Israel as the people of God.' Dahl, 'Abraham', 151.

81. Johannes Munck, *Paul and the Salvation of Mankind* (trans. Frank Clarke; London: SCM Press, 1959), 44.

82. This latter expression is prompted by the recent volume edited by David P. Moessner, *Jesus and the Heritage of Israel: Luke's Narrative Claim upon Israel's Legacy* (Harrisburg, Pa.: Trinity Press International, 1999).

LISTENING TO LUKE

To learn how Luke understands the OT, we have to listen to him, and particularly to the ways in which he appeals to the OT. This study will examine two important ways in which he does so. First, there are 14 statements that summarize OT teaching without citing a particular text (Appendix 1). These are seldom considered in the discussion of the use of the OT in Luke–Acts. Second, there are more than 75 explicit OT citations (Appendix 2). Slightly more than half of them are cited as prophecies and it is these that have attracted the greatest attention. The summary statements and explicit citations focus on five themes: the suffering, death and resurrection of Christ; the attendant eschatological blessings; the rejection of Christ by many Jews; the coming judgement, particularly on unbelief; and the proclamation of forgiveness to all (Jew or Gentile) through Jesus. This twofold witness to Luke's understanding of the OT sheds light on Luke's purpose in writing, as well as on his understanding of the OT and its fulfilment in Christ.

2.1 *Scripture Summaries*

One of the distinctive features of the use of the OT in Luke–Acts is the 14 statements that summarize OT expectation.[1] These statements use language commonly employed in citation formulas, but do not (apparently) cite particular OT texts.

The two summaries in Luke 24 are especially important. Schubert argued that this chapter plays a crucial role in the message of Luke–Acts and he calls particular attention to its emphasis on fulfilled prophecy.[2] First, Jesus instructs two travellers on the road to Emmaus on the interpretation of the OT and its application to himself.

---

1.   Jervell has noted that these summaries are distinctive of Luke's approach to the OT and can find only a few similar statements elsewhere in the NT (Matt. 22.40; 26.56; John 1.45; 5.39, 46; 20.9; Rom. 1.2-3; 3.21; 16.26; 1 Cor. 15.3-4; Heb. 1.1). He calls Luke's summaries 'summary references' and lists nine: Acts 3.18, 24; 10.43; 17.3; 18.28; 24.14; 26.23; Luke 24.26, 46. Jervell, 'Center', 123. Fitzmyer calls these 'global references' and lists seven in Acts: 3.18, 24; 10.43; 17.3; 18.28; 24.14-15; 26.22-23. The present study counts Acts 3.18-26 as a single summary and adds Acts 7.52; 13.27; 28.23 as well as Luke 1.68-75; 18.31-33; 21.20-24; 24.25-27; 24.44-49. I cannot find any attempt by Fitzmyer to identify similar texts in Luke. Fitzmyer, *Acts*, 91. Bock calls them 'summary citations', and lists five: Luke 24.26, 44-47; Acts 3.22-23; 17.2-3; 26.22-23. Darrell L. Bock, 'Scripture and the Realization of God's Promises', in *Witness to the Gospel* (ed. Ian Howard Marshall and David Peterson; Grand Rapids: Eerdmans, 1998), 42.
2.   Schubert, 'Structure and Significance', 167–77.

> And he said to them, 'O foolish men, and slow of heart to believe all that the prophets
> have spoken! Was it not necessary that the Christ should suffer these things and enter
> into his glory?' And beginning with Moses and all the prophets, he interpreted to them
> in all the scriptures the things concerning himself. (24.25-27)

'In *all* the scriptures' (emphasis added) there are things about Jesus. It is not a matter of identifying a few isolated predictions here and there, but of finding Christ throughout the OT. The roadside lesson in OT interpretation prompted an enthusiastic response: 'Did not our hearts burn within us while he talked to us on the road, while he opened to us the scriptures?' (24.32).

Luke 24.44-49 records Jesus' final and fullest recorded summary interpretation of the OT.

> Then he said to them, 'These are my words which I spoke to you, while I was still with
> you, that everything written about me in the law of Moses and the prophets and the
> psalms must be fulfilled.' Then he opened their minds to understand the scriptures, and
> said to them, 'Thus it is written, that the Christ should suffer and on the third day rise
> from the dead, and that repentance and [lit. unto] forgiveness of sins should be preached
> in his name to all nations, beginning from Jerusalem. You are witnesses of these things.
> And behold, I send the promise of my Father upon you; but stay in the city, until you are
> clothed with power from on high.'

Again, there are many things ('everything written') throughout the OT ('the law of Moses, the prophets, and the psalms') to be fulfilled in Jesus. The OT speaks not only of Jesus' suffering, death and resurrection, but also of the implications of these for the proclamation of repentance and forgiveness 'to all the nations' through the Spirit-empowered apostolic witness.[3]

Similar summary statements are found in 12 other passages in Luke–Acts. They refer to the OT in a variety of ways. All refer to either 'the prophets' (11 summaries) or 'the scriptures' or 'what is written' (nine summaries). Moses or 'the law of Moses' occurs in five. Although there are 13 explicit citations from eight Psalms in Luke–Acts, the Psalms are mentioned only once. All of the

---

3. Most commentators conclude the summary of 'what is written' with the proclamation to 'all nations' (or possibly with ἀρξάμενον ἀπὸ Ιερουσαλήμ, if we follow RSV and the substantial number of MSS reading ἀρξάμενον in place of ἀρξάμενοι). Dupont claims that here Luke 'reduces the teaching of the messianic prophecies to three points', the suffering of Christ, his resurrection on the third day and the proclamation to the nations – omitting the apostolic witness and promise of the Spirit. Dupont, 'Salvation', 17. While vv. 48 and 49 are not grammatically part of 'thus it is written', the Spirit-empowered apostolic witness is the means by which the message of repentance and forgiveness is to be preached to the nations. Dennis Johnson has argued that this witness, the Spirit, and 'the ends of the earth' are three themes from the Isaianic servant songs woven together in the 'programmatic' Acts 1.8. Dennis E. Johnson, *The Message of Acts in the History of Redemption* (Phillipsburg, NJ: P&R Publishing, 1997), 34–36. The universal witness and the Spirit belong to a complex of themes that Luke found prophesied in the OT and their presence in this summary of 'what is written' is not accidental. The apostolic witness to Christ's sufferings and resurrection in fact becomes part of the kerygma (Acts 2.32; 3.15; 5.32; 10.39, 41; 13.31; cf. 22.15; 26.16.) Thus, 'all the elements of verses 46-48 fall under the spell of the lead, "thus it is written": the death and resurrection of Jesus, the worldwide proclamation of conversion and forgiveness, the gift of the Spirit to the witnessing community'. Carroll Stuhlmueller and Donald Senior, *The Biblical Foundations for Mission* (Maryknoll, NY: Orbis, 1983), 257.

summaries in Acts appear in speeches to or descriptions of encounters with Jews, who would be expected to know and respect the OT; none appear in addresses to unbelieving Gentiles, who might be less likely to find such an appeal persuasive.[4]

Ten of the summaries focus on *Christ*, and his suffering, death and resurrection. He must be ridiculed, abused, killed and raised again so that 'everything that is written of the Son of man by the prophets will be accomplished' (Luke 18.31-33).[5] In Thessalonica (Acts 17.2-3), Paul argued 'from the Scriptures' that 'it was necessary for the Christ to suffer and to rise from the dead', so that his hearers would believe that 'this Jesus ... is the Christ'. 'What the prophets and Moses said would come to pass' includes the fact that 'Christ must suffer, and ... rise from the dead' (Acts 26.23). 'What God foretold by the mouth of all the prophets' (3.18, cf. 3.21, 24) was 'that his Christ should suffer' (3.18). Other summaries are employed more generally to indicate that 'Jesus is the Christ' (Acts 17.2-3; cf. 18.28) and the expected 'Righteous One' (Acts 7.52; cf. 3.14).

Other summaries describe the *eschatological blessings* of the Messianic age. Zechariah's prayer in Luke 1.68-75 celebrates God's redemption of his people 'as he spoke by the mouth of his holy prophets from of old' in keeping with 'the mercy promised to our fathers, and ... his holy covenant, the oath which he swore to our father Abraham'. Acts 28.23 finds Paul 'testifying to the kingdom of God'. Acts 3.19 speaks of promised 'times of refreshing from the Lord'. These blessings include 'a hope in God ... that there will be a resurrection of both the just and the unjust' (Acts 24.14-15), which is 'nothing but what the prophets and Moses said would come to pass' (Acts 26.22-23).

The sufferings of Christ result from his *rejection* by many Jews. 'Behold, we are going up to Jerusalem ... he will be delivered to the Gentiles' (Luke 18.31-33; cf. Acts 13.27-29). Acts 13.27-29 describes how 'those who live in Jerusalem and their rulers ... did not recognize him and they asked Pilate to have him killed'. Stephen charged this generation with merely following the example of their fathers, who had killed the prophets (Acts 7.52).

Because of this rejection, *judgement* will come. In Luke 21.20-24, distress and desolation will come 'to fulfill all that is written'. This is (in light of Luke 19.37-44) the result of the city's spiritual blindness and refusal to acknowledge Jesus.

Nevertheless, *forgiveness of sins* is offered through the name of Jesus. Acts 10.43 focuses specifically on this gift, asserting that 'all the prophets' testify that 'every one who believes in him receives forgiveness of sins through his name'. Luke 24.44-49 makes forgiveness (with a call to repentance) the central feature

---

4. This is not meant to suggest that the OT was unimportant to Gentile believers, but simply that it was unlikely to be seen as authoritative by most Gentiles. The OT is not cited in speeches addressed to 'true pagans', Gentiles who did not have previous contact with the scriptures of Israel (e.g. Acts 14.14-18; 17.22-31). Paul's reference to the law and the prophets in his hearing before Felix (24.14) is not an appeal to authority but an attempt to present himself as an orthodox Jew guilty only of an intramural disagreement. In Acts 26.22, 27, Paul apparently hopes to win agreement from Agrippa by appealing to the prophets.

5. Luke alone amplifies the third passion prediction this way (cf. Matt. 20.17-19; Mark 10.32-34).

of the apostolic proclamation. Acts 26.22-23 indicates that Christ would, by virtue of his resurrection (and through the apostolic witness), 'proclaim light both to the people and to the Gentiles'.

The summaries all have a Christological focus. They speak not only of his rejection, suffering, death and resurrection, but of the eschatological blessings he brings, warnings of judgement for failure to acknowledge him, and the offer of forgiveness to all (Jew and Gentile) through him. While the summaries do not comprise all that Luke understood of the OT, it is clear that he approached the whole OT Christologically, i.e. with reference to Christ.

2.2 Old Testament Citations

The second way in which Luke appeals to the OT is by explicit citations. Luke employs explicit citations in a variety of ways, as references to provisions of the Mosaic law, to historical events, to doctrinal beliefs, and as prophecies. The prophetic citations focus on the same five themes as the scripture summaries. While the summaries indicate generally *what* Luke believes the OT says about these things, the explicit citations indicate *how* it does so, i.e. his hermeneutic.[6]

Identifying citations is an inexact science and there is little consensus on which texts in Luke–Acts are explicit citations and which are paraphrases or allusions.[7] Although sharing a common text, the two standard editions of the NT differ on OT citations.[8] Neither text agrees with Bratcher's survey of OT quotations, which was also prepared under the direction of the United Bible Societies.[9] Other studies display a similar disparity.[10] Texts marked as citations in NA[27] and UBS[4] generally represent a middle-of-the-road approach (i.e. more citations than some studies, fewer than others). Limiting citations to only those marked with an introductory

---

6. 'If Luke defines the Christian meaning of the OT in ch. 24 of his Gospel, he does not indicate which biblical texts are most apt for this Christological demonstration. It is the citations in Acts which fulfill the program announced in ch. 24.' François Bovon, *Luke the Theologian: Thirty-Three Years of Research (1950-1983)* (trans. Ken McKinney; Allison Park, Pa.: Pickwick, 1987), 85.

7. This three-fold categorization of citations, paraphrases and allusions is employed by Robert G. Bratcher, *Old Testament Quotations in the New Testament* (3rd rev. edn.; Helps for Translators 3; London: United Bible Societies, 1987). For a more detailed scheme, see Franklin Johnson, *The Quotations of the New Testament from the Old Considered in the Light of General Literature* (Philadelphia: American Baptist Publication Society, 1896).

8. In Luke, NA[27] marks 33 passages as quotations, ten of which are not shared with UBS[4]; UBS[4] lists 25 texts as quotations, two of which are not shared with NA[27]. In Acts, NA[27] marks 36 passages as quotations, three of which are not shared with UBS[4]; UBS[4] lists 40 texts as quotations, seven of which are not shared with NA[27].

9. Bratcher, *Quotations*.

10. Charles K. Barrett, 'Luke/Acts', in *It is Written: Scripture Citing Scripture* (ed. Donald A. Carson and Hugh G. M. Williamson; Cambridge: Cambridge University Press, 1988), 231–44; Holtz, *Untersuchungen*; Johnson, *Quotations*; Longenecker, *Biblical Exegesis*, 57–59; Helmer Ringgren, 'Luke's Use of the Old Testament', *HTR* 79 (1986): 227–35; Crawford Howard Toy, *Quotations in the New Testament* (New York: Charles Scribner's Sons, 1884); David McCalman Turpie, *The New Testament View of the Old: A Contribution to Biblical Introduction and Exegesis* (London: Hodder & Stoughton, 1872).

formula would be too narrow, and even then, difficulties and uncertainties would remain (a formula may introduce multiple citations, e.g. Acts 1.20; 3.23).

The development of a consistent rationale for identifying citations and the detailed application of such a methodology to Luke–Acts would be a study in itself. It is possible to gain some idea of Luke's use of the OT by analysing: (1) citations identified in either NA[27] or UBS[4] (the two agree over 80 per cent of the time); and (2) citations prefaced by an introductory formula. Examination of both sets of citations yields strikingly similar results.

Luke employs a considerable variety of formulas with OT citations. Forty formulas introduce 48 citations (several formulas introduce multiple citations). The terminology is generally similar to that found in the scripture summaries (although, since these citations have specific sources, we do not find generalized expressions such as 'the law and the prophets'). The 'written' character of OT revelation is emphasized (18 times), as well as the language of speech (18 times). Speakers include Moses, David, 'the prophet' (i.e. Isaiah) and God himself.

When we look at the sources of Luke's OT citations, the same pattern emerges whether we consider the texts marked as citations by NA[27] or UBS[4] or only those explicitly marked by an introductory formula. The citations come primarily from the Pentateuch, latter prophets and Psalms, with few from the historical narratives. Citations, including those with introductory formulas, are more numerous in Acts, despite the gospel's greater length.

Table 2.1

Citations by source[11]	All citations				Citations with introductory formulas			
	Luke	*Acts*	*Total*	*Per cent*	*Luke*	*Acts*	*Total*	*Per cent*
Pentateuch	13	20	33	42%	10	8	18	38%
History[12]	1	1	2	3%	0	1	1	2%
Latter Prophets	11	10	21	27%	6	10	16	33%
Psalms	10	12	22	28%	3	10	13	27%
Total	35	43	78		19	29	48	
	45%	55%			40%	60%		

Luke cites the OT in a variety of ways.[13] We can identify four general categories:

---

11. Luke 7.27 is taken as a quotation from Mal. 3.1 (not Exod. 23.20); see Gleason L. Archer and Gregory Chirichingo, *Old Testament Quotations in the New Testament* (Chicago: Moody, 1983), 165; Gregg K. Beale and D. A. Carson, eds., *Commentary on the New Testament Use of the Old Testament* (Grand Rapids: Baker Academic, 2007), 300–3; Fitzmyer, *Luke*, 1.674. It is more difficult to choose between Exod. 20.11 and Ps. 146.6 as the source of the quotations in Acts 4.24; 14.15; one quotation each is assigned to the Pentateuch and Psalms above.

12. 'History' here includes the former prophets and the narrative books from the writings (i.e. Joshua–Esther in the English Bible). Apart from the Psalms, there are no quotations from the writings (unless Acts 4.24 is understood as a quotation of Neh. 9.6, but it is more likely a quotation of Exod. 20.11 and Ps. 146.6; cf. also 2 Kgs. 19.15; Isa. 37.16).

13. All of the OT citations in Acts occur in speeches with the exception of Acts 8.32-33, the text being read by the Ethiopian eunuch. Clarke, 'Use', 2.93. None occur as comments by the narrator, in marked contrast to, e.g., Matthew. Cf. Matt. 1.22-23; 2.25, 17-18; 3.3; 8.17; 12.17-21; 13.35; 21.5; 27.9-10.

legal, historical, doctrinal and prophetic.[14] *Legal* citations recite requirements of the OT law, as when Mary and Joseph prepare 'to offer a sacrifice according to what is said in the law of the Lord, "a pair of turtledoves, or two young pigeons"' (Luke 2.24; citing Lev. 12.8), or Jesus reciting the two great commandments (Luke 10.26-27; citing Deut. 6.5; Lev. 19.18). These occur primarily in the gospel, accompanied by introductory formulas. Citations from accounts of *historical* events, with the exception of Acts 13.22, all appear in Stephen's speech in Acts 7. These come primarily from the Pentateuch and refer to foundational events of Israel's history, although a few refer to the establishment of the kingdom or subsequent events.[15] A small number of passages cite OT texts that express *doctrinal* convictions, as when Jesus appeals to the designation of Yahweh as 'the God of Abraham and the God of Isaac and the God of Jacob' to demonstrate 'that the dead are raised' (Luke 20.37; citing Exod. 3.6), or when Paul proclaims in Lystra the God 'who made the heaven and the earth and the sea and all that is in them' (Acts 14.15; citing Exod. 20.11; Ps. 146.6). The majority of citations are employed in a *prophetic* capacity, principally drawn from the prophets and the book of Psalms and applied to events which have been fulfilled in the narrative or which are yet to be fulfilled. These are most often in view in discussions of the OT in Luke–Acts. We summarize these findings in Table 2.2.

Table 2.2

Citations by use	All citations				Citations with introductory formulas			
	Luke	Acts	Total	Per cent	Luke	Acts	Total	Per cent
Legal	11	1	12	15%	9	1	10	21%
Historical	0	17	17	22%	0	7	7	15%
Doctrinal	2	3	5	6%	2	0	2	4%
Prophetic	22	22	44	56%	8	21	29	60%
Total	35	43	78		19	29	48	

We can further categorize the ways in which the prophetic citations are applied. The majority are concerned with *Christology*, as when David 'foresaw and spoke of the resurrection of the Christ' (Acts 2.30-31; citing Ps. 132.11; 16.10) or Jesus applied to himself the words of Isa. 61.1-2 (Luke 4.1-21). Isaiah 61 also includes a broader *soteriological* component, speaking not only of Christ as the Spirit-anointed preacher, but also about the blessings that he will bring. The same is true of the citation of Joel 3.1-5 MT in Acts 2.16-21. Luke also cites OT texts to warn of the coming *judgement*, particularly on unbelief and the *rejection* of Christ by many Jews: 'but for others [the secrets of the kingdom] are in parables, so that seeing they may not see, and hearing they may not understand'

14. The categories were derived from a study of the citations themselves. Although a degree of subjectivity is involved, the overall pattern is not likely to differ greatly from one reader to another. Readers are invited to view the texts in Appendix 2 and make their own judgements.

15. Many of these appear to be cited simply as part of Stephen's relating the story of Israel's history, not as an appeal to authority. (The only other historical citations are the citations of Ps. 89.20 and 1 Sam. 13.14 in Acts 13.22.) Although Stephen may have understood the history he summarizes to be prophetic, there is no indication that individual citations are understood prophetically.

(Luke 8.10; citing Isa. 6.9) and Paul's warning in Acts 13.40-41 of the judgement announced by Habakkuk (1.5). Finally, several citations speak of the *universal* spread of the gospel to include all nations (i.e. Gentiles): 'all flesh shall see the salvation of God' (Luke 3.4-6; citing Isa. 40.3-5) and the promise of blessing, through Abraham's posterity, for 'all the families of the earth' (Acts 3.25; citing Gen. 22.18). We can summarize these in Table 2.3. (Some citations address more than one theme, so the percentages total more than 100. Raw numbers do not necessarily indicate which themes are more important.)

Table 2.3

Prophetic citations	*All citations*				*Citations with introductory formulas*			
	Luke	*Acts*	*Total*	*Per cent*	*Luke*	*Acts*	*Total*	*Per cent*
Christological	10	10	20	48%	4	9	13	45%
Soteriological	5	4	9	21%	4	4	8	28%
Judgement	7	7	14	33%	2	7	9	31%
Rejection	4	5	9	21%	0	5	5	17%
Universal	1	4	5	12%	1	4	5	15%

Whether or not we restrict our analysis to citations with introductory formulas, the same patterns emerge in analysis of the sources of Luke's OT citations, their uses (legal, historical, doctrinal, prophetic), and the various applications of the prophetic citations. This suggests that the methodology for identifying citations does not bias the results, and that however we may look at it, the same picture of Luke's understanding and use of the OT will emerge.

2.3 *Analysis*

Luke's scripture summaries and OT quotations make similar appeals to the OT. Both regard the OT as 'what is written' and 'spoken by the prophets' and focus on five central themes.

Old Testament expectation in the scripture summaries	*Old Testament citations*
The suffering, death, resurrection and exaltation of Christ	Christological
The eschatological blessings	Soteriological
The coming judgement	Judgement
The rejection of Christ by many Jews	Rejection
The proclamation of forgiveness to all (Jew or Gentile) through Jesus	Universal

These themes – Christology, soteriology, judgement, rejection and the universal offer of the gospel – form the prophetic significance of the OT in Luke–Acts.[16]

Why these five themes? Luke is not writing an academic theology of the OT, but presumably with the needs of his intended audience in mind. It is at this point that Christopher Stanley's work (see chapter 1) is helpful. Stanley argues that

---

16. Cf. the analysis of Amsler, who finds four points in the proclamation of Acts attested by OT citations: the coming of the promised prophet-king, the necessity of the suffering and death of Jesus, his resurrection and ascension, and the proclamation of salvation to all men along with the hardening of Israel. Samuel Amsler, *L'Ancien Testament dans l'Eglise: Essai d'herméneutique chrétienne* (Neuchâtel: Delachaux & Niestlé, 1960), 71.

'the decision to introduce a direct quotation into a piece of discourse is a rhetorical act'.[17] As a rhetorical strategy, the use of quotations, particularly as an appeal to authority, offers insight into the author's purposes and expectations of the intended readers. Luke's citations of OT prophecy are appeals to authority intended to secure agreement and end debate. Since authors (generally) appeal to authority only when some issue is in doubt or dispute, Luke's appeals to the OT in these areas highlight issues of concern to the author and/or his intended readers.

In the preface to his gospel, Luke indicates his intention to write for Theophilus ἀκριβῶς καθεξῆς, an 'orderly account', with the goal ἵνα ἐπιγνῷς περὶ ὧν κατηχήθης λόγων τὴν ἀσφάλειαν ('that you may know the truth concerning the things of which you have been informed'). Theophilus[18] has been informed about certain things (presumably the essential elements of the life, death and resurrection of Christ, and perhaps key events in the history of the early church), but lacks 'certainty' (NIV) or 'assurance' (Fitzmyer).[19] Luke's account is καθεξῆς, used also in Acts 11.4 to describe Peter's explanation of his behaviour at Cornelius' house, an account designed to persuade his critics of its appropriateness.[20] Luke–Acts, then, is intended as a persuasive document, to bring Theophilus certainty regarding aspects of the Christian faith about which he has already been informed, but may be in some doubt.[21]

As rhetorical strategies, then, the OT citations and summaries provide a clue about the things of which Theophilus needed assurance or that were in dispute in Theophilus' circles.[22] It appears that Theophilus was in need of assurance about the person and work of Jesus. We know from elsewhere in the NT that the crucifixion of Jesus in particular was a stumbling-block to belief (1 Cor. 1.23), that his resurrection was denied (Matt. 28.12-15), and that his Messiahship was disputed (Matt. 26.63-66).[23] The condemnation and execution of Christ by the Romans

17. Stanley, 'Rhetoric', 57.

18. For the present purpose, it does not matter whether Theophilus was a real individual or a symbolic construct, although the former is more likely. Fitzmyer, *Luke*, 1.299–300. Fitzmyer believes he was probably a catechumen or neophyte. Bock describes him as a 'new believer or one whose faith needs bolstering'. Darrell L. Bock, *Luke* (2 vols.; Baker Exegetical Commentary on the New Testament 3; Grand Rapids: Baker, 1994–96), 1.64.

19. Fitzmyer, *Luke*, 1.300–01. RSV's rendering 'know the truth' is inadequate. See BDAG, s.v. ἀσφάλεια. Alexander prefers 'assured knowledge'. Loveday Alexander, *The Preface to Luke's Gospel: Literary Convention and Social Context in Luke 1.1–4 and Acts 1.1* (SNTSMS; Cambridge: Cambridge University Press, 1993), 140. 'The word conveys the antithesis to unreliable gossip, rumour and doubt.' Willem C. van Unnik, 'Remarks on the Purpose of Luke's Historical Writing (Luke I 1–4)', in *Sparsa Collecta: The Collected Essays of W. C. van Unnik, Part One: Evangelia, Paulina, Acta* (NovTSup 29; Leiden: Brill, 1973), 14.

20. Fitzmyer, *Luke*, 1.299.

21. Robert Maddox, *The Purpose of Luke–Acts* (Edinburgh: T&T Clark, 1982), 22, 182–87.

22. 'The plot of a work can often be illuminated by considering the major conflict or conflicts within it.' Tannehill, *Narrative Unity*, 2.34. The citations in a work are a clue to conflicts present in the author's and/or recipients' surroundings and may therefore illuminate the author's concerns and objectives.

23. 'The first objections to the faith were concerned with the suffering and death of Jesus.' Barnabas Lindars, *New Testament Apologetic* (Philadelphia: Fortress, 1961), 284.

was an obstacle to Jews, as well as an embarrassment to Gentiles.[24] Half of the OT citations and almost all of the scripture summaries in Luke–Acts focus on the suffering, death and resurrection of Christ as the fulfilment of prophecy and the plan of God for the salvation of his people. The more generally soteriological texts also support the claim that Jesus is the Christ, by claiming the arrival of the blessings that attend Messiah's coming.

It also appears that Theophilus was in need of certainty about the church's mission to Gentiles. If he was himself a Gentile, the question would have been of considerable personal significance. Acts indicates that the Gentile mission was a matter of controversy: Jews in Jerusalem listened calmly to Paul's account of his conversion until he claimed that God had sent him to preach good news to the Gentiles (Acts 22.21-24). Jews who believed in Jesus had misgivings as well (Acts 10–11; 15.1-35). In such an environment, Gentile believers would undoubtedly have wondered whether they did in fact now belong to God's people.[25] The OT citations and summaries that speak of the inclusion of Gentiles would encourage those who have believed in Jesus that they have indeed been accepted by God. At the same time, the failure of many Jews to welcome Jesus as their Messiah was a matter of concern, both pastoral and theological (Romans 9–11). In Luke–Acts, citations related to Jewish unbelief (e.g. Luke 8.10; Acts 3.23; 13.40-41; 28.25-27) appear most often in conjunction with an announcement of the Gentile mission. Luke's use of the OT 'is designed to calm any doubts that may have existed in the church either about Jesus' position in the plan of God, or his offering of God's salvation to all men, especially the direct offer of salvation to the Gentiles'.[26]

A comparison of the summaries and the quotations, however, reveals that some elements of the summaries are *not* included in the explicit citations. Consider again Luke 24.46-49:

> Thus it is written, that the Christ should suffer and on the third day rise from the dead, and that repentance and forgiveness of sins should be preached in his name to all nations, beginning from Jerusalem. You are witnesses of these things. And behold, I send the promise of my Father upon you; but stay in the city, until you are clothed with power from on high.

The suffering and resurrection of Christ is the predominant theme in the citations, and the proclamation to the nations is also supported by appeal to the OT. The content of the proclamation (repentance and forgiveness), however, is not supported by OT citation. Although Schubert suggested that the apostolic witness and the gift of the Spirit are part of what 'is written', the apostolic witness is supported by no OT citation and the gift of the Spirit by only one.[27] Then again, these things did not appear to have been topics of dispute. That God forgives sins or

24. Frederick F. Bruce, *The Defense of the Gospel in the New Testament* (Grand Rapids: Eerdmans, 1977), 18, 32, 54–55.

25. Maddox, *Purpose*, 183–84.

26. Bock, *Proclamation*, 279.

27. Acts 2.16-21 (Joel 3.1-5 MT) supports the latter. Isa. 43.10; 55.4 could have supported the former, but is not cited.

would in the last days send his Spirit were not in question, but that he would do so for Gentiles, without circumcision and obedience to the law, apparently was.

Stanley notes that, even though an appeal to scripture might be sufficient to clinch an argument, Paul seldom argues by citation alone. Luke uses his narrative, as well as the appeal to the OT, to make his case. The risen Jesus meets with his unbelieving disciples, persuades them of his resurrection (Luke 24.31, 36-52) 'by many proofs' (Acts 1.3), and ascends bodily into heaven in their sight (Acts 1.9-11). The narrative in Acts documents God's acceptance of the Gentiles through the accounts of Philip's preaching in Samaria (8.4-17), the conversion of the Ethiopian eunuch (8.26-39), the commissioning of Paul for the Gentile mission by divine revelation (9.15; 22.21; 26.17-18), the events at Cornelius' house (10.1–11.18), the reception of the gospel by 'Greeks' (11.21-26), and the Spirit-directed decision of the council of Jerusalem (15.1-35). Luke thus brings two lines of argument to bear: his narrative record of 'the things which have been accomplished among us' (Luke 1.1) and the divinely inspired prophecies of those events in the OT. These two lines of reasoning together provide Theophilus with certainty regarding the things of which he has been informed.

2.4 *Conclusion*

This analysis of Luke's scripture summaries and explicit citations demonstrates that the prophetic significance of the OT in Luke–Acts is found in five themes: the suffering, death, resurrection and exaltation of the Messiah; the attendant eschatological blessings; the coming judgement; the rejection of Christ by many Jews; and the proclamation of forgiveness to all (Jew or Gentile) through Jesus.

Considered as rhetorical devices, these appeals to the OT offer insight into his purpose(s). Luke appeals to the authority of the OT (with other rhetorical strategies) to bring Theophilus certainty concerning the things about which he has been instructed, i.e. that Jesus is the Christ and that God has ordained the proclamation of the gospel to the Gentiles. This line of reasoning does not lead to a new conclusion about the purpose of Luke–Acts, but it does bring new evidence to bear on this question.

We began by noting that recent discussions of the OT in Luke–Acts have focused on Christology. This chapter has argued that there are other themes and emphases in appeals to the OT in Luke–Acts: the blessings of the Messianic reign, the coming judgement, the rejection of Christ by many Jews, and the Gentile mission. It is essential that these themes and texts also be brought into the continuing discussion about the OT in Luke–Acts. In order to contribute to this discussion, we will proceed to examine the four texts in Acts that refer to the Gentile mission.

THE SERVANT AND THE NATIONS (ISAIAH 49.6 IN ACTS 13.47)

The citation of Isa. 49.6 in Acts 13.47 represents a major turning-point in the narrative.[1] In the first 12 chapters, Peter has been the leading character and the gospel has been preached primarily within a few miles of Jerusalem to Jews or to Gentiles somehow connected with Judaism (Samaritans in Acts 8 and the pious Cornelius in 10–11). A few disciples, 'scattered because of the persecution that arose over Stephen' (8.4), began preaching to Gentiles ('Greeks'[2]) in Antioch. The apostles, recognizing the significance of this development, sent Barnabas to investigate (11.19-26).[3] Nevertheless, in the narrative of Acts, the church has not conducted a concerted or intentional programme of preaching to Gentiles. This will now change.[4] From chapter 13 to the end of the book, Paul will be the principal spokesman, and, while he will continue to preach in synagogues to Jews and pious Gentiles, he will increasingly focus on Gentiles. The turning-point takes place in Pisidian Antioch where, frustrated by continued and determined opposition from Jews, Paul appeals to Isa. 49.6 (Acts 13.47) as justification for an intentional mission to Gentiles and, in so doing, sets the agenda for the second half of the book.

This section begins as leaders of the church in Antioch[5] are directed by the Spirit to 'set apart for me Barnabas and Saul for the work to which I have called them' (13.2). What this work is to be is not stated, but it will presumably become evident as the narrative unfolds.[6] There have already been anticipations. God had told Ananias that Paul 'is a chosen instrument of mine to carry my name before

1. Luke Timothy Johnson, *The Acts of the Apostles* (SP 5; Collegeville, Minn.: Liturgical Press, 1992), 225.

2. The term here refers to 'pagan sympathizers of Judaism … in the synagogues in Antioch'. Eckhard J. Schnabel, *Early Christian Mission* (2 vols.; Downers Grove, Ill.: InterVarsity, 2004), 786–87. Acts 15 indicates that those involved were Gentiles (15.19), not merely Greek-speakers, and the issue in 15.1 is circumcision and religious obligation, not language or culture.

3. Charles K. Barrett, 'The Gentile Mission as an Eschatological Phenomenon', in *Eschatology and the New Testament: Essays in Honor of George Raymond Beasley-Murray* (ed. W. Hulitt Gloer; Peabody, Mass.: Hendrickson, 1988), 1.552; Darrell L. Bock, *Acts* (Grand Rapids: Baker Academic, 2007), 424.

4. David Pao speaks here of 'the first sustained effort carried out by Christian missionaries to bring the gospel to the various regions beyond the Land of Israel.' Pao, *Acts*, 98.

5. Barrett notes that there is no indication in the text of the church as a whole being present. Barrett, 'Acts', 1.604.

6. Note the signs of divine guidance directing Paul's ministry, e.g. 13.4, 9; 16.6; 19.21.

the Gentiles and kings and the sons of Israel' (9.15),[7] although thus far, Luke has reported only that Paul has preached to 'the sons of Israel'.[8] After the initial preaching in Antioch (11.20-21), 'a large company was added to the Lord' (11.24) through the ministries of Barnabas and Saul over a period of more than a year (11.26).[9] Both Paul's call and the ministry he shared with Barnabas suggest that 'the work' will involve preaching to Gentiles.

In the subsequent narrative, that is what they do. Although they preach in synagogues to Jews (13.5, 14, 34; 14.1) and to those that 'fear God' (13.16), they typically meet with opposition from Jews (13.45, 50-51; 14.2, 5), while receiving a more favourable response from Gentiles (13.12, 43, 48; 14.2). When they return to Antioch, Luke summarizes their journey solely in terms of their ministry to Gentiles ('how [God] had opened a door of faith to the Gentiles', 14.27; cf. 15.3, 12). The substantial influx of Gentiles into the church becomes the occasion for the council in Jerusalem concerning the basis on which Gentiles will be included.

In these two accounts, coming roughly in the middle of Acts, we find the two explicit OT citations that directly address the Gentile mission: here, when Paul and Barnabas first embark on a deliberate programme of preaching to Gentiles, and at the council in Jerusalem, when James appeals to Amos 9.11-12 to settle the question of the means of Gentile inclusion.

The citation of Isa. 49.6 in Acts 13.47 is also important because there are at least two other allusions to Isa. 49.6 in Luke–Acts (possibly more). In those, the object of the prophecy appears to be Jesus, while in Acts 13.47, Paul applies it to his own ministry, raising questions about the interpretation of the prophecy. Nevertheless, this repeated use of the text indicates its substantial importance for Luke.[10]

3.1 *Text*

Although the phrase גּוֹיִם לְאוֹר (εἰς φῶς ἐθνῶν) appears in both Isa. 49.6 and Isa. 42.6, other language indicates that the citation comes from Isa. 49.6 LXX: τέθεικά σε in 49.6e (42.6d reads ἔδωκά σε) and the purpose clause, τοῦ εἶναί σε εἰς σωτηρίαν ἕως ἐσχάτου τῆς γῆς (49.6g, absent from 42.6).

---

7. The Gentile mission also figures prominently in Paul's accounts of his call in 22.21; 26.17-18. Eckhard Schnabel sees echoes of servant language in Paul's descriptions of his call in Acts 18.9-10 (Isa. 41.10) and 26.16-18 (Isa. 42.6-7, 16). Schnabel, *Early Christian Mission*, 943.

8. In Damascus (9.20) and Jerusalem (9.28-29). Bruce believes Paul was already preaching to Gentiles in Arabia (Gal. 1.17) shortly after his conversion, but there is no indication of this in Acts. Bruce, *Acts* (rev. edn.), 191–92.

9. The text does not indicate how many Gentiles (or Jews) were included in this 'company', but Gal. 2.9 seems to indicate that Barnabas as well as Paul had had a ministry to Gentiles. Bruce, *Acts* (rev. edn.), 267; Fitzmyer, *Acts*, 495.

10. 'Isaiah 49.6, which is explicitly cited in Acts 13.47 and is reflected in Luke 1.79 and 24.47 as well as in Acts 1.8 and 26.20, apparently influenced the shape of Luke's entire work.' Jack T. Sanders, 'Isaiah in Luke', in *Luke and Scripture: The Function of Sacred Tradition in Luke–Acts* (ed. Craig A. Evans and Jack T. Sanders; Minneapolis: Augsburg, 1993), 20. See also Tannehill, *Narrative Unity*, 1.52.

Isaiah 49.6 MT		*Isaiah 49.6 LXX*	*Acts 13.47*
			47a οὕτως γὰρ ἐντέταλται ἡμῖν ὁ κύριος·
וַיֹּאמֶר	6a	καὶ εἶπέν μοι	
נָקֵל מִהְיוֹתְךָ לִי עֶבֶד	b	Μέγα σοί ἐστιν τοῦ κληθῆναί σε παῖδά μου	
לְהָקִים אֶת־שִׁבְטֵי יַעֲקֹב	c	τοῦ στῆσαι τὰς φυλὰς Ιακωβ	
וּנְצִירֵי יִשְׂרָאֵל לְהָשִׁיב	d	καὶ τὴν διασπορὰν τοῦ Ισραηλ ἐπιστρέψαι.	
וּנְתַתִּיךָ	e	ἰδοὺ τέθεικά σε	b τέθεικά σε
לְאוֹר גּוֹיִם	f	εἰς διαθήκην γένους εἰς φῶς ἐθνῶν	c εἰς φῶς ε᾽θνῶν
לִהְיוֹת יְשׁוּעָתִי עַד־קְצֵה הָאָרֶץ	g	τοῦ εἶναί σε εἰς σωτηρίαν ἕως ἐσχάτου τῆς γῆς.	d τοῦ εἶναί σε εἰς σωτηρίαν ἕως ἐσχάτου τῆς γῆς.

Isaiah 42.6 MT		*Isaiah 42.6 LXX*	*Acts 13.47*
			47a οὕτως γὰρ ἐντέταλται ἡμῖν ὁ κύριος·
אֲנִי יְהוָה קְרָאתִיךָ בְצֶדֶק	6a	ἐγὼ κύριος ὁ θεὸς ἐκάλεσά σε ἐν δικαιοσύνῃ	
וְאַחְזֵק בְּיָדֶךָ	b	καὶ κρατήσω τῆς χειρός σου	
וְאֶצָּרְךָ	c	καὶ ἐνισχύσω σε	
וְאֶתֶּנְךָ	d	καὶ ἔδωκά σε	b τέθεικά σε
לִבְרִית עָם לְאוֹר גּוֹיִם	e	εἰς διαθήκην γένους, εἰς φῶς ἐθνῶν	c εἰς φῶς ἐθνῶν
			d τοῦ εἶναί σε εἰς σωτηρίαν ἕως ἐσχάτου τῆς γῆς.

There are several minor textual issues in the MT of Isa. 49.6, but only one occurs in the portion of the text cited (6e–g): 1QIsaᵃ makes the singular קָצֵה ('end') in 6g plural, a distinction that makes no discernible difference in this text.[11]

There are two significant textual issues in the LXX of 49.6e–g. In 6e, some MSS read δέδωκά σε for τέθεικά σε. The former was more frequently used to translate נתן and could be seen as a more literal rendering, but the latter was used frequently enough that it was clearly an acceptable alternative. Although τέθεικά σε may have been read back into the LXX from Acts 13, the fact that the two verbs are interchanged in other texts suggests that the motive here (whichever verb was original) was stylistic.[12] Both Rahlfs and the Göttingen Septuagint conclude that the correct reading in 49.6 is τέθεικά σε. In 6f, some MSS read εἰς διαθήκην

---

11.   The singular is more common (see Isa. 5.26; 42.10; 43.6; 48.20; 62.11; Jer. 25.31; Ps. 46.9; Prov. 17.4) and may indicate a particular location or direction in several texts (Deut. 28.49; Isa. 5.26; Jer. 10.13; 51.16; Ps. 61.2; 135.7). The plural appears only in Isa. 40.28; 41.5, 9; Job 28.24.

12.   At least five other texts show variation between δίδωμι and τίθημι: 4 Kgdms. 5.1; 2 Chr. 3.16; Eccl. 7.22 (21 MT); Ezek. 30.24; 2 Esd. 17.71 (Neh. 7.71). The two verbs appear somewhat interchangeable. HRCS, s.v. τιθέναι.

γένους, although this is absent from the MT and Acts 13. Its inclusion here appears to represent assimilation to Isa. 42.6, where the 'light to the nations' is accompanied by 'a covenant to/for the people'. The reverse appears in 49.8, where some MSS insert 'a light to the nations' following 'a covenant for the people'.[13] Although Rahlfs includes the phrase in 6f, the Göttingen Septuagint rightly omits it.[14]

There are no significant textual variants in the citation in Acts 13.47. Some variation appears in the introductory words in 47a (e.g. οὕτως and οὕτω, ἐντέταλται and other forms including ἐντέταλκε(ν), ἐντέλλεται, etc.), but none significantly affect the meaning. The citation itself includes minor variants, such as an initial ἰδού and τοῖς ἔθνεσιν instead of ἐθνῶν, but none are well attested and none affect the meaning of the text.

The citation follows the MT of Isa. 49.6 more closely than it does the LXX. Except for a few MSS, Acts 13.47 omits the ἰδού present in the LXX. The citation in Acts omits the apparent interpolation from 42.6 (and/or possibly 49.8), εἰς διαθήκην γένους (49.6f), which appears in some LXX MSS. The rest of the citation follows the MT and the LXX exactly, suggesting that Luke (or his source) has either made a fresh translation of the MT that coincides remarkably with the LXX or used an LXX MS closer to the MT than any now extant.

3.2 *Isaiah 49.6*

It is necessary first to place the citation in the context of the servant songs and particularly the similar language that appears in Isa. 42.6. Isaiah will be treated as a literary unit; whatever its compositional history, it was regarded as a single work in the first century.[15]

3.2.1 *The Servant Songs*
Both Isa. 49.6 and Isa. 42.6 have been identified as belonging to the servant songs of Isaiah 40–55. The literature on these texts is immense and only a cursory survey can be given here.[16]

---

13.   However, North believes that לִבְרִית עָם in 49.8 'has been inserted for the purpose of making what was originally an Israel-Song into a Song about the Servant'. Christopher R. North, *The Suffering Servant in Deutero-Isaiah: An Historical and Critical Study* (2nd edn.; London: Oxford University Press, 1956), 129–30.

14.   'The Hebrew text is probably right as against LXX ... in omitting לברית עם (for a covenant of the people) as a gloss from 42.6.' Norman H. Snaith, 'Isaiah 40–66: A Study of the Teaching of Second Isaiah and Its Consequences', in *Studies on the Second Part of the Book of Isaiah* (VTSup 14; Leiden: Brill, 1967), 156.

15.   Luke attributes to Isaiah quotations from 6.9-10 (Acts 28.25-27); 40.3-5 (Luke 3.4-6); 53.7-8 (Acts 8.28-33); 61.1-2 (Luke 4.17-19). Cf. Isa. 9.1-2 (Matt. 4.15-16); 42.1-4 (Matt. 12.17-20); 1.9 (Rom. 9.29); 10.22-23 (Rom. 9.27-28); 11.10 (Rom. 15.12); 53.1 (Rom. 10.16); 65.1-2 (Rom. 10.20-21). A good case can be made for the integrity of the songs as they appear in the MT. North finds that the songs were written 'almost certainly by the same author' as the surrounding prophecies. North, *Suffering Servant*, 188.

16.   'A well-known commentator is said to have abandoned his projected commentary on Isaiah because this part of his subject overwhelmed him.' Henry Wheeler Robinson, *The Cross in the Old*

In the first edition of his Isaiah commentary (1892), Bernard Duhm first identified four texts in the latter portion of Isaiah as 'Servant Songs': 42.1-4; 49.1-6; 50.4-9; 52.13–53.12.[17] Duhm believed these had been written by a single author and inserted into the book by a later editor. Other scholars have suggested that the songs may also include 42.19-21; 48.14-16; 51.4-8; 51.9-16; 61.1-6; and, notably for our purposes, 42.5-9 (or 5-7) and 49.7-13.[18] Other texts in Isaiah 40–55 also speak of Yahweh's 'servant', but have not been viewed as servant songs.[19]

Many have followed Duhm's view that the songs speak of a single servant,[20] but there is less agreement on the servant's identity. The servant has been viewed as an individual (e.g. the prophet, Cyrus, one of the kings of Judah), as a corporate entity (e.g. Israel, a pious remnant within Israel),[21] mythologically (reflecting the Babylonian myth of the dying and rising God), and as the Messiah (possibly combining the servant with the Davidic Messiah in Isaiah 9 and 11).[22] Others have combined these. Kittel and Rudolph argued that the servant was both an anonymous historical figure and a messianic one.[23] Delitzsch famously spoke of a pyramid, with all Israel as the base, the remnant as the centre section, and 'the apex [as] the person of the Mediator of salvation springing out of Israel'.[24]

> The figure of the Servant is a very fluid one; it seems to refer now to one thing, now to another; and any attempt to interpret it too rigidly will do violence to the evidence and

Testament (London: SCM Press, 1955), 66. Still of great help are two older surveys: North, *Suffering Servant*; Harold H. Rowley, *The Servant of the Lord and Other Essays on the Old Testament* (Oxford: Blackwell, 1952), 3–60.

17.   Cf. B. Duhm, *Das Buch Jesaia* (4th edn.; Göttingen: Vandenhoeck & Ruprecht, 1922).

18.   North, *Suffering Servant*, 127–38.

19.   The singular noun, עֶבֶד, appears 20 times in Isaiah 40–55 (41.8-9; 42.1, 19 (2×); 43.10; 44.1-2, 21 (2×), 26; 45.4; 48.20; 49.3, 5-7; 50.10; 52.13; 53.11), only six of which appear in Duhm's account of the servant songs (42.1; 49.3, 5, 6; 52.13; 53.11). The term is absent from Duhm's third song (50.4-9), although it appears in 50.10, as has been noted by Harry M. Orlinsky, 'The So-Called "Servant of the Lord" and "Suffering Servant" in Second Isaiah', in *Studies on the Second Part of the Book of Isaiah*, 90 and Snaith, 'Servant', 168. See also Hugh G. M. Williamson, *Variations on a Theme: King, Messiah and Servant in the Book of Isaiah* (Carlisle: Paternoster, 1998), 131.

20.   A single identity for the servant in these passages had not been insisted on prior to Duhm. North, *Suffering Servant*, 46. So e.g. Calvin understands 42.1 to speak of Christ, but 49.3 to speak of the church. John Calvin, *Commentary on the Book of the Prophet Isaiah* (Calvin's Commentaries 8; Grand Rapids: Baker, 1979; repr. of Calvin Translation Society edn, Edinburgh, 1845–56), 3.284 and 4.11–12.

21.   See especially Henry Wheeler Robinson, *Corporate Personality in Ancient Israel* (rev. edn.; Philadelphia: Fortress, 1980); Robinson, *Cross*, 75–79.

22.   North, *Suffering Servant*, 64–68.

23.   North, *Suffering Servant*, 85–88.

24.   Franz Delitzsch, *Isaiah* (Commentary on the Old Testament; Grand Rapids: Eerdmans, 1975), 2.174. See also Joseph Addison Alexander, *Commentary on the Prophecies of Isaiah* (2 vols.; new and rev. edn.; New York: Charles Scribner's Sons, 1865), 2.128; Walter C. Kaiser, Jr., *Mission in the Old Testament: Israel as a Light to the Nations* (Grand Rapids: Baker, 2000), 56; Edward J. Young, *The Book of Isaiah* (3 vols.; NICOT; Grand Rapids: Eerdmans, 1965–72), 3.109, n. 1.

almost certainly distort what the prophet wished to say … . The figure of the servant oscillates between the individual and the group.[25]

Insisting on a single identity for the servant virtually demands a 'fluid' understanding, since the servant clearly appears in some texts to be an individual but in others to be Israel.

Unfortunately, as North has observed, 'there is no theory that has been altogether immune from criticism'.[26] The absence of consensus suggests that the whole question may need to be reexamined, particularly the isolation of these texts from their present contexts[27] and the assumption that the songs all speak of a single servant. John Goldingay has recently called both assumptions into question, arguing that 'the separation of these passages from their literary contexts seems to have made it impossible to answer the question regarding their reference' and that 'the assumption prevalent since Duhm that the four passages must have the same reference needs to be regarded as an open question'.[28] Such a reexamination is beyond the scope of the present study, but we will follow Goldingay's lead and attempt to read Isa. 42.6; 49.6 in their present contexts, with the servant's identity as an open question.

A scholarly impasse sometimes indicates the need for a fresh look at the data. A cursory survey, summarized in Table 3.1, finds over 100 references to a servant of Yahweh (rather than a human master) in the MT: 'my servant' (עַבְדִּי, with לִי עֶבֶד only in Isa. 44.21; 49.6; cf. Lev. 25.55); 'his servant' (עַבְדּוֹ, with לוֹ עֶבֶד only in Isa. 49.5), 'your servant' (עַבְדְּךָ), and 'servant of Yahweh' (עֶבֶד יְהוָה). (Pronoun antecedents were determined from the contexts.)

Table 3.1

	My	His	Your	Yahweh's	Total
Abraham	1	3			4
Moses	6	5	8	9	28
Caleb	1				1
Joshua		1			1
David	23	4	1	1	29
Solomon		1			1
Hezekiah		1			1
Isaiah	1				1

25. John Bright, *The Kingdom of God: The Biblical Concept and Its Meaning for the Church* (Nashville: Abingdon, 1953), 150.

26. North, *Suffering Servant*, 209.

27. Some scholars have noted important connections between the servant songs and other portions of Isaiah 40–55. Morna D. Hooker, *Jesus and the Servant: The Influence of the Servant Concept of Deutero-Isaiah in the New Testament* (London: SPCK, 1959), 27–30; Johannes Lindblom, *The Servant Songs in Deutero-Isaiah* (Lund: Gleerup, 1951), 52–64.

28. John Goldingay, *The Message of Isaiah 40–55: A Literary-Theological Commentary* (London: T&T Clark, 2005), 150. See also Hans M. Barstad, 'The Future of the "Servant Songs": Some Reflections on the Relationship of Biblical Scholarship to Its Own Tradition', in *Language, Theology, and the Bible: Essays in Honor of James Barr* (ed. Samuel E. Balentine and John Barton; Oxford: Clarendon, 1994), 261–70; Lindblom, *Servant Songs*; Orlinsky, 'Servant', 12–16; Williamson, *Variations*, 130–31, 141.

	My	His	Your	Yahweh's	Total
A prophet		7			7
Job	6				6
Nebuchadnezzar	3				3
Anonymous			2	1	3
Jacob (as individual)	2				2
Israel	11	2			13
The Isaianic Servant	5	2			7
The 'Branch'	1				1
Total					**108**

Clear patterns are evident. Moses and David are the servants of Yahweh *par excellence*, with Israel a distant third and other prophets and kings forming a small part of the background. Viewing these as a whole, we see that Yahweh's servant is chosen for a special role in the accomplishing of his redemptive purposes: 'a master chooses a servant to get a job done'.[29] The servant is typically the object of Yahweh's affection and regard (but see Nebuchadnezzar, Jer. 25.9; 27.6; 43.10).[30] Pending detailed study of any particular text, we would expect these things generally to be true of Yahweh's servant.

3.2.2 *Isaiah 42.6*

'"I will give you for a covenant to the people, to be a light to the nations." This formula is so central, and yet so difficult to grasp in its precise significance!'[31] The expression 'a light to the nations' appears only in Isa. 49.6 and 42.6.[32] At least in the present form of the book, Isa. 42.6 forms part of the background of 49.6.

In 42.1-4, Yahweh addresses his servant, whom he 'upholds' and has chosen, and in whom he delights (1a). The servant has a task to perform, to 'bring forth' (יוֹצִיא) and 'establish' (יָשִׂים) justice (מִשְׁפָּט), through application of God's law ('instruction', תּוֹרָה).[33] These are royal responsibilities and imply that the servant is a royal figure.[34] The goal is universal: the servant is to bring justice 'to the

29.   John Goldingay and David Payne, *A Critical and Exegetical Commentary on Isaiah 40–55* (ICC; London: T&T Clark, 2006), 1.52.

30.   Contrary to the impression given by the literature, the title 'servant' is never applied to Cyrus, who is mentioned by name in Isaiah only in 44.28; 45.1. The same observation has been made by Goldingay, *Isaiah 40–55*, 151; Orlinsky, 'Servant', 96.

31.   Klaus Baltzer, *Deutero-Isaiah: A Commentary on Isaiah 40–55* (trans. Margaret Kohl; Hermeneia; Minneapolis: Fortress, 2001), 131. 'The phrases are rich and suggestive, but their precise intent is unclear.' Walter Brueggemann, *Isaiah* (2 vols.; Westminster Bible Companion; Louisville: Westminster John Knox, 1998), 2.44.

32.   A similar expression appears in Isa. 51.4, where the LXX reads εἰς φῶς ἐθνῶν (although the MT there has עַמִּים instead of גּוֹיִם, and it is not the servant, but God's justice that will be a light). The context shares key terms and expressions with 42.6 and 49.6, including תּוֹרָה (42.4), מִשְׁפָּט (43.1, 4), יֶשַׁע (49.6), and the expectation by 'the coastlands' (cf. 42.4; 49.1). Isaiah 51.4 forms part of the complex of ideas to which Isa. 49.6 and 42.6 belong.

33.   'Justice' is more than exacting legal compliance; it is restorative as things are put right as God intends. B. Johnson, *TDOT*, s.v. מִשְׁפָּט, 92–93.

34.   Williamson argues that מִשְׁפָּט and תּוֹרָה refer to the royal function of 'administering, upholding and even initiating justice', particularly on behalf of 'those least able to defend themselves, such as the orphan and the widow'. Williamson, *Variations*, 135–39. See also Goldingay and Payne, *Isaiah*

nations' (לַגּוֹיִם) and establish justice 'in the earth' (בָּאָרֶץ). Even 'the coastlands (אִיִּים) wait for (LXX ἐλπιοῦσιν) his law'.[35] For this task, the servant has been endowed with Yahweh's Spirit (1b).[36] The servant labours faithfully, despite apparent failure and discouragement, until he accomplishes his mission (4).

Duhm and others terminate the first servant song with v. 4,[37] but others have recently argued that the first song continues through v. 9.[38] In these verses, Yahweh is described in universal terms that match the universal scope of the servant's mission.[39] In v. 6, Yahweh announces four actions with four verbs. First, he has 'called' ('commissioned')[40] his servant 'in righteousness' (6a), i.e. for the righteous, 'saving' purpose of Yahweh.[41] The next two verbs describe Yahweh's care for his servant (6b, c).[42] The fourth verb introduces the servant's mission: 'I have given you' to be 'a covenant to the people, a light to the nations' (6d-e).[43]

40–55, 1.209. However, the focus is more on the task to be performed than on the identity of the servant. 'The passage's own key word is not *'ebed* but *mišpāṭ'*. Goldingay and Payne, *Isaiah 40–55*, 213; Williamson, *Variations*, 146.

35.   Although בָּאָרֶץ could be translated 'in the land', references here to the 'nations' and the 'coastlands' indicate that a broader reference is in view. The 'coastlands' are distant and so here imply a universal application of torah. 'Coastlands' parallel 'the ends of the earth' in 41.5; 42.10; 'peoples from afar' in 49.1; cf. 'the coastland across the sea' (Jer. 25.22).

36.   The Spirit is given in the OT for leadership (Num. 11.25, 29), especially in war (Num. 27.18; Deut. 34.9; Judg. 6.34; Judg. 14.6, 9; 1 Sam. 16.3; cf. Isa. 28.6), service (Exod. 31.3; 35.31; 1 Chr. 12.18), and prophecy (1 Sam. 10.6, 10; 19.23; Mic. 3.8; Neh. 9.20). The Spirit is especially associated with eschatological blessings, including new creation (Isa. 32.15; 44.3; 63.11, 14; Ezek. 11.19; 36.27; 37.14; 39.29; Joel 3.1-2 MT; Zech. 4.6).

37.   North, *Suffering Servant*, 131–35.

38.   Yahweh speaks first about the servant (1-4), then to the servant (5-9). J. Alec Motyer, *The Prophecy of Isaiah* (Downers Grove, Ill.: InterVarsity, 1993), 318. See also Baltzer, *Deutero-Isaiah*, 124–37; Lindblom, *Servant Songs*, 23. For the view that 5-9 is a separate oracle, see Claus Westermann, *Isaiah 40–66* (trans. David M. G. Stalker; OTL; Philadelphia: Westminster, 1969), 98; Roger N. Whybray, *The Second Isaiah* (OTG; Sheffield: JSOT Press, 1983).

39.   Yahweh created the heavens, the earth, and everything (or everyone?) in it (42:5). The Hebrew צֶאֱצָא (RSV 'and what comes from it') is most often rendered 'offspring' (i.e. of men). Of 11 instances in the MT (only Isaiah and Job), BDB proposes 'produce' only here and at Isa. 34.1. In the latter verse Yahweh gives life to all people on earth ('who gives breath to the people upon it and spirit to those who walk in it'), supporting a reference to people rather than produce. Verses 8-9 continue the universal orientation, echoing themes from elsewhere in Isaiah. There is no other god (43.10-13; 45.5-7, 14, 18-21; 46.5-11). Only Yahweh can declare things before they happen (41.21-29; 43.9-13; 44.6-8; 45.18-21; 46.5-11; 48.3-8, 14). He will not share his glory with others (48.11), particularly images (40.18-20; 41.29; 42.17; 44.9-20; 45.16, 20-21; 46.1; 48.5; 57.13; 66.3).

40.   Perhaps 'summoned' or 'invited'. BDB, s.v. קרא, 5.

41.   In this way God's 'righteous purposes are fulfilled'. Motyer, *Prophecy*, 322. 'The servant's mission is rooted and grounded in God's righteousness.' Young, *Isaiah*, 3.118. 'In the book of Isaiah, "righteousness" means help, salvation, and peace for the downtrodden. No one except the Messiah can and will establish it among his people and the nations.' Markus Barth, *Ephesians: A New Translation with Introduction and Commentary* (2 vols.; AB 34–34A; New York: Doubleday, 1974), 796.

42.   To 'hold the hand' is an expression of tender care (Ps 73.23; 139.10). The other verb (וְאֶצָּרְךָ) could be derived from נצר ('to keep') or יצר ('to form'). The former would indicate God's preservation and the latter God's creation of the servant; either way, God's care is evident. Motyer, *Prophecy*, 322; Young, *Isaiah*, 3.119.

43.   'Given' (נתן) with לְ likely bears the sense of 'assign, designate' or 'make, constitute', and is

'People' (עַם) in the expression 'a covenant to the people' is often understood as referring to Israel.[44] This is supported by the consistent use of the singular of עַם for Israel in Isaiah 40–66,[45] the conjunction with 'covenant' (normally associated with Israel), and the application of the same expression to Israel in 49.8. In this case, the twofold character of the servant is highlighted: to Israel (עַם) and the nations (גּוֹיִם). However, עַם may refer to the people of another nation,[46] to people generally (e.g. Isa. 13.4; 25.3), or to all people on earth (e.g. Isa. 24.4).[47] The broader use (for 'all people on earth') in 42.5[48] and the parallel with גּוֹיִם in 42.6 suggest the broader sense here.[49] Either way, the Gentiles are included in the servant's ministry. The phrase לִבְרִית עָם has been variously rendered 'covenant people',[50] an 'obligation' to the world,[51] 'a confederation of peoples',[52] and 'splendour of the people',[53] but more likely indicates the means by which Yahweh's

---

thus roughly parallel to 'call' in 6a. BDB, s.v. נתן, *Qal* 2.d., 3.b. 'We might also compare its use to denote the "appointing" of someone to a position or task (cf. Ezra 8.20).' Goldingay and Payne, *Isaiah 40–55*, 1.227.

44.   As in Isa. 40.7; 42.22; 43.8. Delitzsch, *Isaiah*, 179; Jan Ridderbos, *Isaiah* (trans. John Vriend; Grand Rapids: Zondervan, 1984), 379; Snaith, 'Servant', 158; Young, *Isaiah*, 3.119–20. Some MSS of the LXX seem to share this view, inserting μου after γένους in 42:6. 'My people' would normally suggest Israel. Lindblom believes that 'if the author had meant the nation of Israel, he would surely have written העם or something else unmistakably pointing to Israel'. Lindblom, *Servant Songs*, 21.

45.   Snaith, 'Servant', 157. The only exceptions are Isa. 40.7 (which Snaith believes is a gloss) and 42.5.

46.   E.g. Gen. 19.4; 23.7; Isa. 1.10 (Gomorrah); 14.20 (Babylon); 18.2, 7 (Cush?); 23.13 (Babylon); 33.19 (Babylon?); 34.5 (Edom).

47.   The translation of אֶרֶץ here must be 'earth' rather than 'land', in light of the association of 'heaven' with אֶרֶץ earlier in the verse and the fact that God 'gives breath' not only to Israel, but to all who live (cf. Isa. 2.22).

48.   Julian Morgenstern, 'The Rest of the Nations', *JSS* 2 (1957): 225–31; James Muilenberg, 'The Book of Isaiah: Chapters 40–66', *IB* 5; North, *Suffering Servant*; Charles Cutler Torrey, *The Composition and Date of Acts* (Cambridge, Mass.: Harvard University Press, 1916).

49.   'The referent of "people" (*'am*) is most plausibly the same as that found in the preceding verse, namely, all the inhabitants of the earth, a meaning supported by the parallel "nations" that immediately follows.' Paul D. Hanson, *Isaiah 40–66* (IBC; Louisville: John Knox, 1995), 46. See also Baltzer, *Deutero-Isaiah*, 132; Brevard S. Childs, *Isaiah: A Commentary* (OTL; Louisville: Westminster John Knox, 2001), 326; Lindblom, *Servant Songs*, 21; Motyer, *Prophecy*, 332; Westermann, *Isaiah 40–66*, 99–100; Roger N. Whybray, *Isaiah 40–66* (NCB; London: Oliphants, 1975), 74–75. While עם and גוי are often opposed (e.g. Num. 23.9; Deut. 4.6; 2 Sam. 7.23), they also appear in parallel (e.g. Deut. 3.8; Mic. 5.8; Hag. 2.14; Ps. 96.3; and especially Isa. 2.4; 11.10; 14.6; 25.7; 30.28; 33.3; 49.22; 61.9), including parallels between the singular עם and the plural גוים (e.g. Exod. 34.10; Ps. 18.4).

50.   Israel W. Slotki, *Isaiah: Hebrew Text and English Translation with an Introduction and Commentary* (Soncino Books of the Bible; London: Soncino, 1949), 200. The syntax, however, seems to prevent this reading.

51.   'He is to be the agent who imposes Yahweh's obligations upon them.' Whybray, *Isaiah 40–66*, 75. 'The nations of the world will be obliged to accept Yahweh's sovereignty, of which they will now become aware for the first time (hence *a light*), and will thus be forced to accept the obligation (*bᵉrît* which he imposes on them.'

52.   '"The called" will grow into a large assembly of peoples bound together, of course, by the same faith and a common subjection to Yahweh, Israel's God.' Lindblom, *Servant Songs*, 21.

53.   Deriving בְּרִית in this case from a root meaning 'shine'. North, *Suffering Servant*, 133.

covenant is fulfilled. Goldingay understands the expression as a metonomy comparable to light to the nations or Abraham's becoming a blessing: 'In each case the idea is that the person not only mediates but also embodies the thing.'[54]

Light (6e) is associated throughout Isaiah with Yahweh's salvation and blessing,[55] a fit accompaniment to the joy of those rescued from the darkness of anguish, gloom and oppression (9.2; 59.9). Supernatural brightness, with abundant and life-giving water, accompanies Yahweh's healing of his wounded people (30.26). He gives light to those who are blind and have lost their way in darkness (42.16), metaphors in Isaiah for spiritual ignorance, calamity and judgement.[56] Israel is called to 'walk in the light of the Lord' (2.5), as his law (or instruction) is made known to the nations. Light comes not merely from awareness of Yahweh's will, but from his liberating and restorative justice (מִשְׁפָּט) (51.4; 59.9). Light evokes the glory Yahweh will give to his restored people (58.8, 10; 60.1, 3), which is ultimately the glory of the presence of Yahweh himself ('for the LORD will be your everlasting light', 60.19-20). The servant thus brings deliverance. 'Light to the nations' is thus tantamount to 'salvation to all the world'.

Some have sought to limit the seeming universalism of 'light to the nations'. Rashi applied *goyim* here to Israel.[57] Snaith understands the light as a beacon for Jewish exiles scattered among the nations; Israel will experience salvation while the nations only 'see' it.[58] However, Koole observes that 'in DI גוים always means the other nations and never Israel'.[59] Goldingay notes that texts such as Isa. 45.22; 42.10 envision that the nations experience God's salvation.[60]

In Isa. 42.6, the servant is distinguished from both the nations (cf. 1) and the people (cf. 5). His accomplishments, bringing forth and establishing justice (1, 4), are nowhere predicated of Israel, but are the responsibilities of the king.[61] 'His

54. Goldingay, *Isaiah 40–55*, 164. 'The one commissioned does not form a covenant, but rather embodies a covenantal relationship with the nations.' Childs, *Isaiah*, 326.

55. 'We may take the two ['light' and 'salvation'] as rough synonyms, both of them referring to the full offer of well-being as intended by the creator.' Brueggemann, *Isaiah*, 2.112.

56. Snaith understands blindness and imprisonment to refer to the exile. Snaith, 'Servant', 158. This does not fit Isaiah's use of the terms, however. For blindness and darkness as metaphors for spiritual ignorance, see Isa. 29.18; 35.5; 42.16, 18-19; 43.8; 56.10; 59.10; and as metaphors for judgement, see Isa. 5.20, 30; 8.22; 9.1; 29.18; 45.7; 47.5; 49.9; 50.10; 58.10; 59.9; 60.2.

57. Jan L. Koole, *Isaiah, Part 3* (trans. Anthony P. Runia; 3 vols.; Kampen: Kok Pharos, 1997–2001), 1.233.

58. Snaith, 'Servant', 156–57. Orlinsky argues that the expression 'must be understood strictly within the limits of Judean nationalism' and that 'the verses that precede and follow our own make it amply clear that Israel alone is to benefit from God's actions'. Orlinsky, 'Servant', 111–14. (He does not address the seemingly universal references in 42.1, 4, 5, 10, 12.) 'In a word: Israel will be "a light of nations" in the sense that Israel will dazzle the nations with her God-given triumph and restoration; the whole world will behold this single beacon that is God's sole covenanted people.' Orlinsky, 'Servant', 117.

59. 'Our v., too, must mean that the nations not only perceive Israel's salvation, but also share in the great liberation.' Koole, *Isaiah*, 1.233.

60. John Goldingay, *Isaiah* (NIBCOT 13; Peabody, Mass.: Hendrickson, 2001), 283.

61. Isa. 9.7; 11.3-5; 16.5; 32.1; 2 Sam. 8.15; 1 Kgs. 10.9; Ps. 72.1; Jer. 22.15; 23.5; Prov. 29.4. Williamson argues that the servant is a royal figure, but understands the royal language to apply to Israel's role vis-à-vis the nations. Williamson, *Variations*, 132, 139–46.

law' (תּוֹרָתוֹ) is Yahweh's law, not Israel's. The 'blind' in Isaiah are most often Israel and, if so, cannot be the sight-giving servant as well (42.7). The servant is distinguished from Israel and is most plausibly an individual.[62]

3.2.3 *Isaiah 49.6*

There is no consensus on the boundaries of the unit to which Isa. 49.6 belongs. While many follow Duhm in limiting the song to vv. 1-6,[63] others have extended the song through v. 9a or 13.[64] Many also follow Duhm in isolating the song from its present context,[65] although others have identified important connections to the immediately preceding and following contexts.[66] Verses 1-6 are distinguished by the voice of the servant speaking in the first person, in contrast with the verses that precede or follow.[67] Although in vv. 5-6 Yahweh speaks, this speech is reported by the servant. Yet it appears that Yahweh continues to speak through v. 9a to 'you' (masculine singular), the servant whom he has chosen (7), answered, helped, kept, and given a unique role (8-9a). The following verses (9b-13) then appear to describe those who are brought out of prison and their return to the land. Even then it is not clear that we have reached the end of the text; the following verses (even into the opening verses of Isaiah 50) continue the assurance that Yahweh will restore his people as he promised in 49.9 (continuing the thought, if not the song).[68] Nevertheless, the focus of 49.1-13 is on the servant, while the focus after 49.14 is on Zion and its restoration, and so we can regard 49.1-13 as the primary context for Isa. 49.6.

Following the proclamation of Yahweh's victory over Babylon (chs 46–48), Isaiah 49 issues its call to the 'coastlands' and 'peoples from afar' to listen to the servant's words. The servant has been 'called' and 'named' by Yahweh from before birth (1).[69] The servant is described as a weapon carefully prepared for use – a sharp sword, a polished arrow (2). The reason for concealing the weapons is

---

62.   See the careful argument of Orlinsky, 'Servant', 76–79. His arguments do not, however, establish the individual as the prophet himself. The Targum understands him to be an individual, designating him by adding the word *mšyh*? Goldingay and Payne, *Isaiah 40–55*, 1.213.

63.   Motyer, *Prophecy*, 383; Slotki, *Isaiah*, 239; Whybray, *Isaiah 40–66*, 135.

64.   Ridderbos recognizes a change in speaker with v. 7, but believes that the servant is still in view, as the prophet speaks of him or to him through 9a. Ridderbos, *Isaiah*. Those who extend the text through v. 13, including Hanson, *Isaiah 40–66*, 126–33; Westermann, *Isaiah 40–66*, 213; Young, *Isaiah*, 3.276–83.

65.   Whybray, *Isaiah 40–66*.

66.   For connections to the preceding context, see Motyer, *Prophecy*, 383–84; Huub van de Sandt, 'The Quotations in Acts 13,32-52 as a Reflection of Luke's LXX Interpretation', *Bib* 75 (1994): 51. Lindblom sees 49.1-7 related both to 48.20-21 and to 49.8-21. Lindblom, *Servant Songs*, 27–32.

67.   The later verses are 'a response on the Lord's part to the utterance of the servant'. Young, *Isaiah*, 277.

68.   Curiously, in 50.4-9 (or 4-11?) the third song (the only other one to be written in the first person) also affirms God's eventual vindication despite present suffering. Might the whole of 49.1–50.11 be a single unit?

69.   Cf. Isa. 44.2; Jer. 1.5; Gal. 1.15.

not clear, although protection and preparation have been suggested.[70] At a minimum, these expressions indicate Yahweh's care and preparation.

Despite Yahweh's call and care, the servant's mission proves difficult. 'I have labored in vain, I have spent my strength for nothing and vanity' (4). The cause of frustration is not stated, but there may be a hint in v. 3, which speaks of 'Israel, in whom I will be glorified'. In fact, Yahweh has *not* been glorified through Israel, but 'continually all the day my name is despised' (52.5). Isaiah had also experienced frustration. He was called to

> 'Go, and say to this people: "Hear and hear, but do not understand; see and see, but do not perceive." ... lest they see with their eyes, and hear with their ears, and understand with their hearts, and turn and be healed.' (Isa. 6.9-10)

Israel did not listen (28.12; 30.9; 65.12; 66.4) and, although Isaiah does not reveal his feelings, it cannot have been easy. Jeremiah was sent to preach to an unresponsive people (7.27), and he complained bitterly to Yahweh (20.7-10, 14-18; 15.10, 17-18). Here, Yahweh responds to the servant's complaint with the assurances of 49.5-6.[71]

These assurances include the promise that God will use his servant to restore Israel. His mission is 'to bring Jacob back to him, and that Israel might be gathered to him' (5), 'to raise up the tribes of Jacob and to restore the preserved of Israel' (6), to be 'a covenant to the people',[72] and 'to establish the land, to apportion the desolate heritages; saying to the prisoners, "Come forth", to those who are in darkness, "Appear"' (8-9). The restoration includes return from exile and restoration as a coherent state, but the promised restoration is never merely geographical and/or political;[73] it is primarily about restoring Israel to God himself ('to him' twice in 49.5[74]). The exile had a spiritual cause (faithlessness to Yahweh and his covenant) and was a spiritual punishment (separation from Yahweh, Isa. 54.8; Jer. 52.3). The return is above all a return to blessing in Yahweh's presence as his people.[75]

---

70. Ridderbos, *Isaiah*, 434–35; Young, *Isaiah*, 3.268.

71. Young, *Isaiah*, 3.273.

72. 'The people' here is Israel in light of 'the land', the apportioning of 'desolate heritages', and the summoning of (exiled) prisoners. Koole, *Isaiah*, 1.230; Motyer, *Prophecy*, 322, 391. See also Isa. 42.6 (section 3.2.2 above).

73. Whybray wrongly claims that 'salvation' 'generally in Deutero-Isaiah denotes not spiritual blessings but Yahweh's coming victory over Babylon'. Whybray, *Isaiah 40–66*, 139.

74. In the second instance, *Qere* לוֹ ('to him') in place of לֹא ('not'). Reading לֹא, Calvin saw an indication of Israel's 'rejection', although he granted that 'it cannot necessarily be proved from the context [of Acts 13.47] that Paul affirms that the Gentiles were not to be enlightened until the light had been extinguished for the Jews'. John Calvin, *Acts 14–28* (trans. John W. Fraser; Calvin's New Testament Commentaries; Grand Rapids: Eerdmans, 1995), 391–92. The *Qere* is supported by 1QIsa[a] and other versions. If לֹא is the correct text, Whybray believes the verb 'must not mean "gather" but "sweep away": "that Israel might not be swept away."' Whybray, *Isaiah 40–66*, 139. However, this substitution appears in a number of texts (see BDB, s.v. לֹא, Note.) The parallelism with אֵלָיו in the previous line makes לוֹ here 'undoubtedly correct'. Motyer, *Prophecy*, 387, n. 2.

75. See also the prominence of spiritual restoration in Deut. 30.1-10; Ezek. 36.24-36; Joel 2.18-32.

Grammatically, the interpretation of Isa. 49.6 begins with v. 5, where the speaker of v. 6 is identified. It is Yahweh, who has formed the servant in the womb for his purpose[76] (i.e. to gather and restore Jacob/Israel) and who continues to honour and strengthen his servant. It is Yahweh's regard for the servant that leads to the expanded mission of v. 6. It is, first of all, 'to raise up the tribes of Jacob and to restore (לְהָשִׁיב) the preserved[77] of Israel'. But Yahweh's desire to honour his servant means that it is not enough for the servant only to be the agent of Israel's restoration. That would be נָקֵל, 'trifling' or 'too small or insignificant'.[78] Instead, Yahweh will make his servant a 'light to/for the nations' (לְאוֹר גּוֹיִם).

On the basis of Isa. 42.6, we would expect this expression to refer to release from the darkness of spiritual ignorance and oppression into the salvation of God, a salvation now extended, not only to the descendants of Abraham, but to Gentiles.[79] This is supported by the purpose clause[80] that follows: לִהְיוֹת יְשׁוּעָתִי עַד־קְצֵה הָאָרֶץ ('that my salvation may reach[81] to the end of the earth').[82]

In Isaiah, God's salvation often looks toward both deliverance from the Assyrian threat or Babylonian captivity and a more comprehensive deliverance. In 25.9, God's awaited salvation includes a feast in Jerusalem 'for all nations' and fulfilment of the promise that God 'will swallow up death for ever, and ... wipe away tears from all faces' (25.6, 8). Isaiah 51.4-6 joins three major elements of Isa. 49.6 (light, salvation and the nations): 'a law will go forth from me, and my justice for a light to the peoples' (עַמִּים); 'my salvation has gone forth ...

Young goes too far when he claims 'the reference is not to a return from Babylon, but a spiritual return to God'. Young, *Isaiah*, 3.273–74. Conversely, North wrongly believes the mission of the servant is primarily political. North, *Suffering Servant*, 145–46. The two are intimately related.

76.   Cf. Jer. 1.5; Ps. 22.9; 71.6; 139.13.

77.   'Preserved' translates the *Qere* נְצוּרֵי, the *qal* passive participle of נצר; the *Kethiv* נְצִירֵי, an adjective occuring only here, has the same general meaning. *BHS* margin conjectures נֵצֶרֵי, from נצר ('branch'). The noun is used only four times in the MT (Isa. 11.1; 14.19; 60.21; Dan. 11.7) and never with the sense of 'descendants'. The LXX's τὴν διασποράν may reflect uncertainty about נְצִירֵי and the reasoning that, if Israel was to be 'gathered' (5), it must first be scattered (διασπείρω is used of the 'scattering' of exile in Deut. 4.27; 28.64; 30.3).

78.   BDB, s.v. קלל; *HALOT*, s.v. קלל; Young, *Isaiah*, 3.275. See 1 Kgs. 16.31. What is 'trivial' is not being Yahweh's servant, but being the agent of 'only' the restoration of Israel. Koole, *Isaiah*, 2.21–22.

79.   'The genitive construction אוֹר גּוֹיִם = "light of the nations", means not only that the nations (with the exiles) see salvation, 52.10, but that God's intervention brings about their own salvation, 51.4f.' Koole, *Isaiah*, 2.23.

80.   Bruce K. Waltke and Michael P. O'Connor, *An Introduction to Biblical Hebrew Syntax* (Winona Lake, Ind.: Eisenbrauns, 1990), §36.2.3d; Ronald J. Williams, *Hebrew Syntax: An Outline* (2nd edn.; Toronto: University of Toronto Press, 1976), §520.

81.   Thus RSV's interpretation of לִהְיוֹת, inferring that for God's salvation to 'be' to the end of the earth, it must be extended there. Others personalize the translation: 'that you may bring my salvation' (NIV); 'that thou mightest be my salvation' (Young, *Isaiah*, 3.276).

82.   The expression קְצֵה הָאָרֶץ appears eight times in Isaiah 40–66, three times in the plural (40.28; 41.5, 9) and four others (as in 49.6) in the singular (42.10; 43.6; 48.20; 62.11). The end(s) of the earth are created by Yahweh (40.28); tremble before his judgement (41.5); are the place from which he has gathered (41.9) or will gather (43.6) his people; will hear that he has redeemed his people (48.20; 62.11); and will give him praise (42.10).

my salvation will be for ever, and my deliverance will never be ended'; 'and my arms will rule the peoples (עַמִּים); the coastlands wait for me'. The universality of the promise of salvation in Isa. 49.6 also looks forward to a greater salvation.

The universal dimension of the servant's ministry is not at the expense of Israel. The servant's initial calling is 'to bring Jacob back to him, and that Israel might be gathered to him' (49.5) and 'to restore the preserved of Israel' (49.6) – and this calling will be fulfilled (vv. 8-13). Nor is it prompted by divine rejection of Israel (or the initial fruitlessness of the servant's ministry to Israel), but by God's desire to bestow even greater honour on his servant (49.5–6, especially 6b). The mission to Israel remains first, not only in time, but of necessity, because it is the means by which God will glorify himself and win the worship of the nations.

> Clearly the Servant's work for Israel will affect the whole world. After her redemption Israel will call other nations to her, and they will come running (55.3-5). In response to Yahweh's invitation to turn to him and be saved (45.14, 22), the nations will bow down before the Lord's people (45.14; cf. 49.23), acknowledging that there is no other God than Yahweh and he is certainly with them.[83]

> The final goal will be a redeemed humanity. Israel will be the center of a confederation of peoples, subject to Yahweh, the God of Israel and Creator of heaven and earth ... The realizing of that goal will imply both the glorifying of Yahweh and the exaltation of Israel, the people of Yahweh.[84]

Who is the servant? Verse 3 seems plain enough: 'You are my servant, Israel, in whom I will be glorified' (עַבְדִּי־אָתָּה יִשְׂרָאֵל אֲשֶׁר־בְּךָ אֶתְפָּאָר).[85] Yet, although the language of calling and forming from the womb can be applied to Israel (44.2, 22, 24),[86] its use in 49.1, 5 most naturally suggests an individual (Jer. 1.5). In 49.5-6, the servant seems clearly to be an individual, who is distinguished *from* Israel and given a mission *to* Israel.[87] The comprehensive, universal scope of the mission strongly suggests that the servant is an eschatological figure.[88] If the servant has a broader reference, it is not to Israel, but to those other royal and prophetic servants of Yahweh who contributed to the ultimate fulfilment of the servant's mission.

---

83. Andreas J. Köstenberger and Peter T. O'Brien, *Salvation to the Ends of the Earth: A Biblical Theology of Mission* (New Studies in Biblical Theology 11; Downers Grove, Ill.: InterVarsity, 2001), 48.

84. Lindblom, *Servant Songs*, 53. The citation is from Lindblom's summary of the teaching of the servant songs, not a comment on this text in particular. Lindblom views Israel having been given the calling of the servant 'to mediate welfare to' and 'be a witness among the pagans to faith in Yahweh' (52).

85. Lindblom, who believes that the prophet is addressed in these verses, believes the text should be read 'you, my servant, you are (i.e. symbolize) Israel'. Lindblom, *Servant Songs*, 30.

86. Young, *Isaiah*, 3.273.

87. Some have sought to resolve the difficulty by removing יִשְׂרָאֵל from v. 5, but textual support for the omission is limited to a single medieval manuscript. See the arguments in Orlinsky, 'Servant', 80–89.

88. Dirk H. Odendaal, *The Eschatological Expectation of Isaiah 40–66 with Special Reference to Israel and the Nations* (Nutley, NJ: Presbyterian and Reformed, 1970), 135.

> The return from exile is part of the same redemptive work of God of which Christ's coming in the flesh is the focus. Fundamentally, the work done by men like Zerubbabel, Joshua, and Ezra in bringing Israel back is the work of the Servant of the Lord; they were His instruments, and at the same time they prefigured Him.[89]

3.2.4 *Summary*

On two occasions, and particularly in Isa. 49.6, the Isaianic servant is designated by God as 'a light to the nations'. This light is, in Brueggemann's phrase, a 'rough synonym'[90] for salvation in Isaiah. The servant is to bring this salvation, not only to Israel, but also to the nations. We can note a number of elements common to these texts.

1. The servant is the object of Yahweh's special regard and care (49.1-2, 5-6; 42.1, 6).
2. He has been called and appointed to his task by Yahweh (49.1; 42.1, 6).
3. The servant faces difficult challenges, frustration, and even apparent failure in the fulfilment of his divinely appointed mission to Israel (49.4; 42.3-4). Yet in the midst of this experience, Yahweh assigns his servant a broader, seemingly universal mission (49.6).
4. The results of the servant's ministry are, in the general sense, salvific (49.6): eyes opened (42.7), prisoners released (49.9; 42.7), Israel restored (49.8), a new Exodus (49.10-13).
5. This ministry has a universal scope. In ch. 49, he addresses the 'coast-lands' and 'peoples from afar' (1) and his salvation reaches 'to the end to the earth' (6) in such a way that he receives obeisance from 'kings' and 'princes' (7) while heaven and earth join in praising God (13). In ch. 42, he is called by the creator of 'the heavens' and 'the earth' (5) and brings justice 'to the nations' (1), and 'the coastlands wait for his law' (4).
6. The servant appears to be an individual. In 42, he is distinguished from the nations and called to establish justice (1, 3, 4), a royal responsibility never ascribed to Israel. In 49, he has a mission to both Israel (5-6) and the nations (6).
7. Finally, in both passages and in Isaiah as a whole, the comprehensive nature of the salvation the servant brings strongly suggests the work of an eschatological figure.

In summary, 'the ʿEbed Yahweh is a royal, individual, eschatological figure, who is instrumental in bringing about the royal eschatological dominion of Yahweh'.[91]

---

89.   Ridderbos, *Isaiah*, 437.
90.   Brueggemann, *Isaiah*, 2.112.
91.   Odendaal, *Expectation*, 135.

3.3 *The Expected Servant*

Outside of Isaiah, there are no certain references in the OT to Isaiah's unnamed 'servant'[92] and the figure of the servant apparently does not appear in the apocrypha, pseudepigrapha[93] or (non-biblical) DSS. Nevertheless the Isaianic servant belongs to a larger complex of prophecies of restoration, renewal and conversion of the nations.[94] (Then again, the term 'Messiah' appears fewer than 40 times in the OT, and most of those in historical narratives, but few would deny the prevalence of messianic expectation.) The royal figure of Isaiah 9 and 11 has been associated with the servant of the latter chapters – both are endowed with the Spirit and bring light, justice, righteousness and release to the oppressed. Both David (Ezek. 34.23-24; 37.24-25) and Moses (Deut. 18.18-19), the preeminent OT servants of God, are models for or types of figures to come. Morna Hooker has noted close similarities between key themes in Isaiah 40–55 and those in Jeremiah 30–33 and Ezekiel 34–37.[95] The servant, and others of these themes, are picked up by Luke and other NT authors.

Scholars have found numerous echoes of the servant songs in Luke–Acts.[96] In Luke 4.16-30, Jesus applies the language of Isa. 61.1-2 to himself. Although the term 'servant' is not in Isaiah 61 and it is not commonly identified among the servant songs, Snaith finds that 'the characteristic phrasing is unmistakable'. 'The opening of His ministry, then, is said by Luke to be the fulfillment of that prophecy. This is the advent of the Servant of the LORD.'[97] Snaith also sees servant language in the account of Jesus' healings, particularly Luke 7.18-23,[98] Jesus'

---

92. Hooker, *Jesus and the Servant*, 53.

93. Hooker, *Jesus and the Servant*, 53–54. There is an allusion to Isa. 49.6 in *1 Enoch* 48.4, where the Son of Man (not explicitly the servant) is 'the light of the Gentiles'. Steyn, *Septuagint Quotations*, 197. There are occasional echoes, particularly to Isaiah 53, but these do not refer explicitly to the servant. Bernd Janowski and Peter Stuhlmacher, eds., *The Suffering Servant: Isaiah 53 in Jewish and Christian Sources* (trans. Daniel P. Bailey; Grand Rapids: Eerdmans, 2004).

94. 'This figure [i.e. the Servant of the Lord] embraces the entire messianic hope of the OT in all its depth, and Isaiah was permitted to see in this figure basic and essential features which seem to be based on a typological approach.' Leonhard Goppelt, *Typos: The Typological Interpretation of the Old Testament in the New* (trans. Donald H. Madvig; Grand Rapids: Eerdmans, 1982), 39, n. 99.

95. Israel will be gathered again, from the ends of the earth; Jerusalem will be rebuilt; Yahweh, the creator of all things, will be with his people and will again be their shepherd; Yahweh will make a new covenant with his people. Hooker, *Jesus and the Servant*, 30–40.

96. Isaiah's influence on Luke–Acts is not limited to the servant songs. 'Luke did not merely utilize Isaiah as a source for prooftexts to support his own point of view. Rather Luke had investigated Isaiah extensively and had a deep appreciation for Isaianic themes. His mind was saturated with Isaianic texts and concepts, which shaped his views.' Thomas S. Moore, '"To the End of the Earth": The Geographical and Ethnic Universalism of Acts 1.8 in Light of Isaianic Influence on Luke', *JETS* 40 (1997): 392. See also Pao, *Acts*; Sanders, 'Isaiah in Luke'.

97. Snaith, 'Servant', 205.

98. Recovery of sight and rescue of the oppressed become distinguishing marks of Jesus' ministry. See especially Luke 4.18-19 (citing Isa. 61.1-2); 7.20-22. The gospels record at least six occasions on which Jesus restored sight to blind people: Matt. 9.27; 12.22-23; 15.30-31 par.; 21.14; Mark 8.22-26; Luke 18.35-43 par.; John 9. Saul's spiritual conversion is paralleled by his being blinded by

passion sayings (Luke 9.22; 18.31-34 and pars., reflecting Isa. 50.6; 53.3-6), and Jesus' reference in the upper room to Isa. 53.12 (Luke 22.37). He concludes that 'Jesus deliberately modeled his ministry on the concept of the Servant of the LORD of the Second Isaiah.'[99] Other scholars hear echoes of Isa. 42.1 in the words from heaven, σὺ εἶ ὁ υἱός μου ὁ ἀγαπητός, ἐν σοὶ εὐδόκησα, at Jesus' baptism (Luke 3.22).[100] The application of Isa. 53.7-8 to Jesus in Acts 8.32-35 is also evidence of the church's identification of Jesus with the Isaianic servant.[101] Luke refers to Jesus as God's servant in Acts 3.13, 26; 4.27, 30 (using παῖς, the primary term translating עֶבֶד in Isaiah 40–55).[102] The explicit citations, narrative indications that Jesus fulfilled the responsibilities of the servant (e.g. sight for the blind), and the use of servant terminology demonstrate that Luke saw Jesus as the awaited servant.

While Acts 13.47 is the only explicit citation of Isa. 49.6 in Luke–Acts, two other texts reflect the language of 'light to the nations' and two more contain possible allusions.[103] The first of these is in Simeon's prayer (Luke 2.32). Prompted by God's Spirit (2.27), the aged saint sees Jesus in the temple and adds his testimony to that of the angel (2.10-12): this is the Christ, the Lord's anointed, 'thy salvation which thou hast prepared in the presence of all peoples, a light for

the appearance of Jesus on the Damascus road and the coming of Ananias so that he would 'regain [his] sight and be filled with the Holy Spirit' (Acts 9.17).

99. Snaith, 'Servant', 205–7, 210–14. Moessner describes 'the servant passages of Isaiah as literarily and theologically constitutive for much of the story material in Acts'. David P. Moessner, 'The Ironic Fulfillment of Israel's Glory', in *Luke–Acts and the Jewish People* (ed. Joseph B. Tyson; Minneapolis: Augsburg, 1988), 46–47. See also Strauss, *Davidic Messiah*, 325 (cf. 235–50, 288–92, 324–33).

100. Fitzmyer, *Luke*, 1.486; Walther Zimmerli and Joachim Jeremias, 'Παῖς Θεοῦ', *TDNT*, 5.701–02. See the extended argument in Jeffrey A. Gibbs, 'Israel Standing with Israel: The Baptism of Jesus in Matthew's Gospel (Matt. 3.13-17)', *CBQ* 64 (2002): 511–26.

101. The servant songs are reflected in many NT texts, including Matt. 8.17; 12.18-21 (citing Isa. 42.1-4); John 12.38-41; Rom. 15.21; 2 Cor. 6.2 (citing Isa. 49.8); along with other, less certain, allusions. Vincent Taylor, *The Names of Jesus* (London: Macmillan, 1953), 36.

102. The LXX uses παῖς to translate עֶבֶד 14 times in Isaiah 40–55, including 41.8-9; 42.1, 19a; 43.10; 44.1-2, 21 (2×), 26; 45.4; 49.6; 50.10; 52.13. The six remaining instances of עֶבֶד in these chapters are translated by δοῦλος (48.20; 49.3, 5; 42.19b; 49.7) or δουλεύοντα (53.11). Luke also applies παῖς to Israel (Luke 1.54) and David (Luke 1.69; Acts 4.25). The only other theologically significant use of the term in the NT is the citation of Isa. 42.1-4 in Matt. 12.18-21. It is difficult to sustain the argument of D. L. Jones that the use of παῖς in Acts has 'no particular reference to Deutero-Isaiah'. Donald L. Jones, 'The Title "Servant" in Luke–Acts', in *Luke–Acts: New Perspectives from the Society of Biblical Literature Seminar* (ed. Charles H. Talbert; New York: Crossroad, 1984), 157. See the persuasive case made by Dennis E. Johnson, 'Jesus Against the Idols: The Use of Isaianic Servant Songs in the Missiology of Acts', *WTJ* 52 (1990): 344–45.

103. Additional allusions to Isa. 49.6 have also been suggested: Luke 1.79 by Strauss, *Davidic Messiah*, 325; Luke 24.46-47 by Pao, *Acts*, 84–86; Acts 28.28 by Willem C. van Unnik, '"The Book of Acts" – The Confirmation of the Gospel', in *Sparsa Collecta: The Collected Essays of W. C. van Unnik. Part One: Evangelia, Paulina, Acta* (NovTSup 29; Leiden: Brill, 1973), 364. 'The resultant combination of the Son of Man and the servant of God ... was of decisive significance for Jesus' sense of mission .' Zimmerli and Jeremias, *TDNT*, 5.688.

revelation to the Gentiles, and for glory to thy people Israel'.[104] Simeon's words echo a number of Isaianic texts. He claims (v. 30) to be a participant in the promise of Isa. 40.5 (quoted in Luke 3.6) that 'all flesh will see the salvation of God'.[105] 'Light', 'salvation' and 'glory' are associated in numerous Isaianic texts.[106] Where Isaiah has εἰς φῶς ἐθνῶν (LXX), Luke (2.32) has φῶς εἰς ἀποκάλυψιν ἐθνῶν[107] and adds καὶ δόξαν λαοῦ σου Ἰσραήλ.[108] It is unclear whether δόξαν is in parallel with φῶς or with ἀποκάλυψιν, although the difference in meaning would not appear to be great. More significantly, Simeon's speech reverses the expected order: as he speaks of the salvation prepared by God κατὰ πρόσωπον πάντων τῶν λαῶν ('in the presence of all peoples'), he mentions first the light bringing revelation to the Gentiles before he speaks of glory coming to Israel, making a strong statement about the universal extent of the ministry of Jesus.[109] Luke 2.32 thus links the Isaianic servant with blessing for Gentiles and indicates that this is the purpose for which the servant has come.[110] 'The allusion to Isa. 49.6 … might well be regarded as a thematic statement of Luke's entire narrative: the call of the servant (*pais*) to restore the diaspora of Israel and to be a light to the Gentiles to the end of the earth.'[111]

---

104. Rusam observes that this is the first indication of Jesus' significance for the nations and that 'Jesus wird as σωτήρ Israels (Lk 2,11) auch zum σωτήριον für alle Heiden werden (Lk 2, 29-32).' Dietrich Rusam, *Das Alte Testament bei Lukas* (BZNT 112; Berlin: de Gruyter, 2003), 80, 81.

105. Cf. Isa. 52.10, 'all the ends of the earth shall see the salvation of our God'. Rusam notes that Simeon testifies that his own eyes have seen God's salvation. *Das Alte Testament bei Lukas*, 80.

106. Light and salvation appear in 49.6; 51.4-6 (LXX); light and glory in Isa. 42.6, 8; 58.8; 59.17-19; 60.1-3; salvation and glory in 46.13; and all three in 60.18-21. In Luke–Acts '*phōs* stands for the Christ who acts like the Father and is the Messiah. … it also looks to the suffering servant, salvation, and eschatology'. Robert F. O'Toole, *The Christological Climax of Paul's Defense* (AnBib 78; Rome: Biblical Institute Press, 1978), 64. Light imagery appears elsewhere in the NT: Matt. 4.14-16 (citing Isa. 9.1-6); John 8.12; 9.5; 12.46. Jesus' disciples experience and become light: Matt. 5.14; Eph. 5.8; 1 Thess. 5.5; 1 Pet. 2.9; Col. 1.12). In the NT, as in Isaiah, light is repeatedly a metaphor for salvation (Rom. 13.12; 2 Cor. 4.6; 6.14; Eph. 5.13-14; 1 John 2.8).

107. Plummer believes that 2.32 combines Isa. 49.6 and Ps. 98.2 (LXX Ps. 97.2, ἐγνώρισεν κύριος τὸ σωτήριον αὐτοῦ ἐναντίον τῶν ἐθνῶν ἀπεκάλυψεν τὴν δικαιοσύνην αὐτοῦ). Alfred Plummer, *A Critical and Exegetical Commentary on the Gospel according to S. Luke* (5th edn.; ICC; Edinburgh: T. & T. Clark, 1922), 69.

108. It has been suggested that this phrase depends on Isa. 46.13 (τῷ Ισραηλ εἰς δόξασμα). NA[27]; Fitzmyer, *Luke*, 1.428; Luke Timothy Johnson, *The Gospel of Luke* (SP 3; Collegeville, Minn.: Liturgical Press, 1991), 55.

109. Moore suggests that the order 'raises the possibility that salvation may go to the Gentiles before glory comes fully to Israel'. Thomas S. Moore, 'Luke's Use of Isaiah for the Gentile Mission and Jewish Rejection Theme in the Third Gospel' (Ph.D. diss., Dallas Theological Seminary, 1995), 226. Plummer, however, finds this doubtful. Plummer, *Luke*, 69.

110. As with Isaiah, some have argued that Simeon only says that Gentiles will 'see' God's salvation, not experience it. Green and Marshall attribute this view to G. D. Kilpatrick, 'λαοι at Luke ii.31 and Acts iv.25-27', *JTS* n.s. 16 (1986), 127. Joel B. Green, *The Gospel of Luke* (NICNT; Grand Rapids: Eerdmans, 1997), 148; Ian Howard Marshall, *The Gospel of Luke: A Commentary on the Greek Text* (NIGTC; Grand Rapids: Eerdmans, 1978), 121. The use of Isa. 49.6; 42.6 in Acts 13.47; 26.22 argues against this minimalist view. Light brings revelation, and consequently salvation, to Gentiles.

111. David L. Tiede, *Prophecy and History in Luke–Acts* (Philadelphia: Fortress, 1980), 31.

The second allusion appears in Paul's defence before Agrippa (Acts 26.22-23),[112] where Paul testifies he is 'saying nothing but what the prophets and Moses said would come to pass: that the Christ must suffer, and that, by being the first to rise from the dead, he would proclaim light both to the people and to the Gentiles' (φῶς μέλλει καταγγέλλειν τῷ τε λαῷ καὶ τοῖς ἔθνεσιν). 'The prophets and Moses' had announced the suffering and resurrection of Christ, with the consequent proclamation of 'light' to Jews ('the people')[113] and Gentiles. As in Isaiah, the ministry to the nations (49.6) follows struggle or suffering (cf. Isa. 49.4). However, in Isa. 49.6; 42.6 the servant *becomes* a light to the nations, while here Jesus *proclaims* light. The sermons of Acts spell out the content of this proclamation: forgiveness of sins (2.38; 5.31; 10.43; 13.38), the gift of the Spirit (2.38; 10.44; 15.8), repentance (3.26; 5.31; 17.30; 20.21; 24.25), resurrection (23.6; 24.15), grace for Gentiles (11.17-18; 13.47; 15.13-18), and release from bondage (26.18). The narrative adds healing (3.1-10; 4.10; 5.12-16; 8.6; 9.33-35; 14.8-10; 19.11), sight (9.12, 17-19), resurrection (9.40-42; 14.19-20; possibly 20.9-12), and release from prison (5.18-19; 12.1-19a; 16.23-40). When Jesus, on the basis of his death and resurrection, proclaims light to the nations, he proclaims himself as the one who brings these blessings. The proclamation of light is the proclamation about the one who is light.[114]

Some see an allusion to Isa. 49.6 in Paul's description of his call in Acts 26.18: 'to open their eyes, that they may turn from darkness to light'.[115] Acts 26.18b speaks of 'turning' *people* from darkness to light, while in Isa. 42.16 God 'will make' darkness *into* light. Here, providing light is the function of Paul's own ministry.[116] He has been sent to the Gentiles (26.17) 'to open their eyes' (ἀνοῖξαι ὀφθαλμούς), echoing the mission of the servant in Isa. 42.7 (ἀνοῖξαι ὀφθαλμοὺς τυφλῶν), so 'that they may turn from darkness to light', echoing Isa. 42.16 and possibly 9.2. They will turn 'from the power of Satan to God' (τῆς ἐξουσίας τοῦ σατανᾶ ἐπὶ τὸν θεόν), possibly reflecting the servant's work 'to bring out the prisoners from the dungeon, from the prison those who sit in

---

112. Absent from the marginal notes and table of citations in NA[27], although it is noted in UBS[4].

113. In Luke, 'the people' refers to Israel. Johnson, *Acts*, 264.

114. Paul is appointed a servant (ὑπηρέτην, 26.16) and witness, but ὑπηρέτης is not applied to the Isaianic servant and Acts 26 does not explicitly identify Paul with Isaiah's servant. 'Yet the light that he brings them is Christ (Acts 26.23 = Isa. 49.6), and Paul is only an apostle of Christ. If the prophecy of Isaiah is fulfilled in Paul, it must first have been fulfilled in Christ. Hence Paul's use of this text in connection with his own mission presupposes its prior use for theological purposes.' Dupont, 'Apologetic', 146. O'Toole writes of 'the task of the Suffering Servant begun by Christ carried on by Paul'. 'The resurrected Christ has from the Father a mission which Christ performs. What Paul does can be predicated of Christ. So, the resurrected Christ cannot only be said to be in heaven; he is with and in Paul proclaiming the light.' O'Toole, *Climax*, 69, 119.

115. Schnabel, *Early Christian Mission*, 943.

116. Johnson sees allusions to the servant songs in Paul's accounts of his conversion and call. Johnson, *Message of Acts*, 116. In addition to echoes in Acts 26.18, see also the account in Acts 22: election (Acts 22.15; Isa. 42.1; 49.2); the Righteous One (Acts 22.14; Isa. 53.11; cf. Acts 3.14; 7.52); witness (Acts 22.15; Isa. 41.1-4; 43.8-12; 44.8); refusal to hear his testimony (Acts 22.18; Isa. 53.1); and salvation for Gentiles (Acts 22.15, 21).

darkness' (Isa. 42.7). The allusion is less to one particular text than to the work of the servant generally or to promises of God's salvation.

Finally, some find an allusion to Isa. 49.6 in Acts 1.8, where Jesus says that the apostles will be his witnesses 'to the end of the earth' (ἕως ἐσχάτου τῆς γῆς).[117] The expression is found in the NT only here and in the citation in Acts 13.47. Dennis Johnson finds further echoes of the servant songs here in the promised coming of the Spirit (Isa. 44.1-8), the calling to bear witness (Isa. 41.1-4; 43.8-12; 44.8), and the extension of salvation to the nations.[118] The suggestion that the apostles are described, even at this early point in Acts, in the language of the Isaianic servant is intriguing. The allusion (if there is one), however, is brief, and the expression ('the end of the earth') occurs often enough in the LXX that we cannot assume that readers would have associated the phrase specifically with Isa. 49.6.[119]

3.4 *Acts 13.47*

At the beginning of Acts 13, the setting shifts to Antioch. During a time of worship and fasting, the leaders of the church there were directed by the Holy Spirit to 'set apart for me Barnabas and Saul for the work to which I have called them' (13.2). The two promptly set sail for Cyprus, Barnabas' home (4.36). There they 'proclaimed the word of God in the synagogues of the Jews' (13.5), but Luke says nothing about the response. The single recorded event is the conversion of the proconsul, apparently a Gentile,[120] who had 'summoned Barnabas and Saul and sought to hear the word of God' (13.7). Their preaching was opposed by 'a certain magician, a Jewish false prophet, named Bar-Jesus' (13.6) or 'Elymas' (13.8), who was struck blind for a time because of his opposition. 'Astonished at the teaching of the Lord', the proconsul believed (13.12). The first account in the narrative of the mission thus introduces the themes of Jewish opposition and blindness, along with Gentile responsiveness to the gospel.

---

117. 'The expansion of Christianity "to the ends of the earth" is not a merely geographic movement, but involves a passage out of the Jewish world into the Gentile world. So Rome, as the capital of the pagan world, is really situated "at the ends of the earth."' Dupont, 'Salvation', 19–20. See also Frederick F. Bruce, *The Acts of the Apostles: The Greek Text with Introduction and Commentary* (3rd rev. edn.; Grand Rapids: Eerdmans, 1990), 315; Wilfried Eckey, *Die Apostelgeschichte: Der Weg des Evangeliums von Jerusalem nach Rom* (2 vols.; Neukirchen-Vluyn: Neukirchener, 2000), 1.304; Turner, *Power*, 300–1.

118. Johnson, 'Idols', 346–49. Johnson might also have included Isa. 55.3-5. None of these references appear in what are usually considered to be servant songs. If, however, one understands the songs to be integrally related to their context, rather than separately composed interpolations, Johnson's approach can be seen as sound.

119. The 'end of the earth' appears in the LXX of Deut. 28.49; 1 Macc. 3.9; Ps. 135.7; *Pss. Sol.* 1.4; 8.15; Isa. 8.9; 45.22; 48.20; 62.11; Jer. 6.22; 10.13; 16.19; 27.41; 28.16; 32.32; 38.8. It occurs with ἕως only in the four Isaiah texts; *Pss. Sol.* 1.4; 1 Macc. 3.9 (and apparently nowhere else in Greek literature). Willem C. van Unnik, 'Der Ausdruck ἕως ἐσχάτου τῆς γῆς (Apostelgeschichte I, 8) und sein alttestamentlicher Hintergrund', in *Sparsa Collecta*, 400.

120. Barrett, *Acts*, 1.614.

From Cyprus, they sailed to Pamphylia and moved inland from Perga to Antioch in Pisidia (13.13-14). There, they again went first to the synagogue. After the reading of the scriptures, they were invited to speak (13.14-15). Paul rose and addressed the assembly of 'men of Israel and ... Gentiles who worship God' (13.16; cf. 26).[121] He began by surveying God's dealings with Israel, from the election of Abraham through the establishment of the kingdom under David, from whose 'posterity God has brought to Israel a Savior, Jesus, as he promised' (13.23). He then summarized the ministry of Jesus, from the ministry of John (13.24-25) to his rejection, death and resurrection (13.30-32). 'What God promised to the fathers, this he has fulfilled,' not through David (13.33-37, citing Ps. 2.7; 16.10; Isa. 55.3)[122] or Moses (13.39), but 'by raising Jesus' (13.32). 'Through this man forgiveness of sins is proclaimed to you, and by him every one that believes is freed from everything from which you could not be freed by the law of Moses' (13.38-39). Paul concluded by warning of judgement on those who reject this message (13.40-41, citing Hab. 1.5).[123]

Many Jews and 'devout converts to Judaism followed Paul and Barnabas' from the synagogue (13.42-43). On the next sabbath 'almost the whole city gathered' (13.44). Jealous of the attention that the missionaries received from the Gentiles, 'the Jews' opposed the message (13.45).[124] The missionaries declared that it had been 'necessary that the word of God should be spoken first' to Jews. Paul and Barnabas have now fulfilled their obligation. Since their audience has rejected their message, they are free to turn to a more fruitful field.[125] This is not

121. Dunn notes that the address has from the beginning included Gentiles. James D. G. Dunn, *The Acts of the Apostles* (Valley Forge: Trinity Press International, 1996), 178. Dunn effectively challenges Epp's view that (apart from the distinctive readings in D), evangelization of Gentiles does not begin until 13.47. Eldon Jay Epp, *The Theological Tendency of Codex Bezae Cantabrigiensis in Acts* (SNTSMS 3; Cambridge: Cambridge University Press, 1966), 83–84. These Gentiles, however, are already associated with the synagogue – they both 'worship' and 'fear' God.

122. Dunn (among others) has noted similarities between Paul's first recorded address and Peter's (Acts 2), particularly in the use of David and the argument concerning the resurrection. Dunn, *Acts*, 177.

123. This warning may seem uncalled-for at this point in the narrative, since no opposition has yet been described in Antioch. Nevertheless, Jews elsewhere had rejected the message about Jesus, a fact evident not only in the narrative of Acts, but even in this sermon (13.27-30). The assumption that some Jews will reject the message does not reflect badly on all Jews, any more than the numerous statements about the nations opposing God reflect badly on all Gentiles.

124. That is, 'some Jews'. Witherington, *Acts*, 414. 'No more did "all Gentiles" believe than did all "the Jews" reject.' Dunn, *Acts*, 184. This jealousy may indicate that Jewish efforts to exert spiritual influence on their neighbors had been less successful. 'The fear would be of an untried and untested new sect upsetting and undermining the good standing and good relations which the Jewish community had established for itself within the city (minorities were always anxious about their legal and social standing since local and international politics were so unpredictable).' Dunn, *Acts*, 183. Dunn argues that their privileged position in the plan of God was threatened by the way Paul had from the beginning addressed his message to the Gentiles present, as well as to the Jews. See also John B. Polhill, *Acts* (NAC 26; Nashville: Broadman, 1992), 306; David J. Williams, *Acts* (NIBCNT 5; Peabody, Mass.: Hendrickson, 1990), 238.

125. Paul's obligation to preach first to Jews echoes Peter's application of the promise to Abraham

surprising; Jesus had told the twelve to do this very thing.[126] What is remarkable is that Paul and Barnabas will now 'turn to the Gentiles' (13.46) and appeal to Isa. 49.6 as justification: 'For so the Lord has commanded us, saying, "I have set you to be a light for the Gentiles, that you may bring salvation to the uttermost parts of the earth"' (13.47, citing Isa. 49.6).

The citation is introduced by the words, οὕτως γὰρ ἐντέταλται ἡμῖν ὁ κύριος ('For so the Lord has commanded us'). It provides the rationale (γάρ) for the dramatic step in v. 46. This is not only justified, but required, by the prophecy.[127] The frustration experienced by Paul and Barnabas in fulfilling their divinely appointed mission forms a clear point of contact with the mission of the servant. Just as the servant suffered frustration in his initial calling to minister to Israel, so 'the Jews' now reject the message of Paul and Barnabas. Just as Yahweh expanded the 'trifling' task of 'gathering Israel to himself', God expands the ministry of Paul and Barnabas, directing them to preach to Gentiles.

> Their situation is nevertheless analogous to the position of the servant in Isa. 49.1-6. Just as the servant failed to bring back to God the whole of Israel, so the apostles meet with opposition from 'the' Jews. Both find themselves in difficult circumstances and it is here that Luke actualizes the verse from Isa. 49,6d. In the greater mandate of the servant the preachers perceive a divine command, explicitly addressed to themselves (ἐντέταλται ἡμῖν).[128]

Like the servant, they are to be 'light for the Gentiles' and 'bring salvation to the uttermost parts of the earth'.[129] For the citation to legitimate a Gentile mission, Isa. 49.6 must mean that salvation in Jesus is actually to be extended to Gentiles; the nations will not simply observe the glory and salvation of Israel, but will share in a salvation and glory that is extended to all nations.

The Gentile mission may be occasioned (in both Isaiah 49 and Acts 13) by Jewish rejection of the work of the servant, but this is not its cause. The citation locates the origin of the mission in the prophesied plan of God. Its present justification is

---

in Acts 3.26, 'God, having raised up his servant, sent him to you first, to bless you' (ὑμῖν πρῶτον ἀναστήσας ὁ θεὸς τὸν παῖδα αὐτοῦ ἀπέστειλεν αὐτὸν εὐλογοῦντα ὑμᾶς).

126. Following Jesus' instructions to the twelve (Luke 9.5 ‖ Matt. 10.14; Mark 6.11) and the seventy (Luke 10.11). The twelve were explicitly forbidden to go to the Gentiles or even the Samaritans (Matt. 10.5-6), although this prohibition does not appear in Luke.

127. Some have contended that ὁ κύριος here is Jesus, not Yahweh, who spoke through the prophet, and it is therefore Jesus who has commanded this turning to the Gentiles. Pao, *Acts*, 101; Martin Rese, 'Die Funktion der alttestamentlichen Zitate und Anspielungen in den Reden der Apostelgeschichte', in *Les Actes des Apôtres: Traditions, rédaction, théologie* (ed. Jacob Kremer; BETL 48; Leuven: Leuven University Press, 1979), 78–79; Steyn, *Septuagint Quotations*, 201. It is unlikely that Jewish opponents would have recognized this association or found it persuasive. Appealing to a command from Yahweh would make much more sense in the circumstances.

128. Sandt, 'Quotations', 54.

129. Barrett characterizes the articular infinitive τοῦ εἶναί σε as epexegetical. The 'light' and 'salvation' represent the same blessing. Barrett, *Acts*, 1.657. Rusam notes that the echo of Acts 1.8, ἕως ἐσχάτου τῆς γῆς, serves to place Paul's ministry here as part of the mission of the eleven given there. Rusam, *Das Alte Testament bei Lukas*, 414.

the coming of Christ as the divine servant (Acts 3.13, 26; 4.27, 30).[130] The citation justifies only 'turning to' Gentiles; it does not require 'turning from' Jews, as
the subsequent narrative will make plain.[131]

From this point, the Gentile mission becomes the primary focus of Luke's narrative. Paul and Barnabas go next to Iconium, where they again preach first in the
synagogue. Many Jews and Gentiles believe, but Jewish opposition forces them
to leave the city (14.1-7). In Lystra, they speak to a pagan audience, from which
they win 'a large number of disciples' (14.8-21). They then return to Antioch in
Syria, 'where they had been commended to the grace of God for the work which
they had fulfilled' (14.26) and report 'all that God had done with them, and how he
had opened a door of faith to the Gentiles' (14.27). This characterization clearly
indicates that the previously unspecified work to which God had called them
(13.2) was to bring Gentiles to faith in Jesus.

This pattern ('to the Jew first, but also to the Greek', Rom. 1.16) will be
repeated in each city as Paul speaks first to Jews, experiences substantial (though
not complete) rejection, and then focuses his ministry on Gentiles (e.g. 18.5-6;
19.8-9). Finally, arrested in Jerusalem on false charges (related to his association
with Gentiles, 21.27-36), Paul will preach to governors and kings (24-26), as God
had said to Ananias (9.15). The narrative closes with Paul in Rome, where, again,
many Jews reject the message and Paul again declares (concluding the last speech
in the book), 'this salvation of God has been sent to the Gentiles; and they will
listen' (28.28).[132]

In Pisidian Antioch, the result of Paul's announcement was that 'the Gentiles ...
were glad and glorified the word of God' (13.48). As a result of the subsequent
proclamation to Gentiles, 'as many as were ordained to eternal life believed. The
word of the Lord spread throughout all the region' (13.48-49). Many Gentiles
'saw the light' and, as a result of these events, salvation indeed came to those in
distant parts of the earth.

It is difficult to overstate how remarkable this turn of events is. Rackham
describes it as 'apostasy – for so the Jews would regard it'.[133] In Acts 22, a crowd
in Jerusalem listened patiently as Paul preached about Jesus; the riot began only
when Paul claimed that God sent him to preach to Gentiles (21.21-22). Such a
dramatic change in perspective must be based on clear direction from God. The
question is how Paul found that direction in Isa. 49.6.

Isaiah 49.6 spoke of an individual 'servant' who would be the light and bringer
of salvation to the nations. The singular 'you' of Isa. 49.6 (MT וּנְתַתִּיךָ, NT and

---

130. Jewish refusal is 'a contributory, though not the primary (cf. chs 10–11), cause of the Gentile
mission'. 'The fact that the Gentile mission could be justified from the Old Testament does not
exclude either the prior proclamation of the gospel to the Jews or the possibility that Jewish obduracy
could become an immediate cause of the Gentile mission.' Wilson, *Gentile Mission*, 222.

131. 'In the very next city on his missionary itinerary, he would again begin his witness in the
synagogue (14.1).' Paul continued preaching in synagogues (Acts 17.1, 10, 17; 18.4, 19; 19.8; cf.
16.13 [not, as Polhill has it, 16.12]). Polhill, *Acts*, 308. So also Barrett, *Acts*, 1.656.

132. The rejection of the message by Jews and the subsequent turning to Gentiles in 13.45-49 and
28.25-31 thus form a kind of *inclusio* for this major section of Acts.

133. Richard B. Rackham, *The Acts of the Apostles* (WC; Grand Rapids: Baker, 1978), 221.

LXX τέθεικά σε), which is applied to Jesus in Luke 2.29-32; Acts 26.23, is here applied to 'us' (ἡμῖν) and the promise is understood as a command addressed to Paul and Barnabas. How does the prophecy come to be applied in this way?

First, some hold that the prophecy is applied to Christ and not to Paul and Barnabas. Grelot states that 'En dépit des apparences, ce texte n'est pas transféré du Christ, Serviteur du Seigneur, à ses deux envoyés, Paul et Barnabé',[134] because the grammar of Acts 13.47 and the singular address (σε) in the citation cannot be understood as applying to (plural) Paul and Barnabas. For the same reason, Fitzmyer also ascribes the citation to Jesus:

> Paul seems to be applying the Servant's words to himself (and Barnabas). The difficulty, however, is that the words cited are addressed to 'you' (2nd person singular), which makes them difficult to apply to Paul and Barnabas. So the quoted part of the Servant Song may in reality refer to Christ, who through Barnabas and Paul is making known to the Jews of Pisidian Antioch this 'light of the Gentiles' and 'means of salvation to the ends of the earth,' i.e., a light that will shine on Gentiles and bring salvation everywhere.[135]

Grelot also argues that the application of the same text from Isaiah to Christ in Acts 26.23 prohibits its application in Acts 13.47 to Paul and Barnabas. Instead, we are to understand that Paul and Barnabas have been called by God to preach the Word – as they proclaim Christ as the light to the nations, they bring salvation to the end of the earth. Peter Bolt argues that the prophecy is a commission that Paul and Barnabas share 'indirectly'.[136] This reading does not, however, reflect what Acts 13.47 actually says, and it is unclear on what basis we may privilege the singular σε and constrain the plural ἡμῖν to fit it.

Eric Franklin argues that the citation is not about the servant, but about the salvation Jesus brings. 'The fact that [Luke] can apply this passage to Paul as well as to Jesus suggests that he sees its emphasis as pointing in the first place, not so much to the person of Jesus, as to the saving work of God which is accomplished through him. It is the salvation of God which is his first concern'.[137] Such a subordination of Christ to God's salvation seems unlikely, however, given the centrality of Christology in most readings of Luke–Acts. It is unclear on this reading how the prophecy becomes a personal obligation for Paul and Barnabas.

James Dunn believes that the language of Isa. 49.6 is applied to Israel: 'Israel itself had been given the task of being and bringing light and salvation to the Gentiles (Isa. 49.6). So all Paul and Barnabas were doing was fulfilling Israel's mission.'[138] Witherington writes that Paul and Barnabas 'are assuming the role and

---

134. Pierre Grelot, 'Note sur Actes, XIII, 47', *RB* 88 (1981): 370. Also Jacques Dupont, 'Je t'ai établi lumière des nations (Ac 13, 14, 43–52)', in *Nouvelles Etudes sur les Actes des Apôtres* (Paris: Cerf, 1984), 343–49.

135. Fitzmyer, *Acts*, 521.

136. Peter G. Bolt, 'Mission and Witness', in *Witness to the Gospel: The Theology of Acts* (ed. Ian Howard Marshall and David Peterson; Grand Rapids: Eerdmans, 1998), 211.

137. Eric Franklin, *Christ the Lord: A Study in the Purpose and Theology of Luke–Acts* (Philadelphia: Westminster, 1975), 121.

138. Dunn, *Acts*, 184. 'For some reason not entirely clear, Paul understood that with the death and resurrection of Jesus, the time and possibility had arrived for Israel's responsibility to be a light to the

tasks of the Servant of the Servant Songs, which is to say, the tasks of Israel'.[139] Neither explains, however, how Paul derives a seemingly specific personal command from this commission to Israel.[140]

Others have found a double reference to Christ and the church. 'The double use of the imagery is important ... Paul is a light of the Gentiles only in virtue of the Christ he preaches; Christ is a light to the Gentiles as he is preached to them by his servants.'[141]

> The view that identifies the servant with Israel fails. Israel alone was never the instrument of the world's redemption. Paul's use of this verse (Acts 13:47) supports the identification of the servant as the Messiah and His people. When His people labor in His Name as Paul and Barnabas were doing, He works through them.[142]

Unfortunately, these writers have generally not explained the nature of this connection or the rationale by which this prophecy may be interpreted in a twofold way while other prophetic texts are given an exclusively Christological application.

Finally, the prophecy may simply be applied to Paul and Barnabas here rather than to Christ.[143] But the question then is in what capacity: as individuals?[144] As apostles?[145] Does it extend to others, such as all Christian ministers and/or

---

Gentiles to be fulfilled (Gal. 1.15-16; 3.13-14, 23-29; 4.1-7).' Dunn, *Acts*, 329 (commenting on 28.16).

139. Witherington, *Acts*, 416. 'The present passage asserts that the mission of the Servant is also the task of the followers of Jesus. Thus the task of Israel, which she failed to carry out, has passed to Jesus and then to his people as the new Israel; it is the task of bringing the light of revelation and salvation to all the peoples of the world (*cf.* the clear allusion to Is. 49.6 in Lk. 2.29-32).' Ian Howard Marshall, *The Acts of the Apostles: An Introduction and Commentary* (TNTC; Grand Rapids: Eerdmans, 1980), 230. So also Jacob Jervell, *Die Apostelgeschichte* (KEK; Göttingen: Vandenhoeck & Ruprecht, 1998), 364.

140. Apart from the servant songs, no OT texts suggest that Israel itself was to illumine the nations. One NT text, however, may support the idea that Israel was not only to bring light but to be light: Rom. 2.19 ('and if you are sure that you are a guide to the blind, a light to those who are in darkness'). Texts which speak of Jesus' disciples (the new Israel?) as light (e.g. Matt. 5.14) could perhaps reflect this idea as well.

141. Barrett, *Acts*, 1.658. See also Bruce, *Acts* (rev. edn.), 267; Rackham, *Acts*, 221; John R. W. Stott, *The Message of Acts: The Spirit, the Church and the World* (Bible Speaks Today; Downers Grove, Ill.: InterVarsity, 1994), 227.

142. Young, *Isaiah*, 3.276. 'The present passage asserts that the mission of the Servant is also the task of the followers of Jesus.' Marshall, *Acts*, 320. See also Suzanne Watts Henderson, 'The Messianic Community: The Mission of Jesus as Collective Christology', paper presented at the AAR/SBL Annual Meeting, San Diego, 2007.

143. Gerhard Schneider, *Die Apostelgeschichte* (HTKNT; Freiburg: Herder, 1980–82), 2.146.

144. Witherington, *Acts*, 416.

145. Rackham, *Acts*, 221; Charles S. C. Williams, *A Commentary on the Acts of the Apostles* (HNTC; New York: Harper & Brothers, 1957), 167. Barnabas is apparently referred to as an apostle in Acts 14.14; cf. 14.4, although the use of the term in this chapter has raised questions. Fitzmyer, *Acts*, 526; Witherington, *Acts*, 419–20. See the literature cited in Frederick F. Bruce, *Paul: Apostle of the Heart Set Free* (Grand Rapids: Eerdmans, 1977), 155, n. 22.

missionaries,[146] or to all followers of Jesus and members of his church?[147] The text provides little data on which to base a decision, although it seems to speak only of the actions of Paul and Barnabas, and not those of the church as a whole (cf. similarly Acts 18.6). In Acts, proclamation appears to be a special responsibility of the apostles (Acts 6.2, 5), and it is primarily the eleven who preach[148] (prior to the ministry of Paul).[149] The role of 'witness' to Jesus appears to have been limited to the apostles and others who had seen the risen Jesus (Luke 24.48; Acts 1.8, 22; 2.32; 5.32; 10.39, 41; 13.31).

A second question is by what rationale the prophecy is applied. Some scholars believe that first-century interpreters felt little need to be logical or consistent in their use of the OT (beyond, say, mere verbal correspondences)[150] and consequently assume there is no rationale for the application of the prophecy. This view is unfortunately self-confirming: no rationale will be found if none is sought and such a position should not be held until a thorough review of possible rationales has been conducted.

We saw that some interpreters regard the servant in Isaiah as a fluid concept, sometimes Israel and sometimes distinguished from Israel. It could then be that Luke regards the servant in a similar way. Jesus' actions in bringing sight to the blind and freedom to the captives echo several Isaianic texts (e.g. 42.7) where these signs are associated with the servant. In Acts, we also find the apostles and other divinely appointed representatives performing signs like those of Jesus: healing the lame (3.7; 8.6; 14.8-10); healing the paralysed (8.6; 9.34-35); healing other people and illnesses (5.15-16; 19.11; 28.8); restoring sight (9.17-18); casting out evil spirits (5.16; 8.7; 16.18; 19.11); raising the dead (9.36-42; 20.9-12?); along with unspecified signs, wonders and miracles (2.43; 5.12; 6.8; 8.13; 14.3; 15.12; 19.11).[151] Although these are servant tasks, servant language is not particularly evident; the only instances where servant-related language is explicitly applied to others are Acts 13.47; 26.18. There are reasons to question the presence of a fluid understanding of the servant in Isaiah, however, and it is difficult to see how a clear command for the Gentile mission could be addressed to Paul and Barnabas on this basis.

The principle of *imitatio christi* is evident throughout the NT. As Jesus was to suffer and die, so believers must take up their cross (Mark 8.31-38 and par.). Believers must patiently endure unjust suffering as Jesus did (1 Pet. 2.21). They are to forgive one another and 'walk in love' as Jesus did (Eph. 4.32–5.2). They

---

146. Calvin, *Acts 14–28*, 391. See also Polhill, *Acts*, 307.

147. Bruce, *Acts* (Greek Text, 3rd edn.), 315; *Acts* (rev. edn.), 267; Marshall, *Acts*, 230.

148. Although other believers were εὐαγγελιζόμενοι as well: 8.4 ('those who were scattered'); Acts 8.12, 40 (Philip); 11.20 ('men of Cyprus and Cyrene'); cf. 6.8–7.60 (Stephen); 18.24-28 (Apollos).

149. Paul's letters abound with statements reflecting his calling to preach (Rom. 1.17; 1 Cor. 1.17; 2 Cor. 4.5; Gal. 1.16; Eph. 3.8; 2 Tim. 1.11), yet his only exhortation to anyone else to preach is to Timothy (2 Tim. 4.2).

150. We have noted Jervell's belief that 'obviously, one cannot expect too much logic in the use of Old Testament quotations in New Testament writings'. Jervell, 'Divided People', 52.

151. See also Luke 9.1, 6; 10.9, 18-19.

are to follow Jesus' example and wash one another's feet (John 13.14-15). In Luke–Acts, disciples are called to 'follow me' (Luke 5.27; 9.23, 59; 18.22; see also the implicit call to imitation in Luke 22.26-27; cf. 1 Cor. 11.1). Nevertheless, believers are not to be like Jesus in every way. They do not offer their lives redemptively for others, nor are they all to be, like Jesus, itinerant preachers. The principle of *imitatio christi* is insufficient to explain the rationale for the application of Isa. 49.6 in Acts 13.47.

Calvin argues that the prophecy applies specifically to ministers of the gospel along with Christ: 'many things that Scripture applies to Christ, apply to His ministers', but 'not everything, for certain descriptions are peculiar to the person of Christ'. 'Since He acts through His ministers transferring His own functions to them', Christ's ministers act on his behalf and with his authority, particularly in the preaching of the gospel. It is in this way, Calvin believes, that the prophecy may be appropriately applied to Paul and Barnabas.[152] While this may be true, an underlying rationale for the connection is not offered.

Such a rationale may lie in the Pauline doctrine of the union of Christ and the church. Because of the fundamental connection between Christ and his church, what is true of Christ may also be applied to the church. J. A. Alexander sees here 'confirmation ... that the person here described is not the Messiah exclusively, but that his people are included.'[153]

> *Commanded us* is not an arbitrary transfer or accommodation of the passage, but a faithful reproduction of its original and proper import, as relating both to the Head and the Body, the Messiah and the Church in their joint capacity, as heralds of salvation to the world.[154]

This approach offers a theological explanation for the application of an apparently Christological prophetic text to the mission of Paul and Barnabas, but it may be questioned whether Luke employs this concept.

Robert F. O'Toole concludes that we simply cannot discover the rationale by which Isa. 49.6 is applied to Paul and the Gentile mission.

> Luke never fully elaborates in this chapter or in the whole of Lk-Acts how Christ unites himself with Christians. But, if Christ be the Savior, he must really effect something in the Christians; otherwise, Luke writes nonsense. But since Luke remains vague on the nature of this union, we have no choice but to be vague ourselves.[155]

There is a way in which to understand the application of Isa. 49.6 to both Christ and the ministry of Paul and Barnabas that draws on dynamics indigenous to Luke–Acts. One of the major conclusions of Bock's study on Luke's use of the OT is that Luke's Christology is developed not only from explicit OT prophecies, but also from OT 'patterns'.

---

152. Calvin, *Acts 14–28*, 391.

153. Alexander, *Isaiah*, 2.228.

154. Joseph Addison Alexander, *Commentary on the Acts of the Apostles* (3rd edn.; New York: Scribner, Armstrong & Co., 1875; repr., Grand Rapids: Zondervan, 1956), 504.

155. O'Toole, *Climax*, 159.

Luke sees the Scripture as fulfilled in Jesus in terms of the fulfillment of OT prophecy and in terms of the reintroduction and fulfillment of OT patterns that point to the presence of God's saving work. In referring to patterns, we refer to what is commonly called typology ...[156]

Bock understands typology to refer to 'a pattern within events that is to culminate in a final fulfillment in light of the passage's and the OT's context of hope and deliverance'.[157] Such patterns are sufficiently common that Bock calls 'Luke's use of the OT for Christology, "proclamation from prophecy and pattern"'.[158] This principle is clearly part of Luke's hermeneutical strategy and can shed light on the use of Isa. 49.6 in Acts 13.47.

One of the most significant studies of typology (and one noted by Bock) is that of Richard Davidson.[159] Typology deals with the fulfilment of God's purposes in history, with things that 'must needs be'[160] in the unfolding of God's redemptive programme. Davidson distinguishes three 'aspects' or phases of typological fulfilment: fulfilment in Christ (inaugurated or Christological fulfilment); fulfilment in the eschatological future (consummated or apocalyptic fulfilment); and fulfilment now in the life of the church (appropriated or ecclesiological fulfilment).[161]

An example may help clarify matters. The tabernacle (later the temple) symbolized God's presence with his people. Even within the OT there are hints of a greater future presence of God (e.g. Isa. 7.14). In the NT, John indicates that the promise of the tabernacle was fulfilled in the incarnation (1.14; cf. 2.20-21), but Paul wrote that the church is now the dwelling of God by Christ's Spirit (1 Cor. 3.16;

---

156. Bock, *Proclamation*, 274.

157. Bock, *Proclamation*, 50.

158. Bock, *Proclamation*, 274. Bock finds evidence of Luke's use of OT patterns in the return from the Babylonian exile (Luke 3.4-6: 97–98), the ministries of Elijah and Elisha (Luke 4.17-19: 110–11), Jesus' answer to John (Luke 7.22, 27: 114), the transfiguration (Luke 9.35: 116), etc. Since his focus is on the role of the OT in the development of Luke's Christology, Bock does not explore whether Christ might stand in typological relation to his followers. Likewise, Goppelt's important study, *Typos*, focuses, as the subtitle states, on *The Typological Interpretation of the Old Testament in the New*. Typological development *within* the NT is beyond his scope, although Goppelt notes that 'the NT types are themselves open to a future salvation' (195) and 'the NT knows itself to be ... a prophecy in type concerning the future consummation' (205).

159. Richard M. Davidson, *Typology in Scripture: A Study of Hermeneutical τύπος Structures* (Andrews University Seminary Doctoral Dissertation Series 2; Berrien Springs, Mich.: Andrews University Press, 1981). See also Richard M. Davidson, 'The Eschatological Structure of Biblical Typology', paper presented at the annual meeting of the Evangelical Theological Society, 19 November 1999; 'Is Biblical Typology Really Predictive? Some Possible Indicators of the Existence and Predictive Quality of OT Types', paper presented at the midwestern regional meeting of the Evangelical Theological Society, St. Paul, Minn., 26–27 February 1999; 'Israel Typology', paper presented at the annual meeting of the Evangelical Theological Society, 16 November 2000.

160. Davidson's expression for an essential feature of typological fulfilment. Davidson understands typology not as a merely literary correspondence, but as historical development within the history of redemption in which types ordained by God *must* be subsequently fulfilled. Luke often expresses this necessity with δεῖ (used 40 times in Luke–Acts, including instances of redemptive-historical necessity such as Luke 4.43; 9.22; 13.16, 33; 17.25; 21.9; 22.37; 24.7, 26, 44; Acts 1.16; 3.21; 4.12; 14.22; 17.3).

161. Davidson, *Typology*, 390–97.

2 Cor. 6.16; Eph. 2.21-22; cf. Col. 1.27); and the immediacy of God's presence with his people will eventually be such that no temple is necessary (Rev. 21.22). Christ's incarnation does not exhaust the tabernacle pattern, but becomes the basis for further fulfilment in the present age and the eschaton. We can picture the entire process like this: OT type → Christ (inaugurated) → church (appropriated) → eschaton (consummated). The OT type anticipates Christ, but once Christ has come, subsequent fulfilments in the church and the eschaton may also be expected. Much as the OT presents types of Christ, Christ himself becomes a type of the church and both are types of the eschaton. The patterning does not just run from OT to NT (or to Christ), but also from Christ to the church in the present age (and eventually to the eschaton).

This is the reverse of the 'narrowing' many see in OT expectation, where, e.g., David's dynasty becomes focused in the one king who 'will reign over the house of Jacob forever' (Luke 1.33). Old Testament promises and types 'narrow' and come to a focus in Christ, the one to whom all of God's promises point and in whom they all find their 'yes' (2 Cor. 1.20). But (Davidson argues) flowing out of Christ, the type then expands as these things are fulfilled not only in Christ himself, but also through him in his church and in the consummation.

This multi-layered fulfilment may sound like what is sometimes called the 'double fulfilment of prophecy', but the dynamic is different. In double fulfilment, some prophecies are understood to have a multi-layered fulfilment (e.g. fulfilled both in the return from exile and in the coming of Christ, or both in Christ's first and second comings), while most have only a straightforward single fulfilment ('this is that'), and there do not appear to be any criteria for determining in advance whether a particular prophecy will have a double fulfilment. Davidson offers a potentially richer understanding of fulfilment: *every* prophecy or type is susceptible to a fulfilment in Christ which then anticipates further fulfilments in the church and in the consummation. Apparent instances of double fulfilment are better understood as examples of this multi-layered typology.

There is ample evidence of a typological dynamic in Luke–Acts. We find reflections in Jesus' ministry of the ministries of Elijah and Elisha[162] and of Moses.[163] We find that the ministry of Jesus is a pattern for that of his followers: they, too, 'take up the cross' (Luke 9.22; cf. 23); they go through suffering (Luke 9.22; cf. Acts 9.16; 14.22 – δεῖ appears in all three passages); they are empowered by the Spirit (Acts 10.38; cf. 1.8); the apostles work 'signs and wonders' (Acts 2.22; cf. 2.43; 5.12; 14.3; 15.12). There are striking parallels as well between the ministries of Jesus and Stephen,[164] and Jesus and Paul.[165] The contention is that these are not

---

162. E.g. Craig A. Evans, 'The Function of the Elijah/Elisha Narratives in Luke's Ethic of Election', in *Luke and Scripture: The Function of Sacred Tradition in Luke–Acts* (ed. Craig A. Evans and Jack T. Sanders; Minneapolis: Fortress, 1993), 70–83.

163. E.g. Moessner, *Lord of the Banquet*. See especially Luke 9.31. See also the deliberate parallels between the ministries of Jesus and Moses in Stephen's speech. Tannehill, *Narrative Unity*, 91–92.

164. Tannehill, *Narrative Unity*, 80–101.

165. See their divine commissioning and reception of the Spirit in baptism (Luke 3.21-22; Acts 9.17); their articulation of their commission in the words from Isaiah (Luke 4.16-21; Acts 13.46-47);

merely literary devices, but reflect a divine necessity that things which happened in the ministry of Jesus 'must needs be' mirrored and fulfilled in his followers.

Davidson's appropriated or ecclesiological typology offers a model for understanding Acts 13.47. Typology is a biblical-theological or redemptive-historical category that is native to the demonstration of the fulfilling of God's promises in and through Christ in Luke–Acts. Davidson offers us the opportunity to have our cake and eat it too: we can affirm with Simeon (Luke 2.32) and with Paul (Acts 26.23) that Jesus is the servant who brings light to the nations, while at the same time affirming with Paul and Barnabas (Acts 13.47) that God has commanded these missionaries to be light to the nations. We can hold both to be true because of the typological relationship that exists between Christ and the church. The prophecy of the servant finds fulfilment first of all in Jesus, but also through him in his church – and particularly in those of his church entrusted with the responsibility to take his message to the nations.

Because the promise of the servant's bringing light to the nations has been fulfilled in Christ, it is thus incumbent on Paul and Barnabas to reflect that light on the nations through their own preaching. By virtue of the church's relationship to Christ, and because the promises fulfilled in him are also fulfilled in and through his church, when the servant-Messiah received Yahweh's commission to be light to the nations, so did the church.

3.5 *Summary*

Acts 13 marks a turning-point in the narrative of Acts. Up to this point in the narrative the gospel has been proclaimed primarily to Jews, with Peter as the primary spokesman. Beginning in Acts 13, Peter disappears from sight (except for Acts 15), Paul becomes the primary spokesman for the gospel, and he speaks everywhere to both Jews and Gentiles. The decisive change comes with the citation of Isa. 49.6 in Acts 13.47. The summary of Paul's first journey in 14.27 focuses exclusively on Gentile response to the gospel. The account of Paul's mission leads directly into the account of the council in Jerusalem that would conclusively address questions relating to Gentiles and the church.

Isaiah's prophecy of the 'servant' as 'a light to the nations' is echoed at least three times in Luke–Acts. The allusions in Luke 2.32 and Acts 26.23 are applied to Jesus and the salvation he brings to the Gentiles. Jesus' universal ministry arises in the context of opposition (Luke 2.32) and suffering (Acts 26.23) encountered in his initial ministry to Israel. In the explicit citation in Acts 13.47, the text is applied to the ministry of Paul and Barnabas, and through them to the church. Although the initial point of contact between the servant and the apostolic preachers is their common experience of frustration and failure in ministry to Israel, the Gentile mission is not merely a response to this rejection of the gospel, but derives from the promise of God through Isaiah and is required by the

---

their rejection and arrest by Jewish leaders in Jerusalem; their being delivered by the Jewish officials to Gentiles (Luke 18.32; Acts 21.11).

fulfilment of that promise in Jesus. In light of the servant's calling, Paul and Barnabas cannot *not* preach Jesus to Gentiles. The citation thus demonstrates the necessity of an intentional Gentile mission.

3.5.1 *Text*

The form of the citation is close enough to both the LXX and the MT that it could be derived from either. Luke exactly reproduces wording from the LXX, but does not follow it where it diverges (at least in some MSS) from the MT. There are no substantive textual issues, however, in the portion cited. It is impossible to determine whether the citation reflects a fresh rendering of the MT or an LXX MS closer to the MT than extant LXX MSS.

3.5.2 *Hermeneutic*

Although some have questioned whether Isa. 49.6 envisions the extension of God's saving work to Gentiles, we have seen that this is exactly what the text indicates. Luke's citation of this text in Acts 13.47 to legitimate the Gentile mission is in keeping with the text's original contextual meaning.

Luke employs a Christocentric hermeneutic in his interpretation and application of the prophecy of the servant and his work. Evidence from the rest of the OT leads us to expect that Yahweh's servant will be the object of Yahweh's special regard and play a distinctive role in the accomplishment of his (saving) purposes. In Luke 2.32 and Acts 26.23, the prophecy is applied to Jesus, but in Acts 13.47 to Paul and Barnabas. In the former two verses, we find the Christocentric hermeneutic of Luke 24.44 ('everything written about me in the law of Moses and the prophets and the psalms must be fulfilled'). In Acts 13.47, the same hermeneutic is employed, with the addition of a typological connection between Christ and his church (and particularly to the apostles as his official representatives). Davidson's appropriated/ecclesiological typology provides a conceptual framework that illuminates the way that the text is applied.

3.5.3 *Purpose*

The citation of Isa. 49.6 in Acts 13.47 is employed to demonstrate the legitimacy and necessity of an intentional Gentile mission. Paul appeals to this prophetic text to justify his claim that Christ's messengers have been commissioned by the Lord to preach to Gentiles. While Peter had been directed to preach in Cornelius' house (Acts 10–11) and some had preached to 'Greeks' in Antioch (11.20), this represents the first conscious decision by leaders of the church to preach to Gentiles, at least as recorded in the narrative of Acts. Such a significant and apparently unexpected step would not have been taken apart from divine direction. In Acts 13.47, Paul claims he received just such direction, not through a vision like Peter's (Acts 10), but through the commission of Yahweh to his servant in Isaiah 49.6, to be a light to the nations. Since Jesus had come in fulfilment of that commission, the church's (and particularly Paul's) active engagement in the Gentile mission is now an obligation. Paul (and Luke) uses the citation to demonstrate this; it functions as 'proof from prophecy' of the legitimacy of the Gentile mission.

The citation not only explains Paul's subsequent action in speaking again and again to Gentiles, but it assures readers that this step is in keeping with the plan of God and required by that plan's fulfilment in Jesus. The appeal to scripture legitimates this action both within the narrative and (thereby) for Luke's readers. The subsequent narrative, with the characterization of this missionary journey as one through which God 'had opened a door of faith to the Gentiles' (14.27), supports the interpretation given to the cited text. The citation, with the narrative of the success of this initial Gentile mission, sets the stage for the Jerusalem council in Acts 15, where there will be a final decision on the basis on which Gentiles are to be included among the people of God. That decision will also be based on OT prophecy. The careful crafting and evident focus of this section of Acts, including these two important appeals to OT prophecy, indicate that the legitimacy of the Gentile mission and the basis of Gentile inclusion were matters of importance for Luke and his intended audience.

THE KINGDOM AND THE GENTILES (AMOS 9.11-12 IN ACTS 15.16-18)

The citation of Amos 9.11-12 in Acts 15.16-17 plays a central role in the council that settled a critical theological question: the basis upon which Gentiles were to be admitted to the people of God.[1] Walter Kaiser has rightly called this important passage a 'test passage for theological systems'.[2] The citation has attracted study, but insufficient attention has been paid to the central argument, which is based on the relationship between the restoration of the Davidic kingdom in Christ and the Gentile mission.

4.1 *Text*

Amos 9.11-12 MT		*Amos 9.11-12 LXX*		*Acts 15.16-18 (NA²⁷)*
בַּיּוֹם הַהוּא	11a	ἐν τῇ ἡμέρᾳ ἐκείνῃ	16a	μετὰ ταῦτα
			b	ἀναστρέψω
אָקִים אֶת־סֻכַּת דָּוִיד הַנֹּפֶלֶת	b	ἀναστήσω τὴν σκηνὴν Δαυιδ τὴν πεπτωκυῖαν	c	καὶ ἀνοικοδομήσω τὴν σκηνὴν Δαυὶδ τὴν πεπτωκυῖαν
וְגָדַרְתִּי אֶת־פִּרְצֵיהֶן	c	καὶ ἀνοικοδομήσω τὰ πεπτωκότα αὐτῆς		
וַהֲרִסֹתָיו אָקִים	d	καὶ τὰ κατεσκαμμένα αὐτῆς ἀναστήσω	d	καὶ τὰ κατεσκαμμένα αὐτῆς ἀνοικοδομήσω
וּבְנִיתִיהָ	e	καὶ ἀνοικοδομήσω αὐτὴν	e	καὶ ἀνορθώσω αὐτήν,
כִּימֵי עוֹלָם	f	καθὼς αἱ ἡμέραι τοῦ αἰῶνος		
לְמַעַן יִירְשׁוּ אֶת־שְׁאֵרִית אֱדוֹם	12a	ὅπως ἐκζητήσωσιν οἱ κατάλοιποι τῶν ἀνθρώπων	17a	ὅπως ἂν ἐκζητήσωσιν οἱ κατάλοιποι τῶν ἀνθρώπων τὸν κύριον
וְכָל־הַגּוֹיִם אֲשֶׁר־נִקְרָא שְׁמִי עֲלֵיהֶם	b	καὶ πάντα τὰ ἔθνη, ἐφ' οὓς ἐπικέκληται τὸ ὄνομά μου ἐπ' αὐτούς	b	καὶ πάντα τὰ ἔθνη ἐφ' οὓς ἐπικέκληται τὸ ὄνομά μου ἐπ' αὐτούς,
נְאֻם־יְהוָה עֹשֶׂה זֹּאת	c	λέγει κύριος ὁ θεὸς ὁ ποιῶν ταῦτα.	c	λέγει κύριος ποιῶν ταῦτα
			18	γνωστὰ ἀπ' αἰῶνος.

---

1. 'For here, Luke says, the problem of the Gentiles and the Gentile mission is once and for all decided at a meeting in Jerusalem of all the main figures in the early church.' Wilson, *Gentile Mission*, 178.
2. Walter C. Kaiser, Jr., 'The Davidic Promise and the Inclusion of the Gentiles (Amos 9.9-15 and Acts 15.13-18): A Test Passage for Theological Systems', *JETS* 20 (1977): 97–111.

4.4.1 *Amos 9.11-12*

The MT of Amos 9.11-12 is well attested. BHS identifies no variants in the Hebrew textual tradition.[3] Two non-biblical texts from Qumran substitute the perfect וַהֲקִימֹתִי for the imperfect אָקִים, but this reflects the circumstances of the Qumran texts, not a different textual tradition.[4] BHS proposes changing the pronominal suffixes in 11c (feminine plural, פִּרְצֵיהֶן, '*their* breaches') and 11d (masculine singular, וַהֲרֹסֹתָיו, '*his* ruins') to feminine singular (as in 11e) to correspond with the feminine סֻכָּה in 'David's fallen hut'. In both 11c and 11d the Greek text (both the LXX and the NT) reads αὐτῆς (corresponding to the feminine σκηνή). Commentators have generally followed the Greek and the BHS emendation.[5] But not all commentators find it necessary to emend the pronominal suffixes. Niehaus[6] and Nogalski[7] have independently offered convincing arguments against these emendations, demonstrating plausible (*constructio ad sensum*) readings of the suffixes as they stand and noting that other versions generally support the MT. Their arguments, together with the principle of accepting the more difficult reading, support retaining the suffixes as they stand in the MT. In any case, the suffixes will not affect interpretation of the citation.

The LXX text of Amos 9.11-12 shows more variation. This includes transcriptional or stylistic variants, such as ἐν ταῖς ἡμέραις ἐκείναις for ἐν τῇ ἡμέρᾳ ἐκείνῃ (11a), ἐκζητήσουσιν for ἐκζητήσωσιν (12a), κατεστραμμένα for κατεσκαμμέν, and the addition of ἄν to ὅπως.[8] There are also minor differences from the MT of Amos 9.11-12. In addition to the feminine singular (αὐτῆς) for the feminine plural in 11c and masculine singular in 11d, two distinct verbs (וְגָדַרְתִּי in 11c and וּבְנִיתִיהָ in 11e) are translated by ἀνοικοδομήσω,[9] and the

---

3. Amos 9.11-12 is preserved in only one of the biblical scrolls from Qumran (Mur. 88, col. VIII) and only in a fragmentary form. The only textual question on which the fragment is able to shed any light is in v. 11d, where the masculine singular pronominal suffix clearly appears. Pierre Benoît et al., *Les grottes de Murabba'at* (2 vols.; DJD II; Oxford: Clarendon Press, 1961), pl. LVIII.

4. 4Q174 (4QFlor) and CDᵃ. Both citations are preceded by an introductory formula, כאשר כתוב (4Q174 1 1) or כאשר אמר (CDᵃ, VII, 16). In both סוכת is written fully and, in 4Q174, דויד and הנופלת are written fully.

5. See the list in James D. Nogalski, 'The Problematic Suffixes of Amos IX 11', *VT* 43 (1993): 417, n. 1.

6. Jeffery Niehaus, 'Amos', in *The Minor Prophets: An Exegetical and Expositional Commentary* (ed. Thomas Edward McComiskey; 3 vols.; Grand Rapids: Baker, 1992), 490.

7. Nogalski, 'Suffixes'.

8. Stylistic, possibly archaizing, interests may have prompted the addition of ἄν. Earl Richard, 'The Creative Use of Amos by the Author of Acts', *NovT* 24 (1982): 46; Rusam, *Das Alte Testament bei Lukas*, 426. The general trend is that 'ὅπως has largely lost its ἄν in NT'. James Hope Moulton et al., *A Grammar of New Testament Greek* (4 vols.; Edinburgh: T. & T. Clark, 1996–99), 3.105. See also BDF, §369(5).

9. Francis I. Andersen and David Noel Freedman, *Amos: A New Translation with Introduction and Commentary* (AB 24A; New York: Doubleday, 1989), 890. Ådna notes the repeated pattern ἀναστήσω ... ἀνοικοδομήσω in 11b-c and 11d-e, and argues that the rendering is stylistically motivated. Jostein Ådna, 'James' Position at the Summit Meeting of the Apostles and Elders in Jerusalem (Acts 15)', in *The Mission of the Early Church to Jews and Gentiles* (ed. Jostein Ådna and Hans Kvalbein; Tübingen: Mohr Siebeck, 2000), 129–30.

singular אֹת is rendered as the plural ταῦτα in 12c.[10] The external evidence favours the omission of ὁ θεὸς (leaving λέγει κύριος ὁ ποιῶν ταῦτα) in 12c and so *contra* Rahlfs, the Göttingen Septuagint rightly omits it.[11]

Much more striking and significant differences appear in 12a, where the LXX reads ὅπως ἐκζητήσωσιν οἱ κατάλοιποι τῶν ἀνθρώπων ('so that the rest of mankind will seek'[12]) for לְמַעַן יִירְשׁוּ אֶת־שְׁאֵרִית אֱדוֹם ('that they may possess the remnant of Edom'). While there are minor variants within the LXX tradition, no extant MSS are closer to the MT. Some MSS supply an object for ἐκζητήσωσιν by inserting με after the verb or τὸν κύριον following ἀνθρώπων. These competing 'solutions' suggest that the original lacked the object,[13] a more difficult reading that would readily explain the additions. While the secure text of Acts 15.17 provides an additional witness to τὸν κύριον, it seems most likely that the LXX original lacked the object.

The larger question is why the LXX diverges in this way from the MT. If, with most scholars, we view the LXX reading as derived from the MT, we can distinguish four changes: יִרְשׁ became ἐκζητέω; the object אֶת־שְׁאֵרִית אֱדוֹם became the subject; אֱדוֹם became אָדָם; and the singular שְׁאֵרִית and אָדָם became the plurals οἱ κατάλοιποι and τῶν ἀνθρώπων.[14] The Vulgate, reading *ut possideant reliquias Idumeae*, follows the MT.

Most commentators begin with the verb.[15] It is commonly thought that the translator read יָרַשׁ ('possess', 'inherit', 'dispossess') as דָרַשׁ ('seek', 'enquire'), mistakenly reading *yôd* in place of *dālet*, whether because of their similar appearance[16] or because of an unclear or damaged original (only here have the LXX translators rendered יָרַשׁ as ἐκζητέω). The change may also have been made intentionally by a translator who felt that the usual translation of יָרַשׁ by κληρονομέω was not appropriate here.[17]

10.   This is not uncommon, particularly with a generalizing sense. It appears in four of seven occurrences of אֹת in Amos (2.11; 8.4, 8; 9.11).

11.   Joseph Ziegler, *Duodecim Prophetae* (Septuaginta: Vetus Testamentum Graecum 13; Göttingen: Vandenhoeck & Ruprecht, 1984). 'God' could be understood as implicit in the Hebrew דָרַשׁ, but not in the Greek ἐκζητέω, prompting this 'filling in' of the Greek text. Sabine Nägele, *Laubhütte Davids und Wolkensohn: eine auslegungsgeschichtliche Studie zu Amos 9,11 in der jüdischen und christlichen Exegese* (AGJU 24; Leiden: Brill, 1995), 88.

12.   The translation 'men' has been retained only when explicitly citing RSV. Otherwise, following recent versions (e.g. JB, TEV, ESV) it has been rendered as 'mankind'.

13.   Although ἐκζητέω may occur without an object (e.g. Deut. 17.4; Josh. 2.22; Judg. 6.29; Ps. 9.25, 34), it normally (and much more frequently) takes an object in the accusative.

14.   Despite the assertion of de Waard, there is no evidence that a distinctive *Vorlage* of this section of Amos ever circulated. Jan de Waard, *A Comparative Study of the Old Testament Text in the Dead Sea Scrolls and in the New Testament* (STDJ 4; Leiden: Brill, 1965), 25, 78. Following de Waard is Michael A. Braun, 'James' Use of Amos at the Jerusalem Council: Steps toward a Possible Solution of the Textual and Theological Problems', *JETS* 20 (1977): 116–117.

15.   Barrett, *Acts*, 2.727; Richard Bauckham, 'James and the Jerusalem Church', in *The Book of Acts in its Palestinian Setting* (ed. Richard Bauckham; Grand Rapids: Eerdmans, 1995), 4.455; Bruce, *Acts* (rev. edn.), 294.

16.   'In the history of the transmission of the OT there was a time when *d* and *y* were virtually indistinguishable.' Braun, 'James' Use of Amos', 117.

17.   Karen H. Jobes and Moisés Silva, *Invitation to the Septuagint* (Grand Rapids: Baker, 2000),

The object clause, אֶת־שְׁאֵרִית אֱדוֹם, then became the subject. If the text initially became corrupt through misreading ירש as דרש, ὅπως ἐκζητήσωσιν τὸν κατάλοιπον Ἰδουμαίας would have been puzzling. The post-exilic community would not 'seek' the remnant of Edom in the way it worships and prays to Yahweh.[18] It has been suggested that the translator may have read אֶת as אֶל,[19] read אֶת instead as אֹתוֹ ('him') or אֹתִי ('me'),[20] ignored the object marker[21] or understood it differently.[22] However the change arose, either verb (יִירְשׁוּ or יִדְרְשׁוּ) requires an object; 'that the remnant of Edom will possess/seek' has no clear meaning.

Many commentators assume that אֱדוֹם was misread as אָדָם, due to their supposed identity in the consonantal text. The *wāw*, however, normally appears in 'Edom' and should prevent reading אֱדוֹם as אָדָם;[23] *wāw* is clearly present in extant Hebrew MSS, including the fragmentary copy of Amos among the Dead Sea Scrolls.[24] It may be that the translator's text was defective, or was faded, soiled or damaged, so that the *wāw* was not visible, but this cannot be proven. It is also possible that the translator interpreted the text, believing that 'the remnant of mankind' in 12a was a more natural parallel to 'all the nations' than 'the remnant of Edom',[25] or that Edom, as one of Israel's most persistent enemies, was to be

195. 'Possessing', i.e. 'ruling over', might have seemed more appropriate than 'inheriting' Edom in the context of a revived Davidic kingdom.

18.   The term is used in this sense in about a dozen of three dozen instances in the LXX of the prophets, including Amos 5.4; Isa. 9.12 MT; Jer. 10.21; Hos. 5.6; Zech. 8.21 (the last two translating בקשׁ rather than דרשׁ). The sense of 'searching for something' (e.g. Ezek. 34.8) is possible, if Edom is viewed as destroyed in judgement ('look and see if you can find anything left of Edom'), but it is unlikely that this would apply to 'all the nations who are called by my name'.

19.   Braun, 'James' Use of Amos', 117; Rainer Riesner, 'James's Speech, Simeon's Hymn, and Luke's Sources', in *Jesus of Nazareth: Lord and Christ* (ed. Joel B. Green and Max Turner; Grand Rapids: Eerdmans, 1994), 271. This may make better grammatical sense, but the meaning would still be unclear and we would not find LXX missing the object or trying to complete the thought by supplying με or τὸν κύριον. Ådna, 'James', 137. No LXX MS supplies τὸν θεόν as a missing direct object.

20.   Archer and Chirichingo, *OT Quotations*, 155. Some LXX MSS, versions, and fathers supply the direct object 'me', but this appears to be the result of copyists attempting to improve the sense by supplying the object they expected to find (cf. the similar addition of τὸν κύριον in Acts 15.17a).

21.   Jobes and Silva, *Invitation*, 194.

22.   Some grammarians believe that אֵת occasionally appears, not as the *nota accusativi*, but with the subject (or as an indicator of emphasis), making it possible that אֶת־שְׁאֵרִית אֱדוֹם was genuinely understood to be the subject by the LXX translator(s). *HALOT*, 101; GKC, §117 *i–m*; Christo van der Merwe et al., *A Biblical Hebrew Reference Grammar* (Sheffield: Sheffield Academic Press, 1999), 247; Waltke and O'Connor, *Syntax*, §10.3.2. For the contrary, see Takamitsu Muraoka, *Emphatic Words and Structures in Biblical Hebrew* (Jerusalem: Magnes Press, 1985), 158.

23.   '*Defective* spelling of Edom is unknown in the MT (except for the gentilic form), but it is possible that *ʾdm* survived to the time of the LXX alongside of *ʾdwm*.' Andersen and Freedman, *Amos*, 890. The noun occurs four times earlier in the book (1.6, 9, 11; 2.1), each time appropriately translated as Ἰδουμαία.

24.   Mur. 88. See Benoît et al., *Les grottes*, 188 and pl. LVIII.

25.   McLay suggests that the translation may have been influenced by the 'minor theme of the twelve prophets' that, following the restoration of Israel, the Gentiles would seek Yahweh (cf. Zech. 8.20-23; Mic. 7.17). R. Timothy McLay, *The Use of the Septuagint in New Testament Research* (Grand Rapids: Eerdmans, 2003). The LXX translators frequently interpreted and applied the text. Jobes and Silva, *Invitation*, 21–22, 93–101.

understood as a representative of them all.[26]

Once the object אֶת־שְׁאֵרִית אֱדוֹם has become the subject and אֱדוֹם has become ἄνθρωπος, the change from singular to plural is the least difficult to explain. At least 160 times (over one-quarter of all occurrences), the LXX translates the frequently collective אָדָם as ἄνθρωποι. Similarly, שְׁאֵרִית is translated more than half the time by a plural noun or participle (as here).

Bauckham, Ådna and Nägele have recently argued that the LXX of v. 12a does not depend on a now-lost Hebrew *Vorlage* or on transmissional errors, but must be understood in the context of the exegetical practices of the day as an instance of *'al tiqrē'* or 'implicit' midrash. Bauckham argues that those who think the LXX misreads the Hebrew

> entirely misunderstand the way in which Jewish exegesis of this period treated the biblical text, as the Dead Sea Scrolls in particular have now made clear to us. A Jewish Christian familiar both with the Hebrew and the LXX of this verse would not regard the latter as a misreading of the Hebrew ... . But in a case such as ours, it is scarcely possible to distinguish a variant text which has arisen accidentally in the transmission of the text from one which results from the exegetical practice of deliberately reading the text differently by means of small changes (known as *'al tiqrē'* in later rabbinic terminology). The 'misreading' of the Hebrew text presupposed by the LXX of Amos 9.12 is quite comparable with many examples of deliberate 'alternative readings' (*'al tiqrē'*) in the Qumran pesharim.[27]

The argument, however, cuts both ways. If 'it is scarcely possible to distinguish a variant text from one which results from the exegetical practice known as *'al tiqrē'*", then it is equally possible that we may have a misreading or an alternative original. However, in the absence of an extant Hebrew *Vorlage* that supports the LXX, we must assume that the translators have deliberately interpreted the text for Diaspora readers who might be more interested in a believing 'remnant'

---

26.   Kaiser, 'Davidic Promise', 103.

27.   Richard Bauckham, 'James and the Gentiles (Acts 15.13-21)', in *History, Literature, and Society in the Book of Acts* (ed. Ben Witherington III; Cambridge: Cambridge University Press, 1996), 160–61; Bauckham, 'James and the Jerusalem Church', 455–56. See also Jostein Ådna, 'Die Heilige Schrift als Zeuge der Heidenmission: Die Rezeption von Amos 9,11-12 in Apg 15,16-18', in *Evangelium, Schriftauslegung, Kirche* (ed. Jostein Ådna et al.; Göttingen: Vandenhoeck & Ruprecht, 1997), 1–23; Ådna, 'James', 131; Nägele, *Laubhütte Davids*, 104. 'Implicit midrash' is from Ellis, 'Biblical Interpretation', 703–06; Edward Earle Ellis, 'Midrash, Targum and New Testament Quotations', in *Neotestamentica et Semitica* (ed. Edward Earle Ellis and Max Wilcox; Edinburgh: T. & T. Clark, 1969), 62. 'Many a variant of the LXX may indeed not go back to a variant in the Hebrew texts which was translated, but merely represent an interpretation of that text, yet it must be questioned whether this holds good of all variants and of displacements of texts and parts of texts.' Doeve, *Jewish Hermeneutics*, 117. 'In those instances in which the LXX differs from the received or Masoretic Text, it may have been because of a different text, but it may also have resulted from the translation style, or tendential concerns, or the attempt to harmonize parallel passages.' Jacob Neusner, *What is Midrash?* (GBS; Philadelphia: Fortress, 1987), 24. Others seeing midrashic tendencies in the LXX include Johnson, *Septuagintal Midrash*; Emanuel Tov, 'The Septuagint', in *Mikra: Text, Translation, Reading and Interpretation of the Hebrew Bible in Ancient Judaism and Early Christianity* (ed. Martin Jan Mulder; CRINT 2.1; Assen: Van Gorcum, 1988), 177–78.

from the Gentiles than in the reassertion of political sovereignty over Edom.[28] Still, it is unclear why an interpreter, having already exercised some freedom in rendering the text, would not go ahead and supply the direct object that ἐκζη-τήσωσιν requires. Nevertheless, despite minor variants in the LXX MS tradition, the rendering 'that the rest of mankind may seek' must be regarded as the established LXX text.

4.1.2 *Acts 15.16-18*

Although the citation in Acts 15.16-18 appears to follow the LXX, especially in reading ὅπως ἂν ἐκζητήσωσιν οἱ κατάλοιποι τῶν ἀνθρώπων (adding the object, τὸν κύριον), it also differs from the LXX at a number of points.[29]

We can first dispense with several minor variants. In 16b, only D reads ἐπι-στρέψω for ἀναστρέψω.[30] The alternative readings for κατεσκαμμένα (16d) follow those in the LXX.[31] The evidence for ὁ before ποιῶν in 17c is divided, but the difference is of little consequence. Acts adds ἀναστρέψω (and καί, 16b), substitutes ἀνοικοδομήσω for ἀναστήσω (16c, d)[32] and substitutes ἀνορθώσω for ἀνοικοδομήσω in 16e (cf. Amos 9.11e),[33] but none of these alters the sense. The omission of Amos 9.11f, καθὼς αἱ ἡμέραι τοῦ αἰῶνος, may be due to conscious adaptation. James does not appeal to the prophecy merely to indicate the restoration of things 'as in days of old', but to demonstrate that God is doing something new.[34]

---

28. The LXX reading 'chimes in with the hope of many Jews of the dispersion that Gentiles would seek and find the true God'. Frederick F. Bruce, 'Prophetic Interpretation in the Septuagint', *BIOSCS* 12 (1979): 17.

29. Holtz notes that v. 17 adheres closely to the LXX ('ein ganz genaues Zitat'), while v. 16 departs significantly from it. Holtz, *Untersuchungen*, 23–25. Ellis has noted that all nine of the NT quotations that include λέγει κύριος 'vary, to one extent or another, both from the LXX and the M.T.' Edward Earle Ellis, 'Λέγει Κύριος Quotations in the New Testament', in *Prophecy and Hermeneutic in Early Christianity* (Grand Rapids: Eerdmans, 1978), 182.

30. The verb ἐπιστρέφω is more common, occurring 18 times in Luke–Acts and 18 more in the rest of the NT, while ἀναστρέφω occurs only twice in Acts and seven times in the rest of the NT.

31. This is the judgement of the editors of NA[27] and UBS[4]. However, the different conclusion of Tischendorf, WH and NA[25] necessitates a measure of humility.

32. This may reflect Luke's desire to reserve ἀνίστημι for the resurrection of Christ. Richard notes that the verb is used intransitively nine times in Acts, six with reference to the resurrection of Christ and three with reference to Deut. 18.15. Richard, 'Creative Use', 47; 'Divine Purpose', 206, n. 38. Bauckham argues that the substitution of ἀνοικοδομήσω for ἀναστήσω here clearly shows that Amos 9.11 is *not* employed here as a prophecy of Christ's resurrection (*contra* Haenchen). Bauckham, 'James and the Gentiles', 157. The verb ἀνοικοδομήσω appears to be borrowed from Amos 9.11c, which is omitted in Acts to yield a chiasm. In doing so, Acts breaks the symmetry of the LXX (ἀναστήσω … ἀνοικοδομήσω … ἀναστήσω … ἀνοικοδομήσω). (Bauckham believes 9.11c is omitted because it 'suggests more strongly the walls of a city than those of a temple', although this assumes that LXX is not the basis of the citation. Bauckham, 'James and the Gentiles', 160.)

33. If ἀνοικοδομήσω was substituted for ἀναστήσω for theological reasons, a different word may have been sought in 16e for stylistic reasons. McLay's suggestion that ἀνορθόω reflects the promise regarding David's 'house' in 2 Sam. 7.13, 16 (ἀνορθώσω τὸν θρόνον αὐτοῦ) cannot be substantiated. McLay, *Use*, 26–27.

34. McLay argues that, 'since the new situation brought about through Christ could not have

Some have claimed that the indefinite plural προφητῶν indicates conflation of words from more than one prophet.[35] However, the plural προφητῶν appears in citation formulas in Acts 7.42 (τῶν προφητῶν, citing Amos 5.25-27) and 13.41 (ἐν τοῖς προφήταις, citing Hab. 1.5), where there is no evidence of conflation with other texts. Lake and Cadbury rightly understand Acts 15.15 to refer to 'the roll of the Twelve Prophets'.[36]

Nevertheless, a number of scholars have claimed that portions of the citation are taken from other prophetic texts.[37] Verse 16a has μετὰ ταῦτα in place of the more common ἐν τῇ ἡμέρᾳ ἐκείνῃ (straightforwardly representing MT בַּיּוֹם הַהוּא).[38] Verse 16b (ἀναστρέψω) is an addition to Joel. One proposed source is Hos. 3.5a, which has μετὰ ταῦτα and Δαυιδ (although both occur elsewhere), ἐπιστρέψουσιν (not the less common ἀναστρέψω, which differs in person and number), and ἐπιζητήσουσιν (not the more common ἐκζητήσουσιν). In Hosea, it is the people who return, not Yahweh. Jeremiah 12.15-16 is concerned with the eschatological incorporation of the nations in the people of God; it includes μετά (but not ταῦτα), ἐπιστρέψω (not ἀναστρέψω), and (42 words later) οἰκοδομηθήσονται (not the active and less common ἀνοικοδομέω).[39] Holtz has suggested there may be a reflection of Zech. 1.16,[40] which speaks of the restoration of the temple, but again ἐπιστρέψω is not ἀναστρέψω and other texts also share the word ἀνοικοδομέω.[41] These similarities are too slight to make a convincing case for borrowing or conflation.[42] Barrett and Richard have

existed in a former time ... the reference to *the days of old* would not have contributed to the point being made'. McLay, *Use*, 29.

35.   Ådna, 'James', 133; Witherington, *Acts*, 459.

36.   Frederick J. Foakes Jackson and Kirsopp Lake, eds., *The Beginnings of Christianity, Part I: The Acts of the Apostles* (5 vols.; London: Macmillan, 1920–33; repr., Grand Rapids: Baker, 1979), 4.176. See also Johnson, *Acts*, 264; Marshall, *Acts*, 252. The only citation from the Twelve that is more precisely introduced is the lengthy citation from Joel (Acts 2.16-21). Like other quotations Luke shares with the synoptics, the quotation of Mal. 3.1 (Luke 7.27 ∥ Mark 1.2) does not indicate the source.

37.   Ådna, 'Die Heilige Schrift', 5–8; 'James', 133–34; Bauckham, 'James and the Gentiles', 163–64; Clarke, 'Use', 2.94.

38.   The expression בַּיּוֹם הַהוּא occurs over 100 times in the prophets (translated almost always by ἐν τῇ ἡμέρᾳ ἐκείνῃ or a close variant). The expression μετὰ ταῦτα is used only four times in the LXX of the prophets for the eschatological future, each time as a translation of אַחֲרֵי־כֵן or אַחַר (Hos. 3.5; Joel 3.1; Isa. 1.26; Jer. 21.7; cf. Gen. 15.14). It appears four times in the NT (Acts 7.7; Heb. 4.8; 1 Pet. 1.11; Rev. 20.3).

39.   McLay finds 'no demonstrable lexical dependence of the quote in Acts on the quote in Jeremiah' and judges any connection to be based upon 'extremely tenuous reasoning'. McLay, *Use*, 18.

40.   Holtz, *Untersuchungen*, 25.

41.   Malachi 1.4 also has ἐπιστρέψω, ἀνοικοδομέω and λέγει κύριος, but there what 'God says' is that he will prevent the Edomites from succeeding in their plans to return and rebuild. Jeremiah 1.10 shares ἀνοικοδομέω and κατασκάπτω with Acts 15.16-18, but this simply establishes that these two verbs are naturally associated (as opposites). There is no indication in Acts 15 of borrowing or the conflation of either with Amos 9.11-12.

42.   Thus Nägele's conclusion that 'there are no literal quotations of other Scriptures'. Nägele, *Laubhütte Davids*, 81–82, 229.

observed that the substitution in 16a is reversed in 2.17, where Acts reads καὶ ἔσται ἐν ταῖς ἐσχάταις ἡμέραις in place of μετὰ ταῦτα (Joel 3.1 LXX),[43] suggesting that there was some interchangeability in these expressions.[44] Once we have recognized the likelihood of other stylistic adaptations in the citation, there is no need to explain these differences by strained connections to additional texts. As Richard concludes (in rejecting an allusion to Jer. 12.15), 'Luke's compositional techniques and thematic concerns provide sufficient explanation for this modification.'[45] And the relevance of the text for the argument in Acts 15 does not depend on these particular words.

The concluding words, ταῦτα γνωστὰ ἀπ' αἰῶνος, are somewhat problematic. There are numerous variants.[46] The editors of NA[27] and UBS[4] have wisely chosen the shorter reading as the original text.[47] The words do not appear in Amos 9 in any known MT or LXX MS. It has been suggested that they may be an editorial comment to the effect that 'this has been God's intention all along'.[48] Many find a reference to Isa. 45.21,[49] but ἐποίησεν ταῦτα ἀπ' ἀρχῆς (Isa. 45.21) is not a particularly close parallel and there is no clear reason for its addition here.[50] Others suggest that the phrase is a free adaptation of the otherwise omitted καθὼς αἱ ἡμέραι τοῦ αἰῶνος from Amos 9.11f.[51] No entirely satisfactory explanation has been offered.

It has been argued that Acts 15.16 independently reproduces an alternative Hebrew *Vorlage*, evident in the citations of Amos 9.11 at Qumran (4Q174 1 I and CD[a] VII, 16). 'The text form of the Amos quotation in Acts differs from that of the MT and the LXX, but it is exactly identical with that of 4QFlor.'[52] In fact,

43. Barrett, *Acts*, 2.725; Richard, 'Creative Use', 47. See also the substitution of μετὰ ταῦτα in 7.7 for ἐν τῷ ἐξαγαγεῖν σε τὸν λαόν μου ἐξ Αἰγύπτου from Exod. 3.12.

44. 'The two temporal elements seem to have been interchanged according to the author's needs.' Richard, 'Creative Use', 47, n. 23.

45. Richard, 'Creative Use', 48, n. 27.

46. Reuben Swanson, ed., *The Acts of the Apostles*, in *New Testament Greek Manuscripts: Variant Readings Arranged in Horizontal Lines Against Codex Vaticanus* (Sheffield: Sheffield Academic Press, 1998), 262.

47. 'The reading ... is so elliptical an expression that copyists made various attempts to recast the phrase, rounding it out as an independent statement.' Metzger, *Textual Commentary*, 379.

48. 'Since the quotation from Am 9.12 ends with ταῦτα, the concluding words are James's comment.' Metzger, *Textual Commentary*, 379.

49. Huub van de Sandt, 'An Explanation of Acts 15.6-21 in the Light of Deuteronomy 4.20-35 (LXX)', *JSNT* 46 (1992): 81–84.

50. 'There is little contact between our quotation and Is 45,21 in the LXX.' George D. Kilpatrick, 'Some Quotations in Acts', in *Les Actes des Apôtres: Traditions, rédaction, théologie* (ed. J. Kremer; BETL 48; Leuven: J. Duculot, 1979), 84. So also Barrett, *Acts*, 2.728; McLay, *Use*; Nägele, *Laubhütte Davids*, 88–89.

51. Toy, *Quotations*, 122. 'In free scripture quotation (and that verse of Amos has been freely quoted in vs. 16) Luke and presumably others often transfer a phrase from one part of a quotation to another. The Hebrew parallelism lent itself to such transfer of phrases.' Foakes Jackson and Lake, eds., *Beginnings*, 4.176–77. See also Jacques Dupont, '"Je rebâtirai la cabane de David qui est tombée" (Ac 15,16 = Am 9,11)', in *Glaube und Eschatologie* (ed. Erich Grässer and Otto Merk; Tübingen: J. C. B. Mohr, 1985), 25; Nägele, *Laubhütte Davids*, 85.

52. Waard, *Comparative Study*, 25, cf. 78. See also George J. Brooke, *Exegesis at Qumran:*

the differences are less than are claimed.[53] The introductory formulas differ in the two Qumran texts[54] and are employed commonly enough in Luke–Acts in any case. The adaptation of וַהֲקִימוֹתִי (*wāw* plus perfect) in place of the imperfect אָקִים would only be evident in the καί in Acts 15.16c, which is required in any case by the addition of ἀναστρέψω at the beginning of the quotation (and already present in καὶ ἀνοικοδομήσω in the LXX of Amos 9.11c, which is otherwise omitted from Acts 15.16).[55]

With the exception of v. 18, then, the text of the citation in Acts 15 is relatively secure. The textual form of the citation appears closer to the LXX than the MT. The amendment at the beginning (μετὰ ταῦτα), the addition at the end (γνωστὰ ἀπ᾽ αἰῶνος), and the alterations in v. 16 suggest that the author is citing freely, possibly without a copy of Amos 9 before him.[56]

4.2 *Amos 9.11-12*

The prophecy of Amos is set in the first half of the eighth century BCE, during the reigns of Jeroboam II of Israel and Uzziah of Judah, the 'Silver Age of Israelite history'.[57] The advances of the Assyrian king Adad-nirari III (811–784) had seriously weakened the Aramaean power to Israel's north. Although Israel became tributary to Assyria, neither Adad-nirari nor his successors were able to consolidate their authority over Syro-Palestine. With the weakening of Damascus, both Israel and Judah enjoyed almost unprecedented political and economic prosperity.[58] The period, however, was also one of advanced moral and spiritual bankruptcy. Amos and his contemporary, Hosea, condemned the northern kingdom for murder (Hos. 4.2), adultery (Hos. 4.2, 12-15; Amos 2.7-8), theft and deceit (Hos. 4.2; Amos 5.10), oppression and injustice (Hos. 10.13; Amos 2.6-7; 4.1; 5.11; 8.4-6), bribery (Amos 5.12), drunkenness (Hos. 4.11; Amos 2.8; 4.1; 6.6), superficial spirituality (Hos. 6.6; Amos 4.4-5; 5.21-27), faith in military power (Hos. 10.13),

---

4QFlorilegium in its Jewish Context (JSOTSup 29; Sheffield: JSOT Press, 1985), 210–11; Riesner, 'James's Speech', 271.

53.   F. F. Bruce argues that 'it takes more than the omission of "in that day" and the insertion of "and" before "I will (re)build" to provide an adequate basis for such a conclusion.' Bruce, *Acts* (Greek Text, 3rd edn.), 340. See also Chaim Rabin, *The Zadokite Documents* (2nd rev. edn.; Oxford: Clarendon Press, 1958), 29; Martin Stowasser, 'Am 5,25-27; 9,11f. in der Qumranüberlieferung und in der Apostelgeschichte', *ZNW* 92 (2001): 47–63.

54.   The introductory formula 'as it is written' (present in 4Q174, but 'as he said' in CDᵃ) is common enough. There is no need to hypothesize that a text with this formula must lie behind Acts 15.16.

55.   Ådna argues for an alternative Hebrew *Vorlage* behind Acts 15.17, but concedes that 'on its own' the case is 'very speculative', and is rendered 'more likely' only in light of the supposed *Vorlage* lying behind 15.16 (viewed as established). Ådna, 'James', 138.

56.   Barrett believes this is 'probably a simple gloss rather than an additional quotation'. Barrett, *Acts*, 2.728.

57.   Shalom M. Paul, *Amos: A Commentary on the Book of Amos* (Hermeneia; Minneapolis: Fortress, 1991), 1.

58.   John Bright, *A History of Israel* (Philadelphia: Westminster, 1972), 253–55.

idolatry (Hos. 4.17; 8.4; 10.5-6; 11.2; 13.2; Amos 2.4), and Baal worship (Hos. 2.8; 7.16; 13.1). After announcing judgement on surrounding nations (Damascus, Gaza, Tyre, Edom, Ammon, Moab) in 1.3–2.3, Amos announces God's judgement on Judah and then, at greater length, on Israel for its many sins. 'Thus says the LORD: "For three transgressions of Israel, and for four, I will not revoke the punishment"' (2.6; cf. 7.8-9; 8.9-10; 9.1, 9-10).

Many have questioned whether Amos 9.11-15 is the work of the prophet whose words are recorded in the rest of the book. Although linguistic and other arguments have been advanced,[59] there are two fundamental objections.

First, the hopeful tone of these verses is seen as incompatible with Amos's message – 'Rosen und Lavendel statt Blut und Eisen' as Wellhausen famously declared.[60] This change of tone, however, is not unusual.

> The message of hope and restoration following repeated oracles of doom may be startling to some, but the typical pattern of oracles in the other eighth-century B.C. prophets is that of hope for salvation following oracles of judgment.[61]

> The fact that throughout the book, Amos speaks of doom and judgment, and in the epilogue, of restoration and a bright future, did not create a literary problem for the Rabbis. On the contrary, that was to them characteristic of all the prophets who followed the example of Moses by inaugurating their prophetic utterances with words of reproach and closing them with words of comfort.[62]

If not prominent, the message of hope is not absent from Amos. Yahweh twice averts planned destruction (7.3, 6).[63] Despite warnings that 'not one of them shall escape' (9.1), a few will be saved 'as the shepherd rescues from the mouth of the lion two legs, or a piece of an ear' (3.12). Although 'everyone' dies, those who come to dispose of the bodies find one still alive (6.9-10). Yahweh promises that he will 'not utterly destroy the house of Jacob' (9.8). The message of hope in 9.11-15 is not alien to Amos's message and therefore need not be a later addition.[64]

59.   Shalom Paul contends that 'the arguments for the lateness of the pericope are based on linguistic and ideological grounds, all of which, however, are seriously open to question' and that 'almost all of the arguments for later interpolations and redactions, including a Deuteronomistic one, are shown to be based on fragile foundations and inconclusive evidence'. Paul, *Amos*, 288, 6.

60.   'Ich glaube nicht, dass 9,8-15 von Amos herrührt.' Julius Wellhausen, *Die kleine Propheten übersetzt und erklärt* (4th edn.; Berlin: Vandenhoeck & Ruprecht, 1963), 96. See the references in Gerhard F. Hasel, *The Remnant: The History and Theology of the Remnant Idea from Genesis to Isaiah* (Berrien Springs, Mich.: Andrews University Press, 1972), 207–08, n. 300.

61.   Billy K. Smith, 'Amos', in *Amos, Obadiah, Jonah* (ed. Billy K. Smith and Frank S. Page; NAC 19B; Nashville: Broadman & Holman, 1995), 164. Smith notes the messages of hope following judgement in Hos. 1.10–2.1; Mic. 2.12-13; 4.1-5; and the alternating messages of judgement and hope in Isaiah 1–5 as examples. See also Ronald E. Clements, *Prophecy and Covenant* (SBT 43; London: SCM Press, 1965), 110–14. Andersen and Freedman observe that 'the hope of salvation in the near future was given up completely, but not all hope for the future'. Andersen and Freedman, *Amos*, 8.

62.   Hyman J. Routtenberg, *Amos of Tekoa: A Study in Interpretation* (New York: Vantage, 1971), 169.

63.   William Sanford LaSor et al., *Old Testament Survey* (Grand Rapids: Eerdmans, 1982), 325.

64.   Benson points also to 3.2; 4.11; 5.3, 4-6, 14-15. Alphonsus Benson, '"… From the Mouth of

Second, some have argued that the conditions in these verses did not yet exist in Amos's day. The Davidic kingdom had not 'fallen' and the walls of Jerusalem had not been breached.[65] But this reasoning fails to understand the prophetic perspective. Amos has already announced Israel's defeat; *now* he promises that *after* the Davidic kingdom has fallen into disrepair, God will restore Davidic rule and Israel's prosperity.[66] 'The argument that "abruptness of transition" to a picture of restoration unaccompanied by an announcement of destruction points to a later dating completely misinterprets the purport of the prophetic announcements.'[67] But, then again, 'Amos need not have to look that far into the future to see a ruined Davidic dynasty.'[68] Its division had already diminished the glory of David's kingdom.[69] There are no arguments that compel us to deny the authenticity of these verses.[70]

There are also connections between 9.11-15 and earlier portions of Amos: 'in that day' (9.11a, cf. 8.3, 9, 13); David's 'fallen' hut (11b) and 'fallen ... virgin Israel' (5.2; see also 7.17; 8.14) as well as David's hut (11b); the repeated use of the *hipʿil* of קוּם;[71] the infrequent פֶּרֶץ ('breaches', 4.3; 11c);[72] references to Edom;[73] and the 'remnants' of the Philistines (1.8), Joseph (5.15) and Edom (12a). Although the Davidic kingdom is not usually seen as prominent in Amos, one scholar has recently argued that the division of the kingdom is the northern kingdom's central sin for Amos and its reunification the prophet's goal.[74] It is not unreasonable to view 9.11-12 as the words of Amos. In any case, first-century interpreters would have read them in light of the book.

the Lion": The Messianism of Amos', *CBQ* 19 (1957): 199–212. On 'Amos' Future Hope and Eschatology', see Gerhard F. Hasel, *Understanding the Book of Amos: Basic Issues in Current Interpretations* (Grand Rapids: Baker, 1991), 105–20.

65.   Nogalski, 'Suffixes', 416–17.

66.   Hammershaimb argues that the same issues arise in the prophecies of Hosea, Isaiah, Micah and Jeremiah. 'We cannot therefore conclude from this expression that the prophet lives in or after the exile.' Erling Hammershaimb, *The Book of Amos: A Commentary* (trans. John Sturdy; Oxford: Basil Blackwell, 1970), 137–38.

67.   Paul, *Amos*, 289.

68.   Benson, ' "... From the Mouth of the Lion" ', 210.

69.   Clements argues for an early date for the book on just this basis. Clements, *Prophecy*, 111–12. See also the argument of Max E. Polley, *Amos and the Davidic Kingdom: A Socio-Historical Approach* (New York: Oxford University Press, 1989).

70.   Roberts 'is not convinced the general skepticism [regarding an eighth-century date] is warranted.' Jimmy J. M. Roberts, 'The Old Testament's Contribution to Messianic Expectation', in *The Messiah: Developments in Earliest Judaism and Christianity* (ed. James H. Charlesworth; Minneapolis: Fortress, 1992), 44. So also Gerhard von Rad, *Old Testament Theology* (trans. D. M. Starker; London: Oliver & Boyd, 1965), 2.138. For other scholars who support the authenticity of these verses, see Benson, ' "... From the Mouth of the Lion": The Messianism of Amos', 208, n. 37.

71.   Amos uses the *hipʿil* of קוּם five times in his brief book, as many times as Ezekiel and one fewer than Isaiah.

72.   Only Isaiah, Ezekiel and Amos use this noun, each of them twice.

73.   Amos mentions Edom five times (1.6, 9, 11; 2.1; 9.12a). Edom is mentioned only 28 times in the prophetic books: by Isaiah (4), Jeremiah (8), Ezekiel (7), Joel (1), Amos (5), Obadiah (1) and Malachi (1).

74.   Polley, *Amos*.

4.2.1 *The Booth of David (Amos 9.11)*

Amos 9.11 anticipates בַּיּוֹם הַהוּא, a standard prophetic term for the future,[75] here following the judgement Amos has announced. 'In that day' God will 'raise up the booth of David that is fallen'. The סֻכַּת דָּוִיד, the 'booth of David', has been variously interpreted. At Qumran, its raising was interpreted as the fulfilment of the Torah by the community (CD VII, 12–21) and the appearance of the 'branch of David', who was expected to arise with the 'Interpreter of Torah' (4Q174 1 I, 10–13).[76] The rabbis generally understood it as the restoration of Davidic rule, national sovereignty, the rebuilding of Jerusalem, and the rebuilding of the temple;[77] *Bar Nafle*, 'son of the fallen', was even taken as a title for the Messiah.[78] Early Christian interpreters saw both an historical application of the text to Israel's return from exile and a Christological reading in which the 'tent of David' referred to the body of Christ (i.e. the church). Nicholas of Lyra applied the text to the restoration of the purity of the church (i.e. true worship without idols) and Luther to the 'preaching the Gospel of faith'.[79] Other proposals have included the tents of David's military campaigns,[80] the cities of the Davidic kingdom,[81] the city of Succoth,[82] and a royal or bridal canopy that signifies God's 'covering' his people,[83] the tent David pitched for the ark (2 Sam. 6.17)[84] or the celebration of the feast of tabernacles in Jerusalem.[85] Most recent commentators have understood

---

75. The expression (with rare exceptions) refers to a future (often eschatological) event. BDB, s.v. יום, 7.g. Robertson doubts an eschatological reference here. O. Palmer Robertson, 'Hermeneutics of Continuity', in *Continuity and Discontinuity: Perspectives on the Relationship Between the Old and New Testaments* (ed. John S. Feinberg; Westchester, Ill.: Crossway, 1988), 89.

76. Florentino García Martinéz and Eiblert J. C. Tigchelor, *The Dead Sea Scrolls Study Edition* (2 vols.; Grand Rapids: Eerdmans, 1997–98), 561, 353; Nägele, *Laubhütte Davids*, 225–26.

77. Nägele, *Laubhütte Davids*, 226–28.

78. *b. Sanh.* 96b–97a; Routtenberg, *Amos*, 127.

79. For a thorough survey of the interpretation of the text since Qumran, see Nägele, *Laubhütte Davids*.

80. Andersen and Freedman, *Amos*, 915.

81. The argument is based on the application of the term סֻכָּה to Jerusalem in Isa. 1.8. Nogalski, 'Suffixes', 416–17.

82. Reading סֻכֹּת for סֻכָּה, a city that, although in ruins by Amos's time, Richardson believes to have held a strategic role in David's occupation of Transjordan. H. Neil Richardson, '*SKT* (Amos 9.11): "Booth" or "Succoth"', *JBL* 92 (1973): 377–79. He has been followed by others, including Douglas L. Stuart, *Hosea–Jonah* (WBC 31; Waco: Word, 1987). However, the evidence offered seems exceedingly thin and 'it is not likely that the passage in Amos 9.11 has in mind the restoration and rebuilding of Succoth'. Andersen and Freedman, *Amos*, 915.

83. John Mauchline, 'Implicit Signs of a Persistent Belief in the Davidic Empire', *VT* 20 (1970): 290–91.

84. Philip Mauro, 'Building the Tabernacle of David', *EvQ* 9 (1937): 398–413. The term in 2 Sam. 6.17, however, is אֹהֶל, not סֻכָּה.

85. Nägele associates the feast of tabernacles with the temple (and ultimately Jerusalem) and understands the text both as warning Judah that the temple would not protect them from God's judgement and as promising a harvest from all nations for Yahweh. Nägele, *Laubhütte Davids*, 236–38. However, there is no evidence that the temple was ever referred to by סֻכָּה (193), nor of a link between the feast of booths and the temple (194–95). Motyer believes the king played a prominent

an ironic reference to David's 'house' (i.e. family, dynasty, kingdom), although they have different views of the occasion of its 'fall', including the division following the death of Solomon, Joash's conquest of Judah, or the exile.[86]

A סֻכָּה is a temporary shelter. Jacob built 'booths' for his cattle (at Succoth, Gen. 33.17) and Jonah waited in a 'booth' to see Nineveh's judgement (4.5). A 'booth' was temporary, like the tents of military campaigns (2 Sam. 11.11; 1 Kgs. 20.12, 16). It was also vulnerable and fragile: the house of the wicked is 'like a spider's web, like a booth which a watchman makes' (Job 27.18); 'the daughter of Zion is left like a booth in a vineyard, like a lodge (מְלוּנָה)[87] in a cucumber field, like a besieged city' (Isa. 1.8). It may refer generally to shelter (Isa. 4.6; Ps. 31.20) and (probably in this general sense) to God's heavenly dwelling (2 Sam. 22.12 ‖ Ps. 18.11; Job 36.29). Thirteen of the 31 occurrences of the term refer to the 'booths' in which Israel was to live during the feast of booths (חַג הַסֻּכֹּת), although סֻכָּה alone never refers to the festival.[88] The term never refers to the tabernacle, which is uniformly represented by אֹהֶל or מִשְׁכָּן.[89] Neither the tabernacle nor the feast of booths were associated with David ('booth of Moses' would be more apt for either). David pitched a tent for the ark in Jerusalem (2 Sam. 6.17; 1 Chr. 15.1; 16.1), but the term is אֹהֶל, not סֻכָּה, and there is no other indication that this tent played a lasting role in Israel's thinking or expectation. Neither the tabernacle nor temple are ever described as 'of David' (or even Solomon). It is therefore unlikely that the term in Amos 9.11 refers to the festival, tabernacle or temple.

There is an analogous expression referring to Davidic rule that has received too little attention. Isaiah 16.5 speaks of a 'tent of David' (אֹהֶל דָּוִד, LXX σκηνή Δαυιδ as here): 'then a throne will be established in steadfast love and on it will sit in faithfulness in the tent of David one who judges and seeks justice and is swift to do righteousness'. Admittedly, this is an אֹהֶל, not a סֻכָּה, but the semantic fields of the two overlap.[90] The context (Isaiah 15–16) is an oracle concerning Moab.[91] In distress, Moab appeals to Judah for assistance. God promises that

role at the feast and sees here a hope of the coming of the perfect royal and priestly mediator. J. Alec Motyer, *The Day of the Lion* (Downers Grove, Ill.: Inter-Varsity, 1975), 202–03.

86. Nägele, *Laubhütte Davids*, 231–33, 155–57.

87. Used only here and at Isa. 24.20, where the earth 'is violently shaken' (24.19) and 'sways like a hut'. BDB glosses as 'sim. of frail, insecure structure'.

88. For the festival: Lev. 23.34; Deut. 16.13, 16; 31.10; Ezra 3.4; 2 Chr. 8.13; Zech. 14.16, 18, 19; cf. Neh. 8.14 ('the people of Israel should dwell in booths during the feast of the seventh month'). For the booths themselves: Lev. 23.42 (2×), 43; Ezra 3.4; Neh. 8.15, 16, 17 (2×).

89. It is unlikely that the related סֹךְ in Ps. 76.3 refers to the tabernacle or temple, although the temple is in view in שׂךְ (for סֹךְ as BDB suggests?) in Lam. 2.6. Neither of these, however, is סֻכָּה.

90. In about two-thirds of occurrences, אֹהֶל refers to the 'tabernacle' or 'tent of meeting'. In the remaining third, it simply refers to a tent (e.g. the temporary shelters of soldiers in the field, as in Judg. 6.5; 7.8, 13; 2 Kgs. 7.7, 8, 10; Jer. 6.3), although it was apparently used for 'home', even after Israel began to live in settled communities (e.g. 1 Sam. 4.10; 13.2; 2 Sam. 18.7; 19.8; 20.1, 22; 1 Kgs. 8.66; 12.16; 2 Kgs. 8.21; 14.12; 2 Chr. 7.10; 25.22). The term appears to be used for a city on only two occasions (Jerusalem in Isa. 33.20; and as parallel to 'dwellings', 'city' and 'palace' in Jer. 30.18).

91. Scholars differ on the precise circumstances and date of this oracle. See e.g. John Bright,

Moab's oppression will cease and that a good king 'will sit in the tent of David' and dispense 'justice and righteousness'. No human king of Israel ruled from the tabernacle or temple and Jerusalem is never described as the seat of justice and righteousness. The reference must then refer to one who rules (sits) in David's place, on David's throne, and is of David's line.[92]

The 'booth' is therefore the 'house'[93] or dynasty God promised to build for David (2 Sam. 7.11). The expression is ironic. The formerly great 'house' has become a rundown shack.[94] It has either already fallen from its earlier glory[95] or will soon do so.[96] In any case, it *will* have fallen before God raises it up again. While 'fallen' 'virgin Israel' (5.2; cf. 7.17; 8.14) had 'none to raise her up', Yahweh will 'raise up the booth of David that is fallen' and 'its ruins'.[97] It will no longer be 'fallen', but 'as in the days of old' (11f). While the division of the kingdom is not the primary focus, its reunification is implied: 'David and his promises relate to the entire nation of chosen people, not one part of it.'[98]

4.2.2 *The Remnant of Edom (Amos 9.12)*
In v. 12, the purpose or result (לְמַעַן) of this restoration is expressly stated: 'that they may possess the remnant of Edom and all the nations who are called by my name'.[99] A number of questions have challenged interpreters: why Edom is singled out; what 'the remnant of Edom' means; who will 'possess' it and in what sense; how 'the remnant of Edom' is related to 'all the nations'; what it means that God's 'name is called upon them'.

'Isaiah—I', in *Peake's Commentary on the Bible* (ed. Matthew Black; Sunbury-on-Thames: Thomas Nelson, 1962), 501; Ronald E. Clements, *Isaiah 1–39* (NCB; Grand Rapids: Eerdmans, 1980), 150–51; John Oswalt, *The Book of Isaiah: Chapters 1–39* (NICOT; Grand Rapids: Eerdmans, 1986), 336.

92. Bright, 'Isaiah', 501; Clements, *Isaiah 1–39*, 154; Motyer, *Prophecy*, 149, 152–53; Oswalt, *Isaiah*, 343.

93. Hammershaimb, *Amos*, 140; Carl F. Keil, *Minor Prophets* (trans. James Martin; Grand Rapids: Eerdmans, 1973), 329; Simon M. Lehrman, 'Amos', in *The Twelve Prophets: Hebrew Text, English Translation and Commentary* (ed. Abraham Cohen; Soncino Books of the Bible; Bournemouth: Soncino, 1948), 123.

94. For the 'booth' as representing a diminished or dishonoured state, see Isa. 1.8, 'And the daughter of Zion is left like a booth in a vineyard, like a lodge in a cucumber field, like a besieged city.' However, סֻכָּה need not indicate a humble state, since the term is applied to 'the Lord's heavenly pavilion'. Niehaus, 'Amos', 490. Cf. 2 Sam. 12.22 || Ps. 18.11; Job 36.29.

95. 'After the death of David, Israel's sovereignty declined fast.' Hammershaimb, *Amos*, 141. 'In our view what had fallen was the empire, and that had happened a long time ago.' Andersen and Freedman, *Amos*, 916. Others see a reference specifically to the division after Solomon's death. Clements, *Prophecy*, 111–12; Nogalski, 'Suffixes', 416–17; Polley, *Amos*.

96. The participle may be translated 'falling' or 'fallen'. The LXX translates with the perfect πεπτωκυῖαν. Benson notes that 'the *Qal* participle *nophelet* could mean either, but the context favours "which has fallen"'. Benson, '"... From the Mouth of the Lion"', 210.

97. For similar language of 'ruins' with reference to the defeated kingdom, see Pss. 80.12 (80.13 MT; 79.13 LXX); 89.40 (89.41 MT; 88.41 LXX).

98. Gary V. Smith, *Amos* (rev. edn.; Ross-Shire: Christian Focus, 1998), 379.

99. The expression 'implies an order both in purpose and time'. Robertson, 'Hermeneutics', 91.

Interpretations fall into two major camps. One understands the prophecy to refer to the reestablishment of the Israelite kingdom politically as it had been under David and Solomon. 'The remnant of Edom' is 'that part of Edom which is still independent' (not under Davidic rule).[100] 'They' are Davidic kings who will reassert control over Edom as David had done (2 Sam. 8.13-14) in the final phase of the campaign that secured peace for Israel and established his rule. 'They' would 'possess' 'the remnant of Edom' as Israel 'possessed' the nations of Canaan under Joshua, by dispossession and destruction. 'The conquest of Edom in particular would be understood to be either the final step in the reestablishment of the Davidic kingdom'[101] or an exercise of its restored power. 'All the nations upon which my name is called' are the nations God ruled through David at the height of his power, i.e. Moab, Ammon, Philistia and Syria.[102]

There are at least three difficulties with this view. First, the consistent use of remnant language, and of שארית in particular, suggests that the 'remnant of Edom' refers to 'what is left' 'after the reduction of Edom at some future date',[103] rather than an unconquered portion of Edom. Second, when 'dispossess' is the intended sense, ירשׁ most often appears in the *hiph̄il* with a personal object (e.g. 'nations' or 'them').[104] It appears here in the *qal*, which only rarely has 'nations' or 'them' as the object in the sense of 'dispossess',[105] but nearly 100 times has 'land' or 'it' as the object with the sense of 'possess'.[106] The *qal* generally focuses simply on possessing and enjoying the land (e.g. Ps. 25.13, 'his children shall possess the land').[107] Third, the nations do not bear the name of an earthly monarch (see 2 Sam. 12.28), but of God. The grammatical relationship between the remnant of Edom and the nations is not clear: 'all the nations' may be parallel to 'remnant of Edom' as a second object of יִירְשׁוּ (i.e. 'they will possess the remnant of Edom and possess all the nations')[108] or a second genitive parallel to

---

100. Hasel, *Remnant*, 214; Niehaus, 'Amos', 491. It has been suggested that the port of Elat is particularly in view. Nägele, *Laubhütte Davids*, 214–15, 238. Hammershaimb's suggestion 'Edom down to its last fragment' (inferred from Amos 1.8) seems unlikely and does not appear to have attracted many adherents. Hammershaimb, *Amos*, 141.

101. Andersen and Freedman, *Amos*, 918.

102. Hammershaimb, *Amos*, 141; Hasel, *Remnant*, 214. See also Polley, *Amos*, 55–82.

103. As in Amos 1.11-12; Obad. 18-19. Morgenstern, 'Nations', 225–31; Niehaus, 'Amos', 491.

104. Of the 66 instances of ירשׁ in the [*hiph̄il*, only nine lack a personal object (Num. 14.24; 33.53; Josh. 8.7; 17.12; Judg. 11.24?; Job 13.26; 20.15; Ezra 9.12; 2 Chr. 20.11).

105. Only nine of the 162 instances of the *qal*: Deut. 9.1; 11.23; 12.2, 29; 18.14; 19.1; 31.3; Isa. 54.3; Ezek. 35.10; see also Ps. 105.44.

106. Both forms appear in Josh. 23.5: וְהוֹרִישׁ אֹתָם מִלִּפְנֵיכֶם וִירִשְׁתֶּם אֶת־אַרְצָם (Yahweh 'will ... drive them out of your sight [*hiph̄il* with personal object]; and you shall possess their land [*qal* with land as object]').

107. See also Gen. 15.7; Deut. 1.8; Isa. 57.13; Jer. 30.3; Ps. 37.11, 22, 34; 60.21; 61.7; 65.9; 69.35). In a few cases the context refers to those who formerly possessed the land (e.g. Num. 21.35; Judg. 11.21; Ps. 37.34; 105.44).

108. One might expect a second object marker in this case, as in, e.g. Hos. 2.22 (MT 24); 3.5; Joel 4.8.

'Edom' (i.e. 'the remnant of both Edom and all the nations').[109] (Either is more likely than that 'all the nations' is the subject of the verb יִירְשׁוּ.[110])

The nations are those 'who are called by my name' (RSV) or, more precisely, 'upon whom my name is called'. The *nipʿal* of קָרָא with שֵׁם denotes naming, particularly in the sense of possession or dominion,[111] as in 2 Sam. 12.28, where Joab warns that David must lead the conquest of Rabbah, 'lest it be called by my name'.[112] With עַל,[113] the expression often denotes Yahweh's assertion of ownership 'over' or relationship to his people (Deut. 28.10; Jer. 14.9; Dan. 9.19; 2 Chr. 7.14; cf. Isa. 43.7; 48.1),[114] Solomon's temple (1 Kgs. 8.43; 2 Chr. 6.33; Jer. 7.10, 11, 14, 30; 32.34; 34.15),[115] his prophet (Jer. 15.16), and the city of Jerusalem (Jer. 25.29; Dan. 9.18-19), where his name was to dwell (cf. 1 Kgs. 8.16; 11.36; 14.21; 2 Kgs. 23.27; 2 Chr. 6.5; 12.13). Isaiah 63.19 equates this naming with rule: 'We have become like those over whom thou hast never ruled, like those who are not called by thy name.'[116] Yahweh's possession entails a relation that brings blessing (cf. Num 6.27: 'So [with the Aaronic blessing] shall they put my name upon the people of Israel, and I will bless them', וְשָׂמוּ אֶת־שְׁמִי עַל־בְּנֵי יִשְׂרָאֵל וַאֲנִי אֲבָרֲכֵם).[117] Belonging to God in this way reflects the covenantal

---

109. Ebenezer Henderson, *The Book of the Twelve Minor Prophets* (Boston: Draper, 1859), 181; Paul R. Raabe, *Obadiah: A New Translation with Introduction and Commentary* (AB 24D; New York: Doubleday, 1995), 41; Wilhelm Rudolph, *Joel-Amos-Obadia-Jona* (KAT 13.2; Gütersloh: Gerd Mohn, 1971), 279. In support, Raabe cites Paul Joüon, *A Grammar of Biblical Hebrew* (trans. T. Muraoka; SubBi 14; Rome: Pontifical Biblical Institute, 1991). The expression שְׁאֵרִית הַגּוֹיִם is parallel to Edom in Ezek. 36.5, as Israel's enemies (עַל־שְׁאֵרִית הַגּוֹיִם וְעַל־אֱדוֹם). Ultimately, however, the difference in meaning between a second object and a second genitive may be fairly minor.

110. 'That they – all the nations who are called by my name – might possess the remnant of Edom.' Andersen and Freedman, *Amos*, 918. Lehrman had earlier argued similarly, although for the different reason that he believed that God's name is only called over Israel, the temple and Jerusalem. Lehrman, 'Twelve Prophets', 123. None of the early versions read the text in this way.

111. Sandt, 'Explanation', 89.

112. See also Gen. 46.18, where Jacob took Manasseh and Ephraim as his own sons, saying, 'and let my name be called in them' (my translation), and Isa. 4.1, 'And seven women shall take hold of one man in that day, saying, "We will eat our own bread and wear our own clothes, only let us be called by your name; take away our reproach."'

113. The expression occurs 19 times in the MT. It is represented in the LXX as here with ἐπικαλέω … ὄνομα … ἐπί … , except for four instances: Deut. 28.10 lacks ἐπί; 2 Sam. 12.28 and Isa. 4.1 have καλέω for ἐπικαλέω; and Jer. 25.29 (32.29 LXX) has ὀνομάζω for ἐπικαλέω. This Greek expression is used only one other time, translating קָרְאוּ בִשְׁמוֹתָם עֲלֵי אֲדָמוֹת (the *qal* of קָרָא) in Ps. 49.11.

114. 'A special relationship is implied, a relationship that virtually spells out an identity.' David Allan Hubbard, *Joel and Amos: An Introduction and Commentary* (TOTC; Downers Grove, Ill.: Inter-Varsity, 1989), 241.

115. See also 1 Macc. 7.37; Bar. 2.26. Since the expression is also applied to other things, its application to the temple is not sufficient to establish Nägele's assertion that it is here 'taken from temple terminology'. Nägele, *Laubhütte Davids*, 230.

116. Amos 9.12 appears to be the only text in the MT in which God's name is called over the Gentiles. Jacques Dupont, 'Un peuple d'entre les nations (Actes 15.14)', *NTS* 31 (1985): 324. Dupont understands the idiom differently, as 'consecration' rather than 'ownership': the invocation of the divine name consecrates to the Lord the people of Israel, the ark of the covenant, etc.

117. 'This idiom as an expression of ownership can have both a negative and a positive colouring;

formula, 'I will be your God and you will be my people' (e.g. Gen. 17.7-8; Lev. 26.12; Jer. 31.33; Rev. 21.3).

Other interpreters have proposed a second view. Amos is not here promising merely a restoration of the political kingdom as 'of old',[118] but one in which the nations will be called by God's name in blessing and covenantal fellowship and the 'possession' of the nations is not 'dispossession', but incorporation for blessing.[119] Edom (or 'the remnant of Edom') stands in apposition to 'all the nations', as a symbol for them all[120] or simply as 'one typical nation whose name and location evoke its own fate and that of other nations'.[121] When associated 'with all nations seen as an undifferentiated whole, Edom both represents itself and serves as a special illustration of all nations'.[122] 'Edom' then functions here as do Egypt

i.e. it not only addresses cases of subjugation and dominion, but also, particularly when it is related to God's name, can mean ownership in the sense of care and protection.' Ådna, 'James', 146. However, only in 2 Sam. 12.28 is there any hint of a negative connotation. 'When Yahweh's name is the subject, it also connotes a privileged status. In the Hebrew Bible, only Israelite entities have Yahweh's name pronounced upon them ... That Edom and the nations would be given such a status is quite striking and brings to mind the idea expressed in Isa. 19.24-25.' Raabe, *Obadiah*, 42.

118. 'As in days of old' need not refer to identity in every detail. The reference may refer to particular aspects of the former kingdom, such as its authority, glory, and/or rule by one of David's line, and must be determined by the context.

119. Motyer contends that '*possess* signifies a conquest', but argues that 'the conquest is followed by an equality of citizenship in that it is not their name but the name of their God by which the Gentiles are called'. The church's missionary expansion 'involves a submission followed by an equality'. Motyer, *Day*, 204–05. Raabe believes the verb here 'means "to possess" in the sense of incorporate or own; the statement expresses more the idea of Israel controlling and ruling the survivors of the nations than that of occupying their lands'. The occupation is more religious or spiritual than military. Raabe, *Obadiah*, 40. 'The taking possession referred to here will be of a very different character from the subjugation of Edom and other nations to David. It will make the nations into citizens of the kingdom of God, to whom the Lord manifests Himself as their God, pouring upon them all the blessings of His covenant of grace (see Isa. lvi. 6-8).' Keil, *Minor Prophets*, 332.

120. '*Edom* was used symbolically by the prophets as an embodiment of the hostility of the world to the kingdom of God. This was in keeping with its attitude from the first (*cf.* Nu. 20.14) to the last (*cf.* Am. 1.11). The overthrow of Edom therefore speaks of a real and complete end of all opposition.' Motyer, *Day*, 204. So also Kaiser, 'Davidic Promise', 103; Walter C. Kaiser, Jr., *The Messiah in the Old Testament* (Studies in Old Testament Biblical Theology; Grand Rapids: Zondervan, 1995), 147; Keil, *Minor Prophets*, 331; Smith, *Amos*, 380; Stuart, *Hosea–Jonah*, 398. Robertson has suggested that Amos intended to allude to the prophecy of Balaam in Num. 24.18. Robertson, 'Hermeneutics', 91–92. While RSV renders Num. 24.18 as 'Edom shall be dispossessed', the MT reads וְהָיָה אֱדוֹם יְרֵשָׁה, rendered more neutrally by the LXX as καὶ ἔσται Εδωμ κληρονομία. The noun יְרֵשָׁה occurs only here, but the related form, יְרֻשָּׁה, refers to 'possession', not 'dispossession'. BDB, s.v. יְרֵשָׁה, יְרֻשָּׁה; *HALOT*, s.v. יְרֵשָׁה, יְרֻשָּׁה. Note also the promise that Yahweh would prosper Esau because he, too, is Abraham's 'seed' (Gen. 21.13, 18).

121. Moab is employed as representative of the nations in Isa. 25.10-12. Raabe, *Obadiah*, 33. Raabe specifically refers to Isaiah 34; Ezekiel 35–36 and points to a pattern of movement between the universal and particular in judgement oracles. 'By particularizing universal judgement, the prophets grounded the fate of one place or group of people in a more all-inclusive phenomenon.' Paul R. Raabe, 'The Particularizing of Universal Judgment in Prophetic Discourse', *CBQ* 64 (2002): 671.

122. Raabe, *Obadiah*, 45, cf. 36, 39.

and Assyria in Isa. 19.23-25,[123] Egypt in Zech. 14.18-19, and 'Rahab', Babylon, Philistia, Tyre and Ethiopia in Psalm 87. The focus is not on Edom, but on 'all the nations,' and Amos 9.12 thus repeats the promise that Yahweh will rule over all nations (Ps. 22.8; 2 Chr. 20.6; Isa. 14.26; 40.15-17).[124] 'The remnant of Edom and the nations are to be God's own people, just as the elect of Israel had been in the past.'[125] This reading is supported in at least one (later) Jewish source, *Gen. Rab.* 88.

> 'In that day will I raise up the tabernacle of David,' that the whole world shall become one brotherhood, as it is said, For then I will turn to the peoples a pure language, that they may all call upon the name of the Lord, to serve Him with one consent' (Zeph. 3.9).[126]

The text concludes with a solemn 'says Yahweh, who does this', certifying both that this missionary wonder will be all of grace and that, as a word spoken by Yahweh, it will not fail.[127]

4.3 *The Expected Kingdom*

The Davidic kingdom was not only a political reality for hundreds of years, but an important part of eschatological expectation. According to the scriptural narrative, God had announced the coming kingdom long before its establishment under Saul and (more firmly) David. Abraham was not only promised that he would be 'father of a multitude of nations', but that 'kings shall come forth from you' (Gen. 17.4–6, 16; cf. Gen. 17.20; 36.31; 35.11). Despite the difficult שִׁילֹה ('to whom it belongs'), references to staff and sceptre indicate an expectation of royal authority (Gen. 49.10).[128] The third and fourth Balaam oracles promise that Israel's 'king shall be higher than Agag, and his kingdom shall be exalted' (Num. 24.7).

> I see him, but not now; I behold him, but not nigh: a star shall come forth out of Jacob, and a scepter shall rise out of Israel; it shall crush the forehead of Moab, and break down all the sons of Sheth. Edom shall be dispossessed, Seir also, his enemies, shall be dispossessed, while Israel does valiantly. By Jacob shall dominion be exercised, and the survivors of cities be destroyed! (Num. 24.17-19)

123. Benson, ' "… From the Mouth of the Lion" ', 211; Motyer, *Prophecy*, 170, n. 1; Oswalt, *Isaiah*, 381.

124. 'The whole world ('all the nations') will come under the rule of Yahweh.' Niehaus, 'Amos', 491.

125. Robertson, 'Hermeneutics', 93. 'The restoration will not be for the benefit of the house of David alone. The restored kingdom will consist of Gentiles as well as the chosen people (9,12).' Benson, ' "… From the Mouth of the Lion" ', 210. 'Amos is not announcing the doom of Edom so much as a positive promise of blessing on Edom and all the nations (Gen. 12.3; 28.14) committed to Yahweh (cf. Deut. 28.9-10; Jer. 14.9). They will enjoy the blessings of this restored kingdom just like the remnant of Israel.' Smith, *Amos*, 380.

126. Routtenberg, *Amos*, 127.

127. 'The standard *n 'm yhwh.*' Andersen and Freedman, *Amos*, 918.

128. Victor P. Hamilton, *The Book of Genesis* (2 vols.; Grand Rapids: Eerdmans, 1990–95), 2.658–62; Gerhard von Rad, *Genesis* (trans. John H. Marks; OTL; Philadelphia: Westminster, 1961), 425.

The Mosaic law explicitly provided regulations for the kingship (Deut. 17.14-20). Yet, for many years, there was no king and 'every man did what was right in his own eyes' (Judg. 17.6; 21.25).

When Israel asked for 'a king to govern us like all the nations' (1 Sam. 8.5), it betrayed a rejection of God as king (1 Sam. 8.7). Nevertheless, God directed Samuel to anoint Saul as Israel's first king (1 Sam. 9) and, after Saul's failure, David, the 'man after [God's] own heart' (1 Sam. 13.14; 16), who became the forefather of and model for the kings of the dynasty to come.[129] God's covenant with David (2 Sam. 7.9-16 || 2 Chr. 17.8-14; cf. 2 Sam. 23.1-7; Ps. 89.3-4, 19-37; 132.11-12, 17-18) became the basis for later kingdom expectation. Walter Kaiser has noted the significant parallels between God's covenant with David and the earlier one with Abraham – a name (2 Sam. 7.9; Gen. 12.2), a secure home (2 Sam. 7.10; Gen. 12.1; 15.7, 18-21), descendants (particularly a son, 2 Sam. 7.12; Gen. 15.4; 17.4-21), and 'everlasting' duration (2 Sam. 7.13, 16; Gen. 17.7) – and has argued that the Davidic covenant is simply a development of the foundational covenant with Abraham and the means to its realization.[130] Language describing the ideal king of Psalm 72 ('all nations will be blessed through him, and they will call him blessed', 17b NIV) echoes the promise to Abraham and makes him the means to its fulfilment.

The prophets promised a restoration of the Davidic kingdom following the judgement they announced.[131] A new king will rule on David's throne (Isa. 9.7; cf. Jer. 17.25; 22.4; 33.17, 21) in righteousness and mercy (cf. Isa. 16.5; Jer. 23.5; 33.15; Ps. 72.2, 4, 12-14), ruling in concert with Yahweh himself (Jer. 30.9; Hos. 3.5). He will be from the line of David and his reign will never end (Isa. 22.15; Jer. 33.17; cf. Ps. 110.4); several texts even call him 'David' (Jer. 30.9; Ezek. 34.23-24; 37.24-25; Hos. 3.5). Even the natural world will be transformed in response to his reign (Isa. 11.6-9; Ps. 72.3, 7, 16). While he will rule over Israel (a reunited twelve tribes, Ezekiel 37), his reign is universal: 'from sea to sea, to the ends of the earth' (Ps. 72.8; cf. Ps. 2.8), over 'all kings and all nations' (Ps. 72.11; Isa. 11.10; 55.3-5), and 'as long as the sun' (Ps. 72.5, 17; Isa. 9.7). All this fits in with the more general expectation, not only of judgement, but of blessing

129. For David as the model king, see Jer. 30.9; Ezek. 34.23-24; 37.24-25; Hos. 3.5. For Davidic descent, see Isa. 11.1; 55.3; Jer. 23.5; 33.15, 17, 21-22, 26; Zech. 12.7-8, 10, 12; 13.1; Ps. 89.28, 36-37; 132.11, 17. For David's name applied to the dynasty, see Isa. 9.7; 16.5; Jer. 17.25; 22.4; Amos 9.11.

130. Walter C. Kaiser, Jr., 'The Blessing of David: The Charter for Humanity', in *The Law and the Prophets* (ed. John H. Skilton; Nutley, NJ: Presbyterian and Reformed, 1974), 309. See also M. Weinfeld, 'Covenant, Davidic', *IDBSup*, vol.: 188–92; Polley, *Amos*, 46, 48. By contrast, Clements believes that the account of the Abrahamic covenant has been 'moulded' in light of the Davidic covenant 'as part of a conscious attempt to relate the two'. Ronald E. Clements, *Abraham and David: Genesis XV and Its Meaning in Israelite Tradition* (SBT 2/5; London: SCM Press, 1967), 55.

131. For additional treatment of Davidic expectation in the OT and pre-Christian Judaism, see Eduard Schweizer, 'The Concept of the Davidic "Son of God" in Acts and Its Old Testament Background', in *Studies in Luke–Acts* (ed. Leander E. Keck and James Louis Martyn; Nashville: Abingdon, 1966; repr., Mifflintown, Pa.: Siglar Press, 1999), 186–93; Strauss, *Davidic Messiah*, ch. 2.

for the nations (e.g. Isa. 2.2-4 || Mic. 4.1-3; Isa. 19.23-25; Psalm 87). It is in keeping with these promises that in Isa. 42.6 and 49.6 Yahweh promises to send his royal servant to bring light to the nations.

Apart from ch. 9, there is no explicit kingdom expectation in Amos. The mention of David in 6.5 is a musical reference. Other references to kings, kingdoms and rulers are contemporary, not eschatological. However, Amos's criticism of social injustice is an implied criticism of both king and kingdom. If the ideal king was to dispense justice (contrast Jer. 22.13-17), the appalling injustice in Israel under Jeroboam II was an indictment of his rule and must have aroused hope for a true king who would rule with justice.

Expectation regarding the Davidic kingdom grew during the Second Temple period.[132] Sirach 45.25 and 1 Macc. 2.57 refer to the promise of David's descendants ruling on his throne. In 2 Esd. 12.32, we read of 'the Messiah whom the Most High has kept until the end of days, who will arise from the posterity of David'. *Fourth Ezra* speaks of 'the Messiah who will arise from the posterity of David', who 'will deliver in mercy the remnant of my people' (12.32, 34). Echoing canonical OT texts, *Pss. Sol.* describes at length how the 'son of David',[133] 'the Lord Messiah', will bring judgement and justice to his people Israel (17.21-44) and the subjection of the Gentiles (17.30). Among the Qumran materials, 4Q174 contains an extended *pesher* on portions of 2 Sam. 7.10-14 (with references to Exod. 15.17-18 and Amos 9.11), 4Q252 joins the blessing on Judah (Gen. 49.10) with the 'branch of David', 4Q161 comments on Isa. 11.1-5, CD VII joins Amos 5.26-27 with Amos 9.11 and Num 24.13, 4Q285 refers to the 'shoot from the stump of Jesse', and 4Q504 speaks of 'your covenant with David'.

> All the foundational elements of the promise tradition are present – God's faithfulness to his covenant promises, the raising up of David's 'seed', the reign of this Davidic heir forever on the Davidic throne, his domination of the pagan nations, and a father–son relationship with God.[134]

Strauss has reviewed the rabbinic literature and finds that 'its descriptions agree in general with the portraits of the coming Davidic king found in the writings of the Second Temple period, and especially the *Psalms of Solomon*'.[135] Although the focus is usually on Messiah's rule over Israel, *T. Jud.* combines allusions to several prophetic texts and asserts that 'the Shoot of God Most High is the fountain for

---

132. Jouette M. Bassler, 'A Man for All Seasons: David in Rabbinic and New Testament Literature', *Int* 40 (1986): 156–69; John J. Collins, *The Scepter and the Star: The Messiahs of the Dead Sea Scrolls and Other Ancient Literature* (ABRL; New York: Doubleday, 1995); Dennis C. Duling, 'The Promises to David and Their Entrance into Christianity: Nailing Down a Likely Hypothesis', *NTS* 20 (1973): 55–77; Cleon L. Rogers, Jr., 'The Promises to David in Early Judaism', *BSac* 150 (1993): 285–302; Strauss, *Davidic Messiah*, 38–57.

133. *Pss. Sol.* 17.21 appears to be the earliest witness to this Messianic title. Strauss, *Davidic Messiah*, 42.

134. Strauss, *Davidic Messiah*, 44. In some of these texts we find dual (royal and priestly) messiahs. Duling, 'Promises', 64–67.

135. Strauss, *Davidic Messiah*, 53.

the life of all humanity' and 'the rod of righteousness for the nations, to judge and save all that call on the Lord' (*T. Jud.* 24.4, 6; cf. 22.2-3).

Expectations of the restoration of the Davidic kingdom are evident from the beginning of Luke's gospel.[136] The angel Gabriel is sent 'to a virgin betrothed to … Joseph, of the house of David' (1.27). 'The Lord God will give [her son] the throne of his father David, and he will reign over the house of Jacob for ever; and of his kingdom there will be no end' (1.32-33).[137] At John's birth, Zechariah praises God because

> he has raised up a horn of salvation for us in the house of his servant David, as he spoke by the mouth of his holy prophets from of old … to perform the mercy promised to our fathers, and to remember his holy covenant, the oath which he swore to our father Abraham. (1.68-75)

Angels announced to the shepherds that 'to you is born this day in the city of David a Savior, who is Christ [Messiah] the Lord' (2.11, cf. 2.4). He preached about the kingdom (4.43; 8.1; 9.11), and directed the apostles to do so (9.2, 60, 62; 10.9, 11). He cast out demons as a sign that the kingdom had come (11.20). He taught his disciples to pray for (11.2) and to look forward to his kingdom (6.20; 12.32; 21.31). On his final journey to Jerusalem he answered to 'Son of David' (18.35-43; cf. 20.41-45). On the night he was betrayed, he spoke to his disciples about the kingdom (22.16, 18, 29-30). The thief on the cross asked to be remembered when Jesus came into his kingdom (23.42). Joseph of Arimathea was 'looking for the kingdom' (23.51). Luke 13.28-29 suggests that Gentiles will participate in the eschatological kingdom.[138] Jesus found a believing Roman centurion (7.9) and a thankful Samaritan (17.18). He directed the apostles that 'repentance and forgiveness of sins should be preached in his name to all nations' (24.46).

In Acts, the risen Jesus continues to teach about the kingdom (1.3). In 1.6-8, the disciples ask about the restoration of the kingdom to Israel. Jesus does not change the subject,[139] dismiss the question,[140] or point to the distant future.[141] He answers directly: the coming of the Spirit and their own subsequent testimony to the risen (Lord) Jesus *are* the means by which the kingdom will be restored.[142] The apostles continue to preach about the kingdom (8.12; 14.22; 19.8; 20.25;

---

136. In the mid-1980s, Bovon noted that 'No one to our knowledge has analyzed the figure of David in the writings of Luke.' Bovon, *Luke the Theologian*, 93. Bovon calls attention to the following texts: Luke 1.27, 32, 69; 2.4. This deficiency has now been remedied in Strauss, *Davidic Messiah*.

137. These promises parallel those made to David in 2 Sam. 7. Fitzmyer, *Luke*, 1.338.

138. Wilson, *Gentile Mission*, 33.

139. Cleon L. Rogers, Jr., 'The Davidic Covenant in Acts-Revelation', *BSac* 151 (1994): 71–84.

140. Jesus' answer is not 'a substitute for the disciples' hopes', but 'a pledge of the return of Jesus and of the restoration of Israel of which they are the first-fruits. Israel is now being restored and awaits the gift of the kingdom.' Franklin, *Christ the Lord*, 95–96. See also, e.g. Fitzmyer, *Acts*, 205; Johnson, *Acts*, 29.

141. John A. McLean, 'Did Jesus Correct the Disciples' View of the Kingdom?', *BSac* 151 (1994): 215–27.

142. Jacques Dupont, 'La portée christologique de l'evangélisation des nations', in *Nouvelles Etudes sur les Actes des Apôtres* (Paris: Cerf, 1984), 49.

28.23, 31). David's words anticipated Judas' betrayal (1.16-20, citing Ps. 69.25; 109.8), the opposition of Gentiles (4.24-28, citing Ps. 2.1-2), and (especially) the resurrection (2.25-32; 13.35-37, citing Ps. 16.8-11; 132.11) and ascension of Christ (2.34-36, citing Ps. 110.1). David was the model king 'after God's heart' and the ancestor of Jesus (13.22-23). Both are identified as God's servant (4.25, 27, 30; 3.13, 36). 'God had sworn with an oath to [David] that he would set one of his descendants upon his throne' (2.30). By raising Jesus from the dead, 'what God promised to the fathers, this he has fulfilled to us their children', to 'give you the holy and sure blessings of David' (13.34-36, citing Isa. 55.3). David Ravens has argued that kingdom expectation is central to Luke's purpose.

> With his pastoral purpose in mind [i.e. convincing Jewish believers that they have not forsaken the people of God and assuring Gentile believers that they do in fact belong to the people of God], Luke has devised the following strategy. The first step is to show that Israel remains the people of God and that he has always planned to restore Israel to its pre-Davidic unity. ... The second step is to remind his readers that the prophets look forward to the time of the incoming Gentiles. The Gentile mission is therefore Israel's mission and the route to the fulfillment of Israel's destiny.[143]

Similarly, Max Turner has argued that 'Israel's restoration or salvation is a cardinal theme of Luke-Acts' and that Luke understands this to be 'largely complete by Acts 15'.[144]

4.4 *Acts 15.16-18*

Acts 15 marks a critical point in both the book and the life of the early church.[145] It has been called 'the structural and theological centre of Acts'.[146] The gospel had spread from Jerusalem and Judaea, through Samaria, and on toward 'the end of the earth'. In doing so, it penetrated communities of Diaspora Jews, and even overflowed these communities so that many Gentiles on the fringes of the synagogue had come to believe. But when many Diaspora Jews rejected their message, Paul and Barnabas began preaching more widely to Gentiles, supporting this radical step by appealing to Isa. 49.6 as a command addressed to them (Acts 13.47).

The resulting success of this Gentile mission (14.27; 15.3-4) led to sharp disagreements regarding the way in which Gentile believers were to be admitted to the church, and particularly on circumcision, the Mosaic law, and table

---

143. David Ravens, *Luke and the Restoration of Israel* (JSNTSup 119; Sheffield: Sheffield Academic Press, 1995), 250.

144. Turner, *Power*, 419.

145. It is not necessary to review the complex discussion of the relationship between Acts and Galatians on the matter of Paul's visits to Jerusalem. On this, see e.g. Bruce, *Acts* (rev. edn.); Fitzmyer, *Acts*; Witherington, *Acts*.

146. Strauss, *Davidic Messiah*, 180. Wilson has written that 'Ch. 15 forms a watershed in the book of Acts. It is a, if not the, turning point of the whole narrative.' Wilson, *Gentile Mission*, 192–93. Dupont speaks of the 'centre du livre et pivot du récit des Actes'. Dupont, 'Un peuple', 322. This text 'occupe une place centrale dans les Actes des apôtres'. Taylor, *Commentaire*, 4.197.

fellowship between believers of Jewish and Gentile backgrounds (Gal. 2.11-14). Some came to Antioch from Judaea teaching, 'Unless you are circumcised according to the custom of Moses, you cannot be saved' (15.1). Implicit in the requirement of circumcision was the obligation 'to keep the law of Moses' (15.5; cf. Gal. 5.3). The 'yoke' mentioned in 15.10 was 'the yoke of the commandments' (*m. Ber.* 2.2).[147] What is in view, however, is not the moral obligations of the law (to love God and neighbour, or to refrain from murder, theft, adultery, etc.) but its distinctive ceremonial provisions.[148] After 'Paul and Barnabas had no small dissension and debate with them', a delegation was sent to consult with 'the apostles and elders in Jerusalem' (15.2). On their way to Jerusalem, and once they arrived there, they 'gave great joy to all the brethren' as they reported the conversion of the Gentiles (15.3-4).

Luke's report of the council's deliberations can be divided into three parts. First, following 'much debate', Peter recounted his own role in the initial introduction of the gospel to the Gentiles (15.7-11; cf. chs 10–11). He ascribed the leading role in those events to God (15.7) and drew the following conclusions.[149]

1.   By giving the Holy Spirit, God showed his acceptance of Gentile believers.
2.   In cleansing their hearts by faith,[150] God demonstrated that he made no distinction between Jewish and Gentile believers.
3.   Circumcision and the Mosaic law were a burden that Jews had never been able to bear. To require this burden of Gentile believers would be to test God.
4.   Salvation, for both Jew and Gentile, is by grace (not by circumcision or the law).

Second, Barnabas and Paul (Barnabas regains top billing during the account of the council[151]) recounted for the fourth time in the narrative (15.12; cf. 14.27; 15.3, 4) what God had done among the Gentiles, specifically 'signs and wonders' God had

---

147. Bruce, *Acts* (Greek Text, 3rd edn.), 290–91.

148. Luke 10.25-28; 18.18-20; Matt. 5.17-18; Rom. 13.8-10; Gal. 5.22-23; Eph. 6.1-3. 'Moral rules, such as the Ten Commandments, were already assumed. *All* Christians, Jew and Gentile, lived by them ... Morality was not the issue at the Jerusalem Conference.' Polhill, *Acts*, 331–32. For questions and disputes about ceremonial provisions, see Luke 6.1-11; 11.37-41; 13.10-17; 14.1-6; Acts 6.14; 10.9-16; 11.2-18; 21.21; cf. Gal. 4.8-11; Rom. 14.2-6; Col. 2.16-17.

149. Van de Sandt's assertion that 'the beginning of [Peter's] speech is not connected with what went before' is surprising. Sandt, 'Explanation', 75. It overlooks the relevance of the reception of the Spirit, the abolition of distinction, and the cleansing of the heart to the question of circumcision and the law. In fact, both circumcision (Gen. 17.10-14) and the law were clearly understood to be distinguishing marks of the people of God (Deut. 4.6-8; Eph. 2.14-16). The symbolism of circumcision was of cleansing. True circumcision was thus a cleansing of the heart (Deut. 30.6; Jer. 4.4; 9.25; cf. Rom. 2.28-29). J. P. Hyatt, 'Circumcision', *IDB*, 1: 629–31.

150. Purification figures prominently in Acts 10–11 (10.15, 28; 11.9). Dupont, 'Un peuple', 329.

151. It is 'Barnabas and Saul/Paul' from Acts 11.25 to 13.7, but becomes 'Paul and Barnabas' once the Gentile mission begins. The sequence reverts briefly in 14.12, 14 (when Barnabas gets top billing as 'Zeus' to Paul's 'Hermes' in Lystra) and in 15.12, 22, 25 in Jerusalem, where Barnabas had a longer history and/or was perhaps better regarded than Paul.

done,[152] echoing the 'signs and wonders' associated with the exodus,[153] the signs and wonders prophesied by Joel (Acts 2.19-20), and the 'mighty works and wonders and signs which God did through' Jesus (Acts 2.22). Finally, James spoke.

James characterized the events Peter had described[154] as 'God taking from among the Gentiles a people for his name' (ὁ θεὸς ἐπεσκέψατο λαβεῖν ἐξ ἐθνῶν λαὸν τῷ ὀνόματι αὐτοῦ), anticipating the language of Amos 9.12b (cited later in Acts 15.17b),[155] and echoing language from the exodus (ὁ θεὸς εἰσελθὼν λαβεῖν ἑαυτῷ ἔθνος, Deut. 4.34).[156] With this interpretation of these events, James asserted, 'the words of the prophets agree', citing the text from Amos 9.11-12.[157] As Paul's and Barnabas' decision in Pisidian Antioch was sealed with the citation of Isa. 49.6, the decision of the council here would be settled by James's appeal to Amos 9. 'James' address is the climactic and deciding section of the narrative of ch. 15' and 'the citation of Amos 9.11-12 forms the crux of James' argument'.[158] James concluded that the council should not 'trouble' (παρενοχλεῖν) the Gentiles who are 'turning to God'[159] by requiring them to be circumcised and keep the law (15.1, 4). Instead, he proposed several limited obligations, commonly designated the 'apostolic decree' (15.20, 29; 21.25).

152. In the NT, 'signs and wonders' validate the gospel and its messengers (except in Acts 7.36; see Acts 2.19, 22, 43; 4.30; 5.12; 6.8; 14.3; 15.12; Rom. 15.19; 2 Cor. 2.12; Heb. 2.4; cf. John 4.48 and counterfeits in Matt. 24.24; Mark 13.22; 2 Thess. 2.9).

153. Exodus 7.4, 9; 11.9-10; Deut. 4.34; 6.22; 7.19; 11.3; 26.8; 29.3; 34.11; Ps. 78.43; 105.27; 135.9; Jer. 32.20-21. 'When in the LXX the phrase "signs and wonders" is used, the reference is usually to the emancipation of Israel from Egypt ... From the allusion to Exod. 7.3 in Acts 7.36 (and maybe from 2.19 as well) it is obvious that Luke was acquainted with its reference to the Exodus.' Sandt, 'Explanation', 91. See also Karl Heinrich Rengstorf, 'σημεῖον', TDNT 7.242.

154. It has been questioned whether Συμεών here refers to Simon Peter. Peter is never called Συμεών in Luke–Acts (only in 2 Peter 2.1, where the text is in doubt). In Acts he is called Σίμων only in 10.5, 18, 32; 11.13, where he is 'Simon called (ἐπικαλέω) Peter. Two alternatives have been proposed, based on a statement of Chrysostom (the text of which is in doubt). The shorter text identifies this Συμεών with the 'righteous and devout' man in Luke 2.25-35. Riesner believes that the Nunc Dimittis is in view. Riesner, 'James's Speech'. This view is mentioned, but already discounted, by Foakes Jackson and Lake, eds., Beginnings, 4.175. The longer text suggests that this Συμεών was a third person. Some have suggested Simon Niger, who may have represented the church in Antioch at the council. Fitzmyer, Acts, 552–53. However, 'the logic of the entire narrative demands that we take it as referring to Simon Peter'. Johnson, Acts, 264.

155. Ådna, 'James', 149; Bauckham, 'James and the Gentiles', 171. Dupont has persuasively argued that this anticipatory framing of the citation demonstrates that the Amos citation is not a later addition. Jacques Dupont, 'ΛΑΟΣ ῈΞ ῈΘΝΩΝ (Act. xv. 14)', NTS 3 (1956): 47–50. Dupont particularly has in mind the arguments of J. N. Sanders, 'Peter and Paul in the Acts', NTS 2 (1955/56), 133–43.

156. Sandt, 'Explanation', 88.

157. The starting-point is the events that have been described, which are then interpreted in light of scripture. 'Most testimonia in the New Testament follow the sequence "Current Event → Scripture" rather than "Scripture → Current Event."' Edward Earle Ellis, 'Midrashic Features in the Speeches of Acts', in Prophecy and Hermeneutic in Early Christianity (Grand Rapids: Eerdmans, 1978), 204. This runs contrary to the approach of both evangelicals who seek to maintain the priority of scriptural authority and critical scholars who believe that scriptural narratives have been shaped or even created to conform to earlier scripture.

158. Strauss, Davidic Messiah, 182.

159. The present participle, suggesting that this is ongoing and expected to continue.

The assembly agreed, drafted a letter to the church in Syria (15.23-29), and sent it by a delegation of leaders from the Jerusalem church accompanied by Barnabas and Paul. The letter disavowed those who had disturbed the church in Antioch with their teaching, affirmed the apostles' fellowship with Barnabas and Paul, introduced the delegates Judas and Silas, and outlined the obligations James had proposed.

Acts 15 presents a multilayered argument for the legitimacy of the Gentile mission. (Recall Stanley's observation [section 1.3 above] that Paul does not rest his arguments on the appeal to scripture alone, but also provides other lines of reasoning.) First, there are the arguments advanced in the council as Luke has reported them,[160] including the climactic appeal by James to the prophecy of Amos 9. The narrative of the council itself, with its unanimous decision (15.22) and the favourable reception of that decision by the church in Antioch (15.30-34), underscores the claim that the council's decision had 'seemed good to the Holy Spirit' as well as to the church's leaders (15.28). Finally, Acts 15 is set in the context of the larger narrative of Acts, which supports the Gentile mission throughout, with the commisioning of the apostles as witnesses to Jesus 'in Jerusalem and in all Judea and Samaria and to the end of the earth' (1.8), the account of Paul's conversion (with God's stated intention that Paul would 'carry my name before the Gentiles', 9.15), the accounts of Gentile conversions (Acts 8; 10–11; 13–14; 16–21; see especially 14.27; 15.3-4; cf. also 10.44; 11.17-18, 20-21; 16.9, 14; 18.10), and its conclusion with Paul preaching in Rome.

4.4.1 *As It Is Written*

The citation from Amos 9.11-12 is marked as a quotation by the introductory formula καθὼς γέγραπται.[161] The expression οἱ λόγοι τῶν προφητῶν does not indicate that the citation is a composite, nor is the reference indefinite (see the discussion on p. 62, above).[162]

Commentators have noted that Acts also contains the only other explicit citation from Amos in the NT, the citation of 5.25-27 in Acts 7.42b-43. Portions of both Amos 9.11b and 5.26-27a are also cited (somewhat freely) in CD VII, 14–17, although the interpretation there is quite different. Earl Richard has argued that the citations in Acts are related by the common themes of exile and

---

160. The account is certainly abridged. There had already been 'much discussion' before the first of Luke's recorded comments (15.7). Any arguments that may have been offered by the other side are omitted entirely.

161. In Luke–Acts, γέγραπται introduces a quotation in 12 of 14 occurrences (the exceptions are Luke 10.26; 24.46) and in only one of those 12 is the source not mentioned (23.35). Six are unique to Luke–Acts (Luke 2.23; 4.17; Acts 1.20; 7.42; 13.33; 15.15), one is distinctive (only Luke continues the citation in 3.4-6 to include Isa. 40.4-5); and five are shared with the other gospels (Luke 4.4, 8, 10; 7.27; 19.46).

162. As Calvin proposes, *Acts 14-28*, 46. Again, see 7.42; 13.41. Mauro incorrectly deduces from the substitution of μετὰ ταῦτα for ἐν τῇ ἡμέρᾳ ἐκείνῃ that 'James did not purport to give the exact language of Amos, or of any prophet', but 'to declare the substance of "the voices of the prophets" (not of Amos only) touching the matter under consideration'. Mauro, 'Tabernacle', 401.

tabernacle,[163] but the contexts are dissimilar, the 'tent' in Amos 9 is not the tabernacle (see sections 4.2.1, 4.4.3), and a reference to the exile is not enough to claim a connection. These citations, together with those from Joel 3.1-5 MT (Acts 2.16-21) and Hab. 1.5 (Acts 13.40-41), show that the Book of the Twelve was familiar to Luke.

J. W. Bowker has analysed the speech in light of recognized Jewish homily forms and concluded that James's argument is 'a genuine yelammedenu response'[164] that 'derives from a request for instruction, *yelammedenu rabbenu*, let our teacher instruct us'.[165] The matter before the council is an halakic question (note ἀπεκριθή, 'answered', in 15.13). 'James bases his decision on two grounds, what is known to have happened in the past and on scripture. Those are the two classic grounds for establishing *halakah* ... James issues his decision, using the strong formula, ἐγὼ κρίνω. His decision comes closest to what might technically be called a *taqqanah*.'[166]

4.4.2 *I Will Return (16b)*

Acts 15.16b inserts ἀναστρέψω (which does not appear in the MT or LXX) before ἀνοικοδομήσω. It has been suggested that ἀναστρέψω reflects the idiomatic use of שׁוּב as 'again', in which 'I will return and ...' should be translated as 'I will again ...'.[167] While the Hebrew שׁוּב may convey that sense, ἀναστρέφω does not in the LXX or in any other NT text.[168] In Mal. 1.4, Edom 'will return (ἐπιστρέψωμεν, וְנָשׁוּב) and rebuild (ἀνοικοδομήσωμεν, וְנִבְנֶה) the waste places' (the citation is from the ASV, because more recent English translations subsume the former verb into the latter).[169] Edom has been destroyed and its people have been forced into exile, so they 'return' in order to rebuild.[170] In Zech.

163. 'Luke seems to write in a cumulative way so that later narratives and speeches develop earlier themes.' Richard, 'Creative Use', 49.

164. J. W. Bowker, 'Speeches in Acts: A Study in Proem and Yelammedenu Form', *NTS* 14 (1967): 108.

165. Bowker, 'Speeches', 99.

166. Bowker, 'Speeches', 107–08.

167. Claude E. Hayward, 'A Study in Acts XV. 16-18', *EvQ* 8 (1936): 165. Hayward argues against the dispensational view that 'return' here refers to the return of Christ, as held, e.g. by Willard M. Aldrich, 'The Interpretation of Acts 15.13-18', *BSac* 111 (1954): 322. For a conclusive argument against the latter view, see Strauss, *Davidic Messiah*, 186.

168. BDB, s.v. שׁוּב, *Qal* 8; GKC, §120d; *TWOT*, s.v. שׁוּב. The more common ἐπιστρέφω may, e.g. Jer. 12.15; Hos. 2.9; 14.8; Mic. 7.19, but there is no clear instance of this in the NT. There is certainly a sense of 'restore/build up again' in the repetition of ἀνά (ἀναστρέψω ... ἀνοικοδομήσω ... ἀνοικοδομήσω ... ἀνορθώσω). Walter F. Burnside, *The Acts of the Apostles: The Greek Edited with Introduction and Notes for the Use of Schools* (Cambridge: Cambridge University Press, 1916). Kaiser argues that the repeated ἀνά would make ἀναστρέψω in the sense of 'again' unnecessary. Kaiser, 'Davidic Promise', 105.

169. This passage appears to have been overlooked in the discussion of the meaning of ἀναστρέψω in Acts 15.16a.

170. Joyce Baldwin, *Haggai, Zechariah, Malachi: An Introduction and Commentary* (TOTC; Downers Grove, Ill.: Inter-Varsity, 1972), 223; Eli Cashdan, 'Malachi', in *The Twelve Prophets: Hebrew Text, English Translation and Commentary* (ed. Abraham Cohen; Soncino Books of the Bible;

1.16, Yahweh promises that 'I will return (ἐπιστρέψω, שָׁבְתִּי) to Jerusalem with compassion and my house will be built in it' (ἀνοικοδομηθήσεται, יִבָּנֶה). The active ἐπιστρέψω with the passive ἀνοικοδομηθήσεται prevents reading this as the idiomatic construction for 'again'. God's 'return' is relational, reflecting a change of heart, in this case restoring his compassion for Jerusalem.[171] Rebuilding the temple is a subsequent event that is dependent on this prior restoration of God's favour. In Acts 15.16b, ἀναστρέψω merely highlights the restoration of God's favour that is already implicit in Amos's prophecy and will result in the rebuilding of 'David's fallen tent'.

4.4.3 *The Tent of David (16c)*

As with the סֻכַּת דָּוִיד in Amos 9.11, there is considerable diversity of opinion regarding τὴν σκηνὴν Δαυίδ in Acts 15.16. Haenchen argued that the restored 'booth of David' is a reference to the resurrection of Christ, but few have followed him.[172] Many have understood the 'tent of David' as the dynasty and kingdom of David. Recently, Richard Bauckham and others have argued that the expression refers to the erection of the eschatological temple. [173]

Bauckham argues that '"the dwelling of David" … [is] the place of God's dwelling in the messianic age when Davidic rule is restored to Israel. He will build this new temple so that all the Gentile nations may seek his presence there.'[174] He claims support for this identification in Tobit 13.11; Lam. 2.6; Ps. 42.5.[175] He believes Amos 9.11-12 has been conflated with Hos. 3.5; Jer. 12.15-16; Isa. 45.21 and that these together 'put the main quotation from Amos … in a context of prophecies which associate the eschatological conversion of the Gentile nations with the restoration of the Temple in the messianic age'.[176] Finally, he notes that this reading fits with the early church's understanding of itself as the

Bournemouth: Soncino, 1948), 338; Douglas L. Stuart, 'Malachi', in *The Minor Prophets* (ed. Thomas Edward McComiskey; 3 vols.; Grand Rapids: Baker, 1998), 1287–89.

171. Of the texts cited by BDB for this sense of the term, the following are most relevant: Isa. 63.17; Jer. 12.15; Joel 2.14; Zech. 1.3; Mal. 3.7; Ps. 6.5; 80.15; 90.13; 2 Chr. 30.6. BDB, s.v. שׁוּב, *Qal* 6.g. This relational sense of שׁוּב appears most often of people (re)turning to God. *TWOT*, s.v. שׁוּב.

172. Haenchen, *Acts*, 448. See the response of Bauckham, 'James and the Gentiles', 157.

173. Bauckham, 'James and the Gentiles'; 'James and the Jerusalem Church'; Nägele, *Laubhütte Davids*. Nägele apparently came to this conclusion independently of Bauckham. Ådna depends on both Bauckham and Nägele, Ådna, 'Die Heilige Schrift', 1–23; 'James', 125–61. See also Edward Earle Ellis, 'Isaiah and the Eschatological Temple', in *Christ and the Future in New Testament History* (ed. Edward Earle Ellis; NovTSup 97; Leiden: Brill, 2000), 60; Ellis, 'Λέγει Κύριος', 183; Edward Earle Ellis, *Paul's Use of the Old Testament* (Grand Rapids: Eerdmans, 1957), 107–13; Allan J. McNicol, 'Rebuilding the House of David: The Function of the Benedictus in Luke–Acts', *ResQ* 40 (1998): 25–38. For an earlier expression of this view, see Rackham, *Acts*, 253–54.

174. Bauckham, 'James and the Jerusalem Church', 453–54. See also Bauckham, 'James and the Gentiles', 158–59.

175. Lamentations 2.6, however, employs different words in both the MT (the *hapax* שֹׂךְ) and the LXX (σκήνωμα). Psalm 42.5 has the admittedly 'obscure' בְּסָךְ, which is rendered as σκηνῆς by the LXX.

176. Bauckham, 'James and the Jerusalem Church', 455. See also Bauckham, 'James and the Gentiles', 165.

eschatological temple.[177] While this last is certainly true, it does not establish that the present text shares that understanding, nor does the claim that similar views were held at Qumran. (Nägele notes that at Qumran the nations were to be destroyed, while here they are included.[178]) Even if the evidence for conflation were stronger, neither Hos. 3.5 nor Jer. 12.15-16 refer to the eschatological temple and, as Barrett notes, 'the slight verbal echoes of Jer. 12.15; Isa. 45.21 can hardly count as prophetic sayings that agree or disagree with anything'.[179] Thus in Acts 15 there is no 'context of prophecies which associate the eschatological conversion of the Gentile nations with the restoration of the Temple in the messianic age'.[180] Nor does the frequent association of ἀνοικοδομέω in the LXX with Jerusalem and the temple establish Nägele's claim that these are in view here, particularly as she concedes that the term is also used in connection with the kingdom of Israel.[181] A convincing argument that 'David's tent' refers to the eschatological temple has yet to be made.

Rather, 'the tent of David' must be understood as the (restored, eschatological) Davidic kingdom.[182] Dupont notes that in the NT only Luke employs the phrase 'house of David' (Luke 1.27, 69; 2.4).[183] We have noted the prominence of Davidic and kingdom themes in Luke–Acts. While the physical temple is prominent in Luke, references to the eschatological temple are absent and the charge that Jesus threatened to destroy and rebuild the temple (Matt. 26.61 ‖ Mark 14.58; Matt. 27.40 ‖ Mark 15.29) is omitted. For Luke, the kingdom is restored in the ascension of Christ (Acts 2.34).[184]

4.4.4 *The Rest of Mankind (17a)*

Verse 17 expresses the purpose (ὅπως ἄν)[185] for which God restored 'David's fallen tent'. The restoration of the kingdom is not an end in itself, but is intended to have an effect on 'the rest of mankind'. They are connected, not parallel or separate, events.[186] Those who 'seek the Lord' are 'the rest of mankind … and all the

177. Bauckham cites 1 Cor. 3.16-17; 2 Cor. 6.16; Eph. 2.20-22; Heb. 13.15-16; 1 Pet. 2.5; 4.17; Rev. 3.12; 11.1-2. (Some purported examples from the Apostolic Fathers refer to the individual rather than the church corporately as the dwelling of God.) Bauckham, 'James and the Gentiles', 165–67; 'James and the Jerusalem Church', 457.

178. Nägele, *Laubhütte Davids*, 90–91.

179. Barrett, *Acts*, 2.725.

180. Bauckham, 'James and the Jerusalem Church', 455. See also Bauckham, 'James and the Gentiles', 165.

181. Nägele, *Laubhütte Davids*, 89.

182. See e.g. Bruce, *Acts* (rev. edn.), 293; Johnson, *Acts*, 265; Polhill, *Acts*, 330. Strauss's distinction between the kingdom and the Davidic dynasty is a distinction without a difference. There is no rule without a realm and no realm without rule. Strauss, *Davidic Messiah*, 190.

183. Dupont, 'Ac 15,16', 30.

184. Dupont, 'Ac 15,16', 30.

185. BDAG, s.v. ὅπως; BDF, §369(5); Moulton et al., *Grammar*, 3.105.

186. Nägele has argued that ὅπως ἄν is dependent on ἀναστρέψω, so that two events result from God's return: the restoration of David's tent and mankind seeking the Lord. Nägele, *Laubhütte Davids*, 96–97. There are, however, no grounds in 15.16 for privileging ἀναστρέψω above the other indicative verbs. It is more likely that ἀναστρέψω functions here in lieu of a supplementary or

Gentiles who are called by my name' (17a-b). 'The rest of mankind' are those who are not participants in the initial phase of the restoration of the kingdom. If the restoration of the kingdom begins with Jews (as it did in the ministry of Jesus and the earliest ministry of the church), the 'rest of mankind' would most naturally be Gentiles.[187] In Amos 9.12, it is difficult to be certain whether 'all the nations' is in opposition to 'Edom' only or 'the remnant of Edom', but the case forms in the Greek text clearly identify 'the rest of mankind' and 'all the Gentiles' as parallel expressions.[188]

Braun has claimed that 'remnant' is a technical term which is never 'applied to Gentiles in any soteriological or eschatological sense'.[189] Even if this is so, it is up to Braun to make the case that the term must be seen in this technical sense here. It is, of course, also possible that this text marks a dramatic theological development, as in Isa. 19.25, where other terms normally reserved to Israel are applied to Gentiles: 'Blessed be Egypt my people, and Assyria the work of my hands, and Israel my heritage.' Braun seeks to maintain a dispensational distinction between Jew and Gentile, but is unnecessarily concerned that ethnic Jews who believe in Jesus are absent from the text. Exegetically and historically they comprise the core of the reestablished 'tent of David'. It is difficult to see how 'the rest of mankind' could possibly refer to ethnic Jews (whether or not they believe in Jesus) in light of the underlying MT 'the rest *of Edom'*.

The distinctive LXX reading in the citation has prompted some to question the historicity of the account and the appropriateness of the citation.

> The Hebrew text would be useless for James's argument, and would even contradict it. Nearly every expositor concedes that the Jewish Christian James would not in Jerusalem have used a Septuagint text, differing from the Hebrew original, as scriptural proof. It is not James but Luke who is speaking here.[190]

circumstantial participle (for the construction, see BDF, §471(4)). Aldrich's claim that the text envisions two distinct events, the inclusion of the Gentiles and the future restoration of the kingdom, is prompted by the dispensational commitment to maintain a sharp distinction between Israel and the church. Aldrich, 'Acts 15.13-18', 317, 322. It cannot be supported by grammatical or any other aspects of the text itself. Cole has rightly argued that the restoration of David's hut is either the necessary condition of the ingathering of the nations or synonymous with it. Alan Cole, *The New Temple: A Study in the Origins of the Catechetical 'Form' of the Church in the New Testament* (London: Tyndale Press, 1950), 47.

187. Or, less likely, all who are not believing Jews (i.e. unbelieving Jews plus the unbelieving Gentiles). Nägele, *Laubhütte Davids*, 90–91.

188. 'The conjunction "and" before "all the Gentiles" (v. 17) is epexegetic ... The "residue of men" who are to "seek the Lord" are identical with "all the Gentiles, upon whom my name is called" – *i.e.* the elect from every nation.' Frederick F. Bruce, *Commentary on the Book of the Acts: The English Text with Introduction, Exposition and Notes* (NICNT; Grand Rapids: Eerdmans, 1954), 310. (The statement does not appear in the 1988 edition.) So also Barrett, *Acts*, 2.727; Nägele, *Laubhütte Davids*, 101. Sanders argues that the ' "remainder of people" and "all the Gentiles" are, of course, a *parallelismus membrorum* and synonymous'. Sanders, 'Prophetic Use', 195.

189. Braun, 'James' Use of Amos', 120. 'Doctrinally, the word "remnant" applies strictly to Israel.' Braun, 'James' Use of Amos', 119.

190. Haenchen, *Acts*, 448.

James' argumentation would crumble if it rested on the Hebrew text of Amos 9. The universalism that the brother of the Lord recommends in his speech, can only find Scriptural support in the Greek version of the OT, and it is highly unlikely that James spoke Greek at the conference of Jerusalem.[191]

However, others have responded that it would have been entirely appropriate for James to use the OT in Greek in a meeting with representatives of the church in Antioch.[192] If the letter attributed to James is from the same church leader, that letter may be seen as evidence that James was familiar with Greek.[193] Still others have argued that James has deliberately employed a textual variant (or ambiguity) to find 'mankind' here instead of 'Edom', and thus to make his case by midrashic methods.[194] Although he concludes that James's speech in its current form is a Lukan composition, Bauckham believes that its source 'coheres well with what we know of the Jerusalem church under the leadership of James and his circle'.[195]

Still others believe that the argument can in fact be made from the MT.

But even our Masoretic Hebrew would have served the present purpose admirably, since it predicted that 'the tabernacle of David,' i.e. the church of the Messiah, would 'gain possession of all the nations which are called by the name [of the God of Israel].' Cf. vs. 14, where we are told what this quotation was expected to prove: ὁ θεὸς ἐπεσκέψατο λαβεῖν ἐξ ἐθνῶν λαὸν τῷ ὀνόματι αὐτοῦ.[196]

Polhill has observed that 'the rest of mankind' is not the expression that bears the weight of the argument: 'the key phrase "nations [Gentiles] called by my name" occurs in *both* the Hebrew and Greek texts, and either would have suited James' argument'.[197]

The text is cited in the LXX version rather than the Hebrew, although, since James was speaking Aramaic, he need not have rendered either version exactly. In either version the Gentiles will be brought within the orbit of the new Davidic kingdom. Practically all

---

191. Bovon, *Luke the Theologian*, 85.

192. Ådna, 'James', 127; Witherington, *Acts*, 457.

193. Joseph B. Mayor, *The Epistle of St. James* (3rd edn.; New York: Macmillan, 1912), i–lxv, cclx–cclxxvii. Witherington urges that 'more attention should be paid to the various verbal similarities between what we find in this speech (and in the letter of vv. 23-29) and the Epistle of James' and calls particular attention to Mayor's work. Witherington, *Acts*, 457–58. For a recent assessment of the Greek of the letter, see Luke Timothy Johnson, *The Letter of James: A New Translation with Introduction and Commentary* (AB 37A; New York: Doubleday, 1994), 16–121. See also the succinct summary in Cadbury, 'Speeches', 5.411.

194. Ådna, 'James', 137; Bauckham, 'James and the Gentiles', 160–62; 'James and the Jerusalem Church', 457; Johnson, *Acts*, 265; Nägele, *Laubhütte Davids*, 86. Bowker has argued that the *yelammedenu* form of the speech indicates a Palestinian origin. Bowker, 'Speeches', 182.

195. Bauckham, 'James and the Gentiles', 182.

196. Torrey, *Composition*, 39.

197. Polhill, *Acts*, 329, n. 93. Similarly, Bauckham notes (also with reference to 15.17b) that 'Even the MT could easily have been understood by a Jewish Christian as predicting the extension of Israel's covenant status and privileges to the Gentile nations. The LXX merely makes this clearer.' Bauckham, 'James and the Gentiles', 169.

NT commentators agree that St. James correctly understands this prophecy when he sees its fulfillment in the conversion of the Gentiles.[198]

Neither the language nor form of the citation prevents us from holding that Luke's account represents substantially what James said at the council. And the complex textual questions raised by 17a turn out to be of relatively little importance as we seek to follow the argument.

4.4.5 *All the Gentiles upon whom My Name Is Called (17b)*

The expression in v. 17b ('all the nations upon whom my name is called' [my translation], πάντα τὰ ἔθνη ἐφ᾽ οὓς ἐπικέκληται τὸ ὄνομά μου ἐπ᾽ αὐτούς) is awkward,[199] but it represents the Hebrew accurately and its meaning is clear. As noted earlier, the Hebrew idiom expresses ownership and dominion[200] and is applied in the OT to the temple, to Jerusalem and to Israel. Barrett observes that the relative clause could be read either as 'over all those particular Gentiles (not all) over whom my name has been called', or 'all the Gentiles, in that my name has been called over all of them'. The course of the narrative will indicate the author's intent. As it became apparent in Acts 13.48-50 that some Gentiles believed (and some did not), so here it will become apparent that some bear God's name and some do not.[201] 'All' here should therefore be understood as distributive, rather than inclusive ('every individual Gentile'). (Note also 15.14: 'to take *out of them* a people for his name', λαβεῖν ἐξ ἐθνῶν λαὸν τῷ ὀνόματι αὐτοῦ.)

Bauckham believes that the calling of God's name over the Gentiles (Acts 15.17b; Amos 9.12b) is the decisive point in James's argument. 'The nations *qua* Gentile nations belong to YHWH .... precisely as "all nations" they are included in the covenant relationship. It is doubtful whether any other OT text could have been used to make this point so clearly.'[202] It is not clear, however, in what way Amos 9 asserts that Gentiles belong to Yahweh 'as Gentiles' or 'without becoming Jews', or how it does so any more aptly than other prophetic texts that envision inclusion of Gentiles among the people of God. Bauckham suggests that the language here, as in Jas. 2.7 (τὸ καλὸν ὄνομα τὸ ἐπικληθὲν ἐφ᾽ ὑμᾶς), refers to Christian baptism;[203] James's argument would then be that Gentiles are to be

198. Benson, ' "... From the Mouth of the Lion" ', 210–11.

199. The masculine plurals, οὓς and αὐτούς (when one would expect the neuter), should be understood as a *constructio ad sensum*, ' "the Gentiles" signifies a multiplicity of individual human beings'. Barrett, *Acts*, 2.727. See also Moulton et al., *Grammar*, 3.40.

200. Dupont understands the idiom here somewhat differently: it is the invocation of the divine name that consecrates to the Lord the people of Israel, the ark of the covenant, etc. This understanding enables him to connect the consecration involved in the Spirit's cleansing of the Gentiles' hearts (vv. 8-9) with that indicated by the invocation of the divine name. Dupont, 'Un peuple', 324. See the discussion of Amos 9.12 above.

201. Barrett, *Acts*, 2.727.

202. Bauckham, 'James and the Gentiles', 169. Ådna concurs that 'these Gentiles shall be called into the people of God *qua* Gentiles'. Ådna, 'James', 150.

203. A baptismal reference in Jas. 2.7 is supported by Peter H. Davids, *The Epistle of James: A Commentary on the Greek Text* (NIGTC; Grand Rapids: Eerdmans, 1982), 113; Mayor, *James*, 89.

admitted simply on the basis of baptism, without circumcision or the obligation of the law.[204]

Rusam connects the expression here with that in Acts 2.21 (Joel 3.5) and argues that the citation indicates that circumcision and keeping the law no longer matter, but only faith ('calling on the name of the Lord').[205] However, Wall notes that the use of the passive in v. 17 reverses the usual form of the verb in Acts (as in 2.21), shifting the focus from the believer's call to God to 'God's effective calling of a people into Israel'.[206]

4.4.6 *The Argument*

Bauckham has, however, correctly identified the issue before the council. The issue was not whether Gentiles could be accepted into the people of God – that had been settled, certainly by the end of Acts 11 – but whether they could do so without 'becoming Jews',[207] i.e. without circumcision and keeping the law of Moses. The question was not whether, but how – on what 'condition' (van de Sandt) or in what 'manner' (Robertson).[208]

James had characterized Peter's account as how 'God first visited the Gentiles, to take out of them a people for his name' (πρῶτον ὁ θεὸς ἐπεσκέψατο λαβεῖν ἐξ ἐθνῶν λαὸν τῷ ὀνόματι αὐτοῦ).[209] This characterization squarely attributes these events to the activity of God. The terminology James employs is astounding: 'the term *laos* ('people') is used by Luke almost exclusively in reference to Israel as the "people of God."'[210] It is OT language that normally refers to God's choice of Israel to be uniquely his own in distinction from the nations.[211] Yet James applies this language to Gentiles, Gentiles who have not become Jews by

204. Bauckham, 'James and the Gentiles', 169–70. See also Eckey, *Apostelgeschichte*, 1.333.

205. 'Wichtig is nicht die Erfüllung des Gesetzes, sondern die Anrufung des Namens des Herrn.' Rusam, *Das Alte Testament bei Lukas*, 430.

206. Robert Wall, 'Israel and the Gentile Mission in Acts and Paul: A Canonical Approach', in *Witness to the Gospel: The Theology of Acts* (ed. Ian Howard Marshall and David Peterson; Grand Rapids: Eerdmans, 1998), 451.

207. Bauckham, 'James and the Gentiles', 168.

208. Robertson, 'Hermeneutics', 106; Sandt, 'Explanation', 94.

209. Wall notes that the expression 'combines two important Lucan catchwords': λαός and ὄνομα. Wall, 'Israel', 451.

210. Johnson, *Acts*, 264. 'Insofern sonst im [lukanische] Doppelwerk der λαός (Volk Israel) stets von ἔθνη (Heiden) unterschieden wird, wirkt dieser Vers paradox.' Rusam, *Das Alte Testament bei Lukas*, 427. Luke's consistent use of the term makes unlikely Wilson's suggestion that its use here 'may simply be due to Luke's carelessness'. Wilson, *Gentile Mission*, 225. 'The fundamental theological correspondence between James' anticipatory statement and the prophecy of Amos is, however, comprised in the one word λάος ('people').' Ådna, 'James', 149. See also Jack T. Sanders, 'The Jewish People in Luke–Acts', in *Luke–Acts and the Jewish People* (ed. Joseph B. Tyson; Minneapolis: Augsburg, 1988), 56.

211. Dupont has argued that this language (MT סְגֻלָּה, LXX περιούσιος) lies behind λαὸν τῷ ὀνόματι αὐτοῦ in Acts 15.14. Dupont, 'ΛΑΟΣ', 47–50. However, Dahl finds a more likely basis for the expression in the Targums. Nils A. Dahl, 'A People for His Name (Acts XV.14)', *NTS* 4 (1958): 320–22. Nevertheless, Dahl in essence agrees with Dupont's characterization '"pour son Nom", c'est-à-dire pour lui-même, pour sa gloire'. Dupont, 'ΛΑΟΣ', 49.

undergoing circumcision or taking up the obligation to keep the Mosaic law. It seems clear, as Peter said (15.9), that God no longer distinguishes between Jew and Gentile. 'God places the Gentiles on the same level of honour as the Jews, when He wishes His name to be invoked upon them.'[212]

God has done this, not through the proclamation of the Mosaic law, but by the proclamation of Jesus and faith in him. Luke Timothy Johnson observes that to require circumcision for salvation (15.1) 'flies in the face of Luke's whole previous narrative, which made the emphatic point that Gentiles could and did receive salvation through the principle of *faith*'.[213] And they did so without circumcision or obedience to the law.[214]

It is precisely with this that the citation from Amos 9 agrees. In it, God claims 'all the nations/Gentiles who are called by my name' (πάντα τὰ ἔθνη ἐφ' οὓς ἐπικέκληται τὸ ὄνομά μου ἐπ' αὐτούς). This expression makes Amos 9.12 uniquely appropriate to James's argument,[215] connecting the prophecy with James's characterization of Peter's report to the council.[216] It also underscores the activity of God, who calls his name over the Gentiles, making this text more suitable than texts such as Zech. 2.11 (15 MT), which simply promises that 'many nations shall join themselves to the LORD'.[217] The much-discussed wording of Acts 15.17a, 'that the rest of mankind may seek the Lord' (differing from the MT), adds little to the argument.

There is a second, more important way in which the citation from Amos is uniquely appropriate to James's argument and the issue before the council. The citation explicitly links the restoration of the kingdom and the inclusion of the Gentiles. All in the council would have agreed that in Jesus the kingdom is being (or has been) restored[218] and that OT prophecies indicated that at some time and

212. Calvin, *Acts 14-28*, 46. Similarly, 'they are included in the covenant relationship (God's name has been invoked over them).' Bauckham, 'James and the Jerusalem Church', 458.

213. Johnson, *Acts*, 272.

214. 'The outward signs of continuity and identity of Israel, law and circumcision, are replaced by the continuity of saving faith produced by the Holy Spirit' (my translation). Jürgen Roloff, *Die Apostelgeschichte* (NTD; Göttingen: Vandenhoeck & Ruprecht, 1981), 232.

215. The argument offered here challenges the assertion that there are 'many far more apposite passages' from which one might make the argument, as claimed by Richard S. Cripps, *A Critical and Exegetical Commentary on the Book of Amos* (New York: SPCK, 1929), 323.

216. Or rather, James employs this in beginning his speech, because it will be key to his argument. Robertson, 'Hermeneutics', 106.

217. Bauckham correctly notes that 'in most cases such texts *could* be taken to mean that these Gentiles would be proselytes, undergoing circumcision as the corollary of their conversion to the God of Israel'. Bauckham, 'James and the Jerusalem Church', 458.

218. 'The kingdom is already here ... David's kingdom has already been rebuilt (cf. Acts 15.16 with Amos 9.11).' Goppelt, *Typos*, 124. 'James' declaration that God had returned to rebuild the fallen tent of David so that the Gentiles might seek the Lord (Acts 16.16f.) shows that Luke saw the restoration of Israel not as something to be effected only at the parousia, but as actually in progress.' David Seccombe, 'The New People of God', in *Witness to the Gospel: The Theology of Acts* (ed. Ian Howard Marshall and David Peterson; Grand Rapids: Eerdmans, 1998), 351. 'The Cornelius story is cited as proof that the restoration of the fallen house of David has already occurred, as well as the Gentiles seeking the Lord.' Jervell, 'Divided People', 51–52. 'Israel's restoration is an established

in some fashion some Gentiles would be joined with God's people.[219] Amos 9 explicitly connects these. James's argument turns on ὅπως ἄν in 15.17a: the purpose for which God has restored the kingdom is to claim the nations as his own.[220] The inclusion of Gentiles is a necessary consequence of the rebuilding of David's fallen tent. Since the kingdom has been restored, the time for Gentile inclusion is now. It does not belong still to the distant future or depend on the prior completion of Jewish evangelization.[221] Indeed, without the incorporation of the Gentiles, God's messianic project would be incomplete.

> And this [the proclamation to the Gentiles] is required in order that the messianic prophecies may be fulfilled in their entirety. For the passion and resurrection of Jesus do not constitute the entire work of the Messiah. For the complete accomplishment of that work, it is necessary that Paul announce salvation to the Gentiles and carry the Gospel message to Rome, the city that rules the nations.[222]

Dupont writes, 'The Scriptures themselves justify the Christian mission among the pagans, for they require this mission as the continuation of the salvific work of Jesus, the Christ.'[223] More strongly, Calvin argues, 'The Kingdom of Christ can only be established if God is invoked everywhere throughout the whole world, and the Gentiles united into His holy people.'[224] If the Gentiles are prevented from coming in, God's purpose will fail.

Therefore, James argues that the council 'should not trouble those of the Gentiles who turn to God' (μὴ παρενοχλεῖν τοῖς ἀπὸ τῶν ἐθνῶν ἐπιστρέφουσιν ἐπὶ τὸν θεόν, 15.19). Peter has already declared that it would be 'testing God' to impose a burden on these Gentile believers that Jews had been unable to bear (15.10). The council dare not oppose what is clearly God's purpose (as indicated by both God's providential actions and prophecy) and, in so doing, defeat the

---

fact.' Jacob Jervell, 'The Twelve on Israel's Thrones: Understanding the Apostolate', in *Luke and the People of God: A New Look at Luke–Acts* (Minneapolis: Augsburg, 1972), 92. 'The Jerusalem Council was faced with indisputable evidence. The ultimate blessing of the covenant, the possession of the Holy Spirit, had come in fullness on the Gentiles. This point was not a matter of debate. Neither was it being debated whether or not the "tent of David" had yet been restored.' Robertson, 'Hermeneutics', 105–06. More tentatively 'Israel's restoration is underway, but is far from established.' Craig A. Evans, 'Prophecy and Polemic: Jews in Luke's Scriptural Apologetic', in *Luke and Scripture: The Function of Sacred Tradition in Luke–Acts* (ed. Craig A. Evans and James A. Sanders; Minneapolis: Fortress, 1993), 207, n. 145; 'The Twelve Thrones of Israel: Scripture and Politics in Luke 22.24-30', in Evans and Sanders, eds., *Luke and Scripture*, 155, n. 2. Dupont believes that the 'tent of David' was restored by the ascension of Christ (Acts 2.34). Dupont, 'Ac 15,16', 30.

219. Even if some Jews did not expect the inclusion of some Gentiles in the future, the teaching of Jesus would have required such an expectation by the apostles. See e.g. Joachim Jeremias, *Jesus' Promise to the Nations* (trans. S. H. Hooke; SBT 24; Naperville, Ill.: Allenson, 1958), 40–54.

220. 'The restoration of the fallen tent of David (16) is best understood of Jesus as the Davidic seed who has now been installed as Christ and Lord, with the Gentile influx (17) occurring as a consequence.' Bolt, 'Mission', 204. See also Jervell, 'Divided People', 51–53.

221. Munck, *Paul*, 236, 239, 255–259.

222. Dupont, 'Salvation', 19.

223. Dupont, 'Salvation', 33.

224. Calvin, *Acts 14-28*, 47.

purpose for which God sent his Messiah. How ironic if the church (rather than the Sanhedrin, Acts 6.39) were to be found 'opposing God' in this way!

In this light, the restored kingdom differs from David's in important ways: it includes Gentiles (even Israel's historic enemies); it is extended by the Spirit through Christ's appointed witnesses, not military conquest (Acts 1.8); the temple loses its prominence (Luke 21.6; Acts 6.13-14); and the law is seen as 'a yoke ... which neither our fathers nor we have been able to bear' (Acts 15.10). If it were merely reconstituted as before, Gentiles would be conquered, or at most be admitted only on the basis of circumcision and obedience to the law. Amos 9.11f ('as in days of old') may be omitted from the citation to avoid confusion on this point.[225]

The conclusion of the citation (15.17c-18) underscores that this has been God's intention all along: 'says the Lord who makes these things known from of old' (λέγει κύριος ποιῶν ταῦτα γνωστὰ ἀπ᾽ αἰῶνος). 'The eschatological restoration of Israel was always intended to attract the Gentiles to seek God.'[226] The ancient prophecy of Amos is ample testimony to this, and the concluding words, γνωστὰ ἀπ᾽ αἰῶνος (15.18), add nothing new; it is better to see them as a free adaptation than unnecessarily posit conflation with Isa. 45.21. Barrett captures the thought when he says that 'God has not suddenly thought of the inclusion of the Gentiles; it has always been his intention, and he has long made his intention known.'[227]

4.4.7 *The Result*

Lest the Gentiles who are coming to faith be 'troubled' unduly, James proposes only certain minimal requirements for them. The apostolic decree (15.20, 28-29; 21.25) is beyond the scope of the present study. Some have found the origin of the decree in the so-called Noahic regulations, but this view has not found wide acceptance.[228] Nägele has argued that the provisions of the decree correspond 'to the minimal requirements which are binding for Jews even in life-threatening situations ... (cp. *bShevu* 7b; *bSan* 57b)',[229] but it is unclear why only 'emergency' stipulations would be applicable to Gentile believers, and not the whole of the law. Many have argued that the four requirements of the decree correspond to four stipulations in Leviticus 17–18 that are applied to 'the strangers that sojourn among' the people of Israel; the decree is intended to make table fellowship in the

---

225. Sandt, 'Explanation', 92.

226. Witherington, *Acts*, 459. 'That was, after all, the purpose of Israel's restoration: *that the remnant of men may seek the Lord*' (emphasis his). William J. Larkin, *Acts* (IVP New Testament Commentary Series 5; Downers Grove, Ill.: InterVarsity, 1995), 224. Bovon speaks of 'a schema which is dear to Luke (and Paul): the reestablishment of Israel (first phase) which leads to the opening up to the nations (second phase)'. Bovon, *Luke the Theologian*, 99.

227. Barrett, *Acts*, 2.728.

228. These were seven prohibitions supposed to have been given through Noah and required of all mankind: idolatry, blasphemy, murder, incest, stealing, perverting justice, and eating meat with blood in it. Evidence is lacking that these had been formulated at this point in the first century. Fitzmyer, *Acts*, 557; Witherington, *Acts*, 464. See also Bauckham, 'James and the Gentiles', 174.

229. Nägele, *Laubhütte Davids*, 231.

church possible between observant Jews and non-observant Gentiles.[230] Bauckham has refined the argument, proposing that James connects the God-seeking Gentiles of the *eschaton* (Jer. 12.16 and Zech. 2.11 [15 MT]) with the Gentiles 'in the midst' of Israel in Leviticus 17–18 by means of *gēzerâ šawâ* (the shared expression בְּתוֹךְ, 'in the midst').[231] However, Nägele has correctly noted that 'the Amos quote served to settle the overall controversial issues, not just the question of table fellowship'[232] – the issue was that 'Unless you are circumcised according to the custom of Moses, you cannot be saved' (15.1). Witherington has found that the alleged similarities between the decree and Leviticus 17–18 are overstated, and has suggested that worship (particularly feasts) in pagan temples are in view,[233] activities that would be in conflict with God's ownership of Gentile believers ('called by my name'). A satisfying explanation of the decree has not yet been offered.

The concluding statement of James's speech has also puzzled scholars: 'For from early generations Moses has had in every city those who preach him, for he is read every sabbath in the synagogues' (v. 21). Dibelius observed that 'although straightforward from the linguistic and textual points of view, in context and meaning it is one of the most difficult verses in the New Testament'.[234] Lake and Cadbury commented that 'the explanations offered by commentators are numerous and unsatisfactory'.[235] Daniel R. Schwartz has found two main interpretations of the verse.[236] The first suggests that the long proclamation of the Mosaic law justifies the imposition of the decree's requirements, as things that were only to be expected by anyone who knew the law, or that would be necessary for table fellowship.[237] Opponents have questioned why only these few requirements of

---

230. Johnson, *Acts*, 273; Polhill, *Acts*, 332. For an earlier statement of this argument, see Burton Scott Easton, *The Purpose of Acts* (*Theology* Occasional Papers 6; London: SPCK, 1936), 16–17. The prescriptions are said to be found in Lev. 17.8 (sacrifices not to Yahweh, i.e. 'pollutions of idols'); 17.10, 12, 13 ('blood' and 'what is strangled'); 18.26 ('unchastity'). It should be noted that these comprise only a small portion of Leviticus 17–18 and that they are not particularly distinguished in the text from other prescriptions found there. For textual issues, see Witherington, *Acts*, 460.

231. Bauckham, 'James and the Gentiles', 175–77. While the expression ('in your midst') occurs five times in Leviticus 17–18 (Lev. 17.8, 10, 12, 13; 18.26), it also appears in many other texts. It is unclear on what basis we are to connect the expression here with Leviticus 17–18 rather than these other texts. Bauckham concedes that 'Luke's summary has obscured the exegetical argument on which the terms of the apostolic decree are based', but what is so well concealed may not actually be there. Bauckham, 'James and the Jerusalem Church', 458. It is unlikely that readers would grasp 'obscured' textual allusions without more explicit clues. Barrett believes that 'one would expect at least a trace of the אל תקרא form of argument' if one is present here. Barrett, *Acts*, 2.728.

232. Nägele, *Laubhütte Davids*, 231. Note also the claim already made in Acts 15.9, that God has already ceased making any 'distinction between us and them' and that he has 'cleansed [the Gentiles'] hearts by faith'. Nägele, *Laubhütte Davids*, 229.

233. Witherington, *Acts*, 460–67. Cf. 1 Cor. 10.14-22.

234. Dibelius, *Studies*, 97.

235. Foakes Jackson and Lake, eds., *Beginnings*, 4.177.

236. Daniel R. Schwartz, 'The Futility of Preaching Moses (Acts 15,21)', *Bib* 67 (1982): 276–81.

237. Bauckham, 'James and the Gentiles', 177–78; Fitzmyer, *Acts*, 558; Johnson, *Acts*, 267; Gerhard A. Krodel, *Acts* (Augsburg Commentary on the New Testament; Minneapolis: Augsburg, 1986); Marshall, *Acts*, 254; Johannes Munck, *The Acts of the Apostles* (AB 31; Garden City, NY:

the Mosaic law are judged to apply to Gentiles and objected that it is not merely table fellowship that is at issue, but the salvation of Gentiles (15.1). The second proposes that the long and widespread proclamation of the Mosaic law makes it possible to limit the requirements at this time to only a few points, since the whole law is regularly being preached by others.[238] Again, however, the issue was not the preservation of the law of Moses, but the insistence that Gentiles obey the law in order to be saved. Schwartz offers his own proposal:

> James means that it would be wrong to impose Mosaic law upon converts to Christianity, for experience shows that only a few would be willing to accept the worship of the true God under such a condition. The Mosaic law is thus an obstacle to the acceptance of the true religion, and, since God wants the Gentiles to worship him (as the quote from Amos in vv. 15-17 shows), it follows that the law is not to be imposed.[239]

Although Moses had long been preached everywhere, few Gentiles had been drawn to God, but now, through the proclamation of Jesus, many Gentiles were seeking the God of Abraham. In light of the specific emphasis on circumcision as the issue before the council (15.1, 5), it is worth noting the observation of Jeremias that 'the greatest obstacle to the conversion of Gentiles was the demand that they should be circumcised'.[240] Schwartz links the Amos citation and the repeated assertion in Acts that not even the Jews had been able to keep the law (Acts 15.10; cf. 7.53; 13.38-39). His proposal deserves further study. The fulfilment of God's announced purpose for the nations required a different and more effective approach.[241]

James's proposal was accepted by the council with 'one accord' (15.25), remarkable considering the στάσεως καὶ ζητήσεως οὐκ ὀλίγης in Antioch (15.2) and the πολλῆς ζητήσεως with which the council had begun (15.7). This was not merely the judgement of the apostles and elders at the council, but also 'seemed good to the Holy Spirit and to us' (15.28). When the letter and the delegation sent by the council arrived in Antioch, the congregation there 'rejoiced' in

---

Doubleday, 1967), 140; Polhill, *Acts*, 332. 'He warns that it is not possible for the ceremonies to be abolished so quickly, as if at one fell swoop, because the Jews had already been accustomed to the teaching of the Law for many generations, and Moses had his preachers; that agreement therefore must be gained for a short time until the freedom, procured by Christ, should gradually be more clearly understood; in other words, as the common saying goes, that the ceremonies had to be buried with some decency.' Calvin, *Acts 14-28*, 51–52.

238. Bowker, 'Speeches', 108; Bruce, *Acts* (rev. edn.), 296; Burnside, *The Acts of the Apostles: The Greek Edited with Introduction and Notes for the Use of Schools*, 176; Rackham, *Acts*, 254.

239. Schwartz, 'Futility', 27. Schwartz summarizes the view of J. K. L. Gieseler, 'Über die Nazaräer und Ebioniten', *Archiv für alte und neue Kirchengeschichte* 4 (1818–20), 311–12. Schwartz has now been followed by Fitzmyer, *Acts*, 558.

240. Jeremias, *Promise*, 15.

241. Treatments of this text from the standpoint of contextualization expound on the need for adaptability in the service of mission, but fail to grapple with the Mosaic law not merely as a matter of human culture, but as given to Israel by God. David K. Strong, 'The Jerusalem Council: Some Implications for Contextualization', in *Mission in Acts: Ancient Narratives in Contemporary Context* (ed. Robert L. Gallagher and Paul Hertig; American Society of Missiology Series, 34; Maryknoll, NY: Orbis Books, 2004), 196–208.

the council's decision and exhortation (15.31) and the Jerusalem delegates were, after a time, 'sent off in peace' (15.33). In his subsequent travels, Paul 'delivered ... the decisions which had been reached by the apostles and elders who were at Jerusalem' and 'the churches were strengthened in the faith, and they increased in numbers daily' (16.4-5). The episode thus concludes with God's evident blessing on the church as a result of its decision.[242]

4.5 *Summary*

4.5.1 *Text*

The textual issues involved in this citation are complex. The LXX appears to represent an interpretive reading of the text (or, less likely, a lost Hebrew MS tradition or a misreading of the MT). The NT citation appears to be a free citation of the text. Nevertheless neither the LXX nor NT citation diverge at any essential points from the general intent of the MT. The argument does not, as is often suggested, depend particularly on the form of the LXX text, but can be made from the MT as well. The citation of the LXX form of the text does not call into question the historicity of the speech. There is no persuasive evidence that the words of Amos 9.11-12 are conflated with other texts.

4.5.2 *Hermeneutic*

The text of Amos 9.11-12 is used in a way that is consistent with its original contextual meaning. Despite the questions regarding 'the rest of mankind' or 'remnant of Edom', the argument depends instead on the promise that 'all the Gentiles who are called by my name' will come under the merciful care of Yahweh. There is no convincing evidence of conflation with other texts or of arbitrary exegetical strategies.

James employs a Christocentric hermeneutic. The key to the use of Amos 9.11-12 in Acts 15.16-18 is the relationship between the restoration of the Davidic kingdom and the ingathering of the Gentiles. The kingdom has been restored (at least in principle) in Jesus, who now reigns as 'Lord and Christ' (Acts 2.36). Yet according to Amos, the purpose for which God had restored the kingdom is that his saving rule might be extended to Gentiles. The council has already heard 'what signs and wonders God had done through [Barnabas and Paul] among the Gentiles' (15.12), as well as how Gentiles first came to 'hear the word of the gospel and believe' (15.17). James described the latter as God's having taken from the Gentiles 'a people for his name', echoing God's election of Israel and anticipating similar language in the citation. The citation, James says, 'agrees with' this understanding of events. This 'agreement' is the agreement of the prophecy with its intended fulfilment: what God announced through Amos, God has now accomplished through Jesus. The kingdom had been reestablished in Christ, as all in the council would agree. And, just as the prophecy said, Gentiles are coming to God,

---

242. Luke regularly highlights God's continued blessing on the church at the conclusion of episodes within the narrative, e.g. 2.47; 4.32-33; 5.12-16, 42; 9.31.

but through the preaching of Jesus by the apostles, rather than the preaching of Moses in the synagogue.

4.5.3 *Purpose*

The citation is employed as 'proof from prophecy'. It not only interprets the events Peter had narrated, but establishes divine authorization for the manner of Gentile inclusion by demonstrating that the inclusion of the Gentiles is God's design.[243]

The question before the council is whether Gentiles must be circumcised (and keep the law of Moses) in order to be saved. The events at Cornelius's house had made it clear that God had cleansed the hearts of Gentiles by faith (15.9), that the ceremonial cleansing of circumcision was unnecessary – salvation is by faith. What matters is not the law, but God's calling his name over Gentiles in covenant relationship and blessing – salvation is by grace. To require that Gentile believers undergo circumcision and obey the law would 'test God' by imposing a burden that Jews themselves had not been able to bear (15.10). Above all, the church must not 'trouble' Gentiles in such a way as to frustrate God's purposes, for the reestablishing of the kingdom requires the successful incorporation of Gentiles. Acts 13 addressed the necessity of the Gentile mission and Acts 15 its mode of operation; both are now settled questions for the church. (The Gentile mission remained controversial for Jews who did not acknowledge Jesus as the Messiah, Acts 22.21-22.)

The argument does not rest on the citation alone, but is advanced on three levels. First, the account of the deliberations allows readers to follow the council's reasoning and reach its conclusion. Second, the account of the council invites readers to share its own conclusion that it has been guided by the Spirit. Third, the narrative of Acts as a whole shows God's initiative in launching the Gentile mission and his blessing on both the council's decision and the mission itself.

The place of this account in the narrative indicates that not only the appropriateness of the Gentile mission but the manner in which the Gentiles were to be included were matters of importance to Luke and his audience. The multilayered argument (scripture and providence, citation and narrative) provides confidence that God has indeed accepted Gentiles into the people of God without circumcision or obedience to the law of Moses.

---

243. 'Historische Ehrfahrung und Schriftbeweis fliessen zusammen; die Schrift bestätigt die Ehrfahrung des Petrus, und die Ehrfahrung des Petrus bestätigt die Schrift.' Jervell, *Apostelgeschichte*, 395.

THE SPIRIT AND ALL FLESH (JOEL 3.1-5 MT IN ACTS 2.17-21)

The key role played by OT citations in establishing the legitimacy of the Gentile mission is clear from the foregoing examination of the citations in Acts 13.47; 15.16-18. These citations appear in contexts that are explicitly concerned with the Gentile mission and are introduced for the purpose of addressing questions about that mission.

The survey of OT citations in chapter 2 found two additional texts containing language that appeared to refer to the inclusion of the Gentiles in the promises of God. The citations of Joel 3.1-5 MT (Acts 2.17-21) and Gen. 22.18 (Acts 3.25) figure prominently in the first two sermons in Acts and play a significant role in introducing major themes of the book.[1] In their immediate contexts, Peter cites these texts to establish the proclamation about Jesus, not to address the Gentile mission, which had not yet begun. The speeches of Acts, however, have two audiences: *in* the narrative, Peter addresses these sermons to Jewish audiences in Jerusalem; *through* the narrative, Luke addresses his readers.[2] What may be of little importance to, or escape the notice of, one audience may be important to the other. While there is no indication in the narrative that Peter's original audience attended to the implications of these citations for Gentile ministry, Luke's Gentile readers might well be expected to see themselves in the apparently universal language of these citations. The implications of these citations for the Gentile mission become clear in the larger context of the narrative and its use of the OT. References to Gentiles in the citations of Joel 3.1-5 MT and Gen. 22.18 may be anticipatory rather than explicit, but they nevertheless contribute to Luke's legitimation of the Gentile mission from the OT.

---

1. Hans F. Bayer, 'The Preaching of Peter in Acts', in *Witness to the Gospel: The Theology of Acts* (ed. Ian Howard Marshall and David Peterson; Grand Rapids: Eerdmans, 1998), 260. Similarly the two speeches are 'complementary' and 'we must view the two speeches together in order to understand Peter's message in its full scope', Tannehill, *Narrative Unity*, 2.58.

2. 'Luke does not place his speeches randomly but rather strategically, in order to provide his readers at key moments with an interpretation of the story he is narrating. In this sense his speeches are a form of authorial commentary.' Johnson, 'Idols', 10. The failure to recognize this dual audience lies behind assertions such as the following: 'Peter delivers his address to the Jews gathered in Jerusalem for the Feast ... Therefore, this text is to be understood as ecclesiastically particularistic to the Jewish nation. Peter's message is not intended for a universalistic interpretation.' John Strazicich, *Joel's Use of Scripture and Scripture's Use of Joel: Appropriation and Resignification in Second Temple Judaism and Early Christianity* (Leiden: Brill, 2007), 273. This narrow argument is striking in a study devoted to the 'resignification' of the text.

The quotation of Joel 3.1-5 MT (English 2.28-32) in Acts 2.16-21 has been called 'the most discussed explicit quotation in Ac',[3] due to its programmatic significance as the initial citation in the first Christian sermon in Acts.[4] Three parts of the citation appear related to the Gentile mission: Joel 3.1b (Acts 2.17c), 3.5a (Acts 2.21) and 3.5d (2.39).

Joel 3.1a-b MT	*Joel 3.1a-b LXX*	*Acts 2.17a-c*
וְהָיָה אַחֲרֵי־כֵן 1a	καὶ ἔσται μετὰ ταῦτα	17a καὶ ἔσται ἐν ταῖς ἐσχάταις ἡμέραις,
		b λέγει ὁ θεός,
אֶשְׁפּוֹךְ אֶת־רוּחִי b עַל־כָּל־בָּשָׂר	καὶ ἐκχεῶ ἀπὸ τοῦ πνεύματός μου ἐπὶ πᾶσαν σάρκα	c ἐκχεῶ ἀπὸ τοῦ πνεύματός μου ἐπὶ πᾶσαν σάρκα

Joel 3.5 MT	*Joel 3.5 LXX*	*Acts 2.21, 39*
וְהָיָה כֹּל אֲשֶׁר־יִקְרָא 5a בְּשֵׁם יְהוָה יִמָּלֵט	καὶ ἔσται πᾶς ὃς ἂν ἐπικαλέσηται τὸ ὄνομα κυρίου σωθήσεται	21 καὶ ἔσται πᾶς ὃς ἂν ἐπικαλέσηται τὸ ὄνομα κυρίου σωθήσεται.
כִּי בְּהַר־צִיּוֹן b וּבִירוּשָׁלַ͏ִם תִּהְיֶה פְלֵיטָה	ὅτι ἐν τῷ ὄρει Σιων καὶ ἐν Ιερουσαλημ ἔσται ἀνασωζόμενος	
כַּאֲשֶׁר אָמַר יְהוָה c	καθότι εἶπεν κύριος	
		39a ὑμῖν γάρ ἐστιν ἡ ἐπαγγελία
		b καὶ τοῖς τέκνοις ὑμῶν
		c καὶ πᾶσιν τοῖς εἰς μακράν,
וּבַשְּׂרִידִים אֲשֶׁר יְהוָה קֹרֵא d	καὶ εὐαγγελιζόμενοι οὓς κύριος προσκέκληται	d ὅσους ἂν προσκαλέσηται κύριος ὁ θεὸς ἡμῶν.

The omitted verses describe the effects of the outpouring of the Spirit in prophecy, visions and dreams (Joel 3.1c-2 MT; Acts 2.17d-18) and accompanying signs and wonders (Joel 3.3-4 MT; Acts 2.19-20). While these are important for the interpretation and application of the prophecy within Peter's speech, we do not need to consider them in detail for our present purpose.

5.1 *Text*

The Hebrew text of Joel 3 is not in doubt: BHS lists no extant variants and no citations from Joel have been identified in the DSS. Some recent translations (e.g.

---

3.   Steyn, *Septuagint Quotations*, 72.

4.   Robert Wall has argued that the citations from Joel 3 (Acts 2) and Amos 9 (Acts 15) play an important role in 'organizing the entire composition' (i.e. Acts). Wall, 'Israel', 441. Van de Sandt has argued that Joel plays a prominent role, not only in Acts 2, but also in other important texts in Acts. However, his intertextual argument, relying on slender verbal allusions, is ultimately too tenuous to be completely persuasive. Huub van de Sandt, 'The Fate of the Gentiles in Joel and Acts 2: An Intertextual Study', *ETL* 66 (1990): 55–77.

JB, NEB) have amended 3.5b to וּבִשְׂרִידִים שְׂרִידִים to create the parallel 'in Mount Zion those who escape … and in Jerusalem survivors', but this proposal is without MS support. The LXX textual tradition shows more variation, including four minor variants in Joel 3.1b, 3.5a and 3.5d (2.39),[5] but none are well attested and none affect the meaning of the citation in Acts. There are no well-attested variants in the NT MS tradition for Acts 2.17c, 21, 39.[6] There are minor differences between the MT and the LXX, and more substantial differences between the LXX and the text of Acts,[7] but none affect Joel 3.1b (Acts 2.17c) or 3.5a (Acts 2.21). There are also differences in 3.5d (2.39), but there Joel appears to be echoed rather than cited. Steyn concludes that Luke's source 'was probably a LXX text' but notes some points at which it appears more similar to the Hebrew.[8]

5.2 *Joel 3.1-5 MT*

The prophecy of Joel provides few clues regarding either its author or the historical period in which he prophesied. The book has been variously dated from the ninth century to as late as 200 BCE.[9] 'Happily, Joel's message does not hinge on the date.'[10] Debate over the identity of Joel's 'locusts' is more challenging. They have been understood as a literal locust plague,[11] as invading armies,[12] as apocalyptic imagery,[13] or as a combination of these.[14] While important for the

---

5.   In Joel 3.1b (Acts 2.17c), some MSS read τὸ πνεῦμα in place of ἀπὸ τοῦ πνεύματός. In Joel 3.5b (Acts 2.21), several MSS have the future (ἐπικαλέσεται) or present (ἐπικαλῆται) in place of the aorist ἐπικαλέσηται. In Joel 3.5d (Acts 2.39), some MSS have the singular εὐαγγελιζόμενος for the plural εὐαγγελιζόμενοι, some have the active προσκέκληκε (or the middle προκέκληται) for the middle προσκέκληται, and some reverse κύριος and προσκέκληται.

6.   Eldon Epp has noted a number of variants in D that 'universalize' the citation. Only πάσας σάρκας (2.17c) is part of the citations we are considering here. Epp believes that the Gentiles cannot be in view here because Peter is speaking to Jews, 'that the Gentile mission first began later with Cornelius', and that no hints of it appear before Acts 10. Epp, *Theological Tendency*, 66–70.

7.   'Previous studies of this quotation, although numerous, have not provided satisfactory explanation for all the textual changes between the Ac reading and that in existing manuscripts from the LXX.' Steyn, *Septuagint Quotations*, 76, cf. his detailed analysis, 74–90.

8.   Steyn, *Septuagint Quotations*, 99.

9.   See e.g. the survey of views presented in Raymond Bryan Dillard, 'Joel', in *The Minor Prophets: An Exegetical and Expositional Commentary* (ed. Thomas Edward McComiskey; 3 vols.; Grand Rapids: Baker, 1992), 242–43. See also the summaries in Roland K. Harrison, *Introduction to the Old Testament* (Grand Rapids: Eerdmans, 1969), 876–79; LaSor et al., *Survey*, 438–39.

10.   LaSor et al., *Survey*, 439.

11.   E.g. Leslie C. Allen, *The Books of Joel, Obadiah, Jonah, and Micah* (NICOT; Grand Rapids: Eerdmans, 1976), 29–31; Harrison, *Introduction*, 875–76; Hubbard, *Joel and Amos*, 21; Simon M. Lehrman, 'Joel', in *The Twelve Prophets: Hebrew Text, English Translation and Commentary* (ed. Abraham Cohen; Soncino Books of the Bible; Bournemouth: Soncino, 1948), 57–58; Stuart, *Hosea–Jonah*, 232–34.

12.   Henderson characterizes this as 'the more ancient opinion' and attributes it to 'the Targum, the Jews whom Jerome consulted', Ephraem the Syrian, Theodoret, Cyril of Alexandria, Hugh of St Victor, Luther and others. Henderson, *Minor Prophets*, 91.

13.   Most notably by Adalbert Merx. See LaSor et al., *Survey*, 440.

14.   Henderson believes that the plague of ch. 1 is literal, while that of ch. 2 describes the destruction

interpretation of the book as a whole, the identity of the locusts is not crucial for the interpretation of 3.1-5 MT.

The overall flow of thought in the book is clear, even if some commentators differ on details. Joel 1 describes the devastation from a (current) locust plague and calls for repentance. Joel 2 speaks of the locust plague in terms of the day of Yahweh (or vice versa, 2.1-11) and issues a second call to repentance (2.12-17). The message then turns from judgement to restoration: material/economic (2.18-27) and military/political (with the destruction of Judah's enemies, 4.1-21 MT), with Joel 3.1-5 MT between these.

Joel 3.1-5 MT begins with the words וְהָיָה אַחֲרֵי־כֵן ('and it shall come to pass afterward'), indicating a shift from the preceding verses. Most interpreters view the transition as a temporal one. The expression אַחֲרֵי־כֵן occurs 45 times in the MT and is typically translated temporally as 'afterward' or 'after this'.[15] Dillard believes the expression 'seems unambiguously to signify temporal sequence' and finds that 'it is hard to escape the fact that the prophet intends his readers to understand 3.1-5 [2.28-32] as sequential to 2.18-27'.[16] Hubbard believes that it marks the transition from the repair of the old order to the inauguration of the new.[17] Achtemeier believes that the events of 3.1-5 MT take place in 'that indefinite time of the coming of the day of the Lord'.[18] VanGemeren believes that this expression, like בַּיָּמִים הָהֵמָּה ('in those days', 3.2 MT), simply means 'when'.[19] Chapman has argued that discourse analysis indicates the expression is 'used to create major discourse level transitions' and argues that the transition is best understood as one from expected to unexpected blessings.[20]

---

of Judah by its political enemies. Henderson, *Minor Prophets*, 91–92. So John Calvin, *Commentaries on the Twelve Minor Prophets* (Calvin's Commentaries 14; Grand Rapids: Baker, 1979; repr. of Calvin Translation Society ed., Edinburgh, 1845–56). Others see Yahweh's army in ch. 2. James L. Crenshaw, *Joel: A New Translation with Introduction and Commentary* (AB 24C; New York: Doubleday, 1995), 15, 116–17, 128–31; Dillard, 'Joel', 278. Still others find apocalyptic creatures in ch. 2, e.g. Robert H. Pfeiffer, *Introduction to the Old Testament* (New York: Harper & Brothers, 1941), 574; Hans Walter Wolff, *Joel and Amos* (trans. Waldemar Janzen et al.; Hermeneia; Philadelphia: Fortress, 1977), 42.

15. The expression with וְהָיָה occurs only here, although the similar וַיְהִי אַחֲרֵי־כֵן occurs 11 times in narrative contexts in the MT (Judg. 16.4; 1 Sam. 24.6; 2 Sam. 2.1; 8.1; 10.1; 13.1; 15.1 (וַיְהִי מֵאַחֲרֵי כֵן); 21.18; 2 Kgs. 6.24; 1 Chr. 18.1; 19.1). *HALOT*, s.v. אַחַר.

16. Dillard, 'Joel', 294. Dillard understands 2.1-11 to refer to an apocalyptic judgement on Judah and believes 3.1-5 answers to that threat (as 2.18-27 answers the temporal threat of 1.1-20).

17. Hubbard, *Joel and Amos*, 68.

18. Elizabeth Achtemeier, 'The Book of Joel: Introduction, Commentary, and Reflections', *NIB*, 7.326.

19. Willem VanGemeren, *Interpreting the Prophetic Word* (Grand Rapids: Zondervan, 1990), 123–24; 'The Spirit of Restoration', *WTJ* 50 (1988): 84–90.

20. David W. Chapman, 'A Superabundance of Blessing: The Discourse Intent of Joel 3.1-5 and Its Canonical Implications', M.A. thesis, Trinity Evangelical Divinity School, 1996, 129. 'The difference between the two stages is not that the first is material and the second spiritual but that the first is the restoration of old damage and the second is the inauguration of a new era in God's dealings with his people.' Hubbard, *Joel and Amos*, 68. In a like vein also Wolff: 'Not only will earlier conditions be restored (v 23), they will be exceeded.' Wolff, *Joel and Amos*, 65.

Joel 4.1 MT has another temporal indicator, כִּי הִנֵּה בַּיָּמִים הָהֵמָּה וּבָעֵת הַהִיא ('for behold, in those days and at that time'). It sounds a 'somewhat similar chronological note' to 3.1,[21] but the transition seems primarily to be to another blessing: 'not only will I [God] do this, but at the same time, I will also …'.[22] The focus changes from blessing on Judah to judgement on the nations. Joel 3.1-5 MT may thus be viewed as a distinct section within the message of restoration and salvation for Judah that begins in 2.18.

This cited text can be further divided into three sections: the outpouring of God's Spirit (3.1-2 MT), cosmic signs (3.3-4 MT), and the deliverance of all who call on the name of Yahweh (3.5 MT).[23] Of these three, the first ('all flesh') and the third ('everyone who calls' and 'everyone whom the LORD calls') are relevant to the present study. The apocalyptic signs of 3.3-4 MT are important as 'indicators that God is at work',[24] but the focus is on the gift of the Spirit and deliverance.

5.2.1 *All Flesh (Joel 3.1b MT)*

God promises to do much more than restore Judah's agricultural prosperity. 'And it shall come to pass afterward, that I will pour out my spirit on all flesh' (וְהָיָה אַחֲרֵי־כֵן אֶשְׁפּוֹךְ אֶת־רוּחִי עַל־כָּל־בָּשָׂר), paralleled in a chiasm by בַּיָּמִים הָהֵמָּה אֶשְׁפּוֹךְ אֶת־רוּחִי, 'in those days, I will pour out my spirit' in 3.2b MT). The focus of this outpouring is not new obedience as in Ezek. 36.26-27, or refreshment and renewal, as in Isa. 32.15; 44.3.[25] The Spirit here brings revelation: prophecy (נִבְּאוּ), dreams (חֲלֹמוֹת יַחֲלֹמוּן) and visions (חֶזְיֹנוֹת יִרְאוּ).[26] 'In the Old Testament, the Spirit of God is preeminently the spirit of prophecy'.[27] Many see here the fulfilment of Moses' wish (Num. 11.29), 'Would that all the LORD's people were prophets, that the LORD would put his spirit upon them!'[28] Wolff dismisses the view that this gift of prophecy consists in ecstatic experience[29] or prophetic proclamation. Rather it refers to the relationship to God, 'which has become completely new in the new creation through the outpouring of the spirit', 'similar to Jer. 31.33-34: everyone will stand in a relationship of immediacy to

---

21. Dillard, 'Joel', 300.
22. The three other appearances of the expression are in Jer. 33.15; 50.4, 20. Crenshaw, *Joel*, 173.
23. Allen, *Joel*, 97. So also Chapman, 'Superabundance', 200; Crenshaw, *Joel*, 170–71.
24. Hubbard, *Joel and Amos*, 71.
25. Wolff, *Joel and Amos*, 66.
26. There is no particular significance to the attribution of visions to young men and dreams to old men. The association of the forms of revelation with the groups who receive them appears merely 'rhetorical'. Julius A. Bewer, 'Commentary on Joel', in *A Critical and Exegetical Commentary on Micah, Zephaniah, Nahum, Habakkuk, Obadiah and Joel* (ICC; Edinburgh: T&T Clark, 1911), 122. So Crenshaw, *Joel*, 165.
27. Dillard, 'Joel', 294–95. He calls attention in particular to Num. 11.25-29; 1 Sam. 10.6-10; 18.10; 19.20-33; 1 Kgs. 22.22-23 (2 Chr. 18.21-22); 2 Kgs. 2.15; Neh. 9.30; Ezek. 13.3; Zech. 7.12; 13.2.
28. Crenshaw, *Joel*, 171; Duane A. Garrett, *Hosea, Joel* (NAC 19A; Nashville: Broadman & Holman, 1997), 368.
29. As claimed by Bewer, 'Joel', 122.

God',[30] i.e. all will receive intimate and direct knowledge of God such as came previously only to prophets.[31]

The Spirit is poured out on כָּל־בָּשָׂר ('all flesh'). Most limit the expression here to Judah. 'There can be little doubt in this context that Joel intends *all flesh* to refer to Israel alone – the phrase *all flesh* is explicated as *your* sons and daughters, slaves, young and old; the fortunes of Judah are contrasted to those of the Gentiles (4.1-17 [3.1-17]).'[32] It is more likely, however, that כָּל־בָּשָׂר is a universal reference. Keil believes '"all flesh" signifies all men'[33] and Kaiser understands it as 'a synonym for the "nations"', arguing that 'seldom if ever may "all flesh" be reserved and restricted to all Israel'.[34] The expression appears 45 times in the MT and almost always has a universal sense, referring either to all living things (17 times, especially in the flood narrative)[35] or to all humankind (21 times, not counting Joel 3.1 MT).[36] A number among the latter explicitly include other nations (e.g. Zech. 2.13; Isa. 66.16, 23, 24). (We will argue below that the expressions in 3.5 MT also bear a universal sense.) 'All flesh' here must refer to 'all humankind'. Just as the promised blessings in Joel 3 vastly exceed the earlier devastation, so the recipients of those blessings vastly exceed Judah.

Even if we conclude that the context focuses the reference on Judah, there are two indications that the promise is broader than it may at first appear. First, the Spirit will be poured out without distinction: 'sons ... daughters ... old men ... young men ... menservants and maidservants' – merisms meant to indicate the

---

30. Wolff, *Joel and Amos*, 66–67. Wolff compares the use of 'prophesy' with the 'nation of priests' in Exod. 19.5-6, believing both represent 'immediacy to God'. See also Garrett, *Hosea, Joel*, 368; Norman F. Langford, 'The Book of Joel: Exposition', *IB*, 6.752.

31. This would not exclude the existence of a distinctive prophetic gift, just as God's making Israel 'a kingdom of priests' (Exod. 19.6) did not eliminate a distinct priestly office. There remain prophets in Acts (11.27; 13.1; 15.32; 19.6; 21.9-10), despite the fulfilment of Joel 3.

32. Dillard, 'Joel', 295. '*All flesh* may mean all mankind, and we should interpret it thus, if the following context did not restrict it to the Jews.' Bewer, 'Joel', 123. See also Allen, *Joel*, 98; John A. Thompson, 'The Book of Joel: Introduction and Exegesis', *IB*, 6.752.

33. Keil, *Minor Prophets*, 210.

34. Walter C. Kaiser, Jr., 'The Promise of God and the Outpouring of the Holy Spirit', in *The Living and Active Word of God: Studies in Honor of Samuel J. Schulz* (ed. Morris Inch and Ronald Youngblood; Winona Lake, Ind.: Eisenbrauns, 1983; repr., with revisions, in *The Uses of the Old Testament in the New*, Chicago: Moody, 1985: 89–100), 119. An analysis of the 44 instances of the expression outside Joel (Kaiser's count of 32 instances must combine adjacent references) does not support the claim that in a majority of instances 'the expression refers to Gentiles alone' in distinction from 'all mankind'.

35. All 12 occurrences in Genesis 6–9 plus Lev. 17.14 (3×); Num. 18.15; and possibly Ps. 136.25. In Gen. 7.21-23, 'all flesh' (כָּל־בָּשָׂר) is explicated as 'birds, cattle, beasts, all swarming creatures that swarm upon the earth, and every man; everything on the dry land in whose nostrils was the breath of life'. Cf. Gen. 6.17 ('all flesh in which is the breath of life ... everything that is on the earth') and Num. 18.15 ('all flesh, whether man or beast').

36. Num. 16.22; 27.16; Deut. 5.26; Isa. 40.5; 49.26; 66.16, 23, 24; Jer. 12.12 (the sole negative, 'no flesh'); 25.31; 32.27; 45.5; Ezek. 20.48; 21.4-5; Zech. 2.11; Ps. 65.2; 145.21; Job 12.10; 34.15; Dan. 4.9. In the remaining six occurrences, it has a pronominal suffix and refers to 'his whole body' (Lev. 4.11; 13.13; 15.16; Num. 8.7; Ezek. 10.2; Prov. 4.22).

whole people of God.[37] '*All* of God's people will have *all* they need of God's Spirit', without 'societal restrictions'.[38] 'No exclusion will be made on the basis of gender, age or social station.'[39] But the locust plague affected only the residents of Judah, not all of God's people, scattered as they were across the ancient world. It is one thing to understand the blessing of agricultural restoration to apply only to the inhabitants of the land, but another to suggest that Jews living outside the land would be excluded from the larger blessings of the outpoured Spirit and divine deliverance of Joel 3–4 MT.[40]

Second, the 'menservants and maidservants' (3.2 MT) specifically included among those who receive the gift of the Spirit would likely have included Gentiles. Walter Kaiser has argued that the promise indicates that 'even Gentile slaves in Jewish households would benefit from this outpouring'.[41] It is clear that from early times Israel held Gentile slaves.[42] While 'your' might limit 'sons and daughters' to Jews, 'your menservants and maidservants' suggests the overflow of blessing to Gentiles. In addition, there were apparently always free Gentiles living within the borders of Israel: Rahab (Josh. 6.25), Ruth, Doeg the Edomite (1 Sam. 22.9), Araunah the Jebusite (2 Sam. 24), Uriah the Hittite (2 Sam. 11), Solomon's wives (1 Kings 11), and the 'foreign' women married by some in the post-exilic community (Ezra 9–10; Neh. 13.23-27). These were 'strangers' (גֵּר) or 'sojourners' (תּוֹשָׁב) recognized in the Mosaic law, provided with certain protections, and held to many of the same requirements as ethnic Israelites (Exod. 12.49; Lev. 24.22; Num. 15.15-16). A number are presented as believers in the God of Israel (e.g. Rahab, Ruth). All in Judah (servants, strangers and sojourners) would have suffered from the plague and presumably all would have shared in the agricultural renewal of 2.18-27. Would not, then, these Gentiles, slave and free, also participate in the greater blessing of Joel 3 MT?

Some have noted in this context the coming judgement on the nations in Joel 4 MT. Wolff notes that 'concerning other nations a completely different message is coming (4.1ff)'.[43] Joel, however, is painting with a broad brush, as biblical prophets regularly do. The promise of deliverance for Israel does not mean that every Jew, however wicked or impious, will be saved. Nor does the destruction of the nations mean that no Gentiles will be saved, particularly if they have taken

---

37. Hubbard, *Joel and Amos*, 69. The appearance of such particulars may reflect the same kind of particularizing of universals that Raabe finds in judgement oracles (although here they occur in a promise of blessing). Raabe, 'Particularizing', 652.

38. Garrett, *Hosea, Joel*, 260–61.

39. Hubbard, *Joel and Amos*, 69.

40. Hubbard, while insisting that 'Israel, not the whole world is in view', still contends that in its broad extent, this promise 'readies the people for a new era of oneness, when superficial distinctions are set aside and even outcasts become core members of God's new fellowship'. Hubbard, *Joel and Amos*, 69.

41. Kaiser, 'Promise', 119.

42. E.g. 1 Chr. 2.34-35 and possibly Josh. 9.27; Num. 31.18 (slaves or wives?). The law explicitly distinguished between Jewish slaves and slaves from the nations (e.g. Lev. 25.44-46). Israelites were also enslaved in other lands (e.g. 2 Kgs. 5.2; Amos 1.6, 9).

43. Wolff, *Joel and Amos*, 67.

refuge in the God of Israel. The general use of the expression and the presence of Gentiles (slave and free) in Judah support a universal understanding of 'all flesh' in Joel 3 MT.

5.2.2 *Everyone Who Calls (Joel 3.5a MT)*

The opening וְהָיָה ('and it shall come to pass') echoes the וְהָיָה of 3.1a. As in 3.1-2, there is an *inclusio*: the clause כֹּל אֲשֶׁר־יִקְרָא בְּשֵׁם יְהוָה ('all who call upon the name of the LORD') in 5a is balanced by אֲשֶׁר יְהוָה קֹרֵא ('those whom the LORD calls') in 5d.

Joel promises 'escape' (פְּלֵיטָה, 5b), that those who call on Yahweh 'shall be delivered' (יִמָּלֵט, 5a),[44] whether that is understood to be from the effects of the plague (Joel 1), the cosmic distress (3.3-4), or the coming judgement on the nations (4). Many see the unusual expression in 5b, כַּאֲשֶׁר אָמַר יְהוָה ('as the LORD has said'), as indicating a citation of Obad. 17.[45]

בְּהַר־צִיּוֹן וּבִירוּשָׁלַ͏ִם תִּהְיֶה פְלֵיטָה	Joel 3.5b MT	in Mount Zion and in Jerusalem there shall be those who escape [lit. there will be escape]
וּבְהַר צִיּוֹן תִּהְיֶה פְלֵיטָה	Obad. 17	but in Mount Zion there shall be those that escape [lit. there will be escape]

Obadiah, like Joel, promised escape in Mount Zion in the יוֹם־יְהוָה, 'the day of the LORD' (15; cf. Joel 2.11), which not only threatened Edom, but 'is near upon all the nations'.

The promise of escape (Joel 5a) is given to כֹּל אֲשֶׁר־יִקְרָא בְּשֵׁם יְהוָה ('all who call upon the name of the LORD'). 'To call on the name of the Lord (v. 32) … means to worship God (Gen. 12.8), to acknowledge that one belongs to God (Ps. 105.1; Isa 12.4; 44.5; Zech 13.9), and to depend on God for one's life (Prov 18.10; Zeph 2.3).'[46] It also 'means veneration through worship generally (Gen 12.8), especially the confessing of Yahweh among those of other faiths (Is 41.25; 44.5), worshiping him in the midst of the world of nations (Is 12.4; Ps. 105.1; Zech 13.9)'.[47] Finally, it entails 'agreeing to keep YHWH's statutes and to render exclusive loyalty to him.'[48] Deliverance, then, is promised to all who give allegiance and trust to Yahweh – salvation is by faith. This deliverance includes 'not every Jew simply because he is a Jew, but every God-fearing Jew who trusts in Yahweh and calls on him for help'[49] – salvation is by faith alone.

---

44.   The verb 'indicates survival in the face of grave danger', e.g. 3× in Amos 2.14-15. Crenshaw, *Joel*, 169.

45.   Bewer, 'Joel', 124–25; Crenshaw, *Joel*, 169; Wolff, *Joel and Amos*, 68. The argument depends, of course, on the relative dating of these two books, neither of which can be dated with certainty.

46.   Achtemeier, 'Joel', 7.328. Curiously, in the 'Reflection' section of the commentary, Achtemeier adds that 'to "call on the name of the Lord" means, in the scriptures, to tell others what God has done (Ps. 105.1; Isa. 12.4)'.

47.   Wolff, *Joel and Amos*, 68.

48.   Crenshaw, *Joel*, 169. Similarly also Hubbard, *Joel and Amos*, 72; Stuart, *Hosea–Jonah*, 261.

49.   Bewer, 'Joel', 124.

Might Gentiles be included if they call on the name of Yahweh? Gentiles are commonly characterized as 'nations that know thee not, and ... peoples that call not on thy name' (Jer. 10.25; cf. Ps. 79.6), but Garrett notes an 'implicit universality of "everyone"' here and understands the reference to Zion, not as limiting salvation to Jews, but requiring identification with the God of Israel.[50] Throughout the OT there are Gentiles who offer their allegiance to Yahweh,[51] even if they are not said specifically to 'call on his name'.[52] Boaz blessed the Moabite Ruth for her allegiance to and trust in Yahweh, 'under whose wings you have come to take refuge!' (Ruth 2.12; cf. 1.16, 'your people shall be my people, and your God my God'). The Syrian general Naaman vowed not to worship 'any god but the LORD' (2 Kgs. 5.17). In his prayer at the dedication of the temple, Solomon anticipated this very eventuality:

> When a foreigner, who is not of thy people Israel [הַנָּכְרִי אֲשֶׁר לֹא־מֵעַמְּךָ יִשְׂרָאֵל], comes from a far country for thy name's sake (for they shall hear of thy great name, and thy mighty hand, and of thy outstretched arm), when he comes and prays toward this house, hear thou in heaven thy dwelling place, and do according to all for which the foreigner calls to thee; in order that all the peoples of the earth may know thy name and fear thee, as do thy people Israel, and that they may know that this house which I have built is called by thy name. (1 Kgs. 8.41-43)

The prophets and Psalms speak of nations 'turning to' Yahweh, if not explicitly by 'calling on his name'.[53] Would they not share in Yahweh's promised salvation?

5.2.3 *Everyone the LORD Calls (Joel 3.5d MT)*

Joel 3.5d MT closes the chiasm with אֲשֶׁר יְהוָה קֹרֵא ('those whom the LORD calls'). The RSV distinguishes two groups: 'and among the survivors shall be those whom the LORD calls', but most commentators and recent translations equate the two (the survivors and those Yahweh calls).[54] Although some believe that the text shows evidence of earlier editing,[55] our present concern is with the text as it stood in the first century and that text seems secure.

There are surprisingly few instances in the MT where Yahweh is said to call anyone; far more often, people call (to or upon) Yahweh (as in Joel 3.5b). In two instances, Yahweh 'calls' someone to fulfil a task, Bezalel (Exod. 35.30-31) and the Isaianic servant (Isa. 49.1). Most often, Yahweh calls to people to get their attention: e.g. Adam (Gen. 3.9), Moses (Exod. 3.4) or Samuel (1 Sam. 3.4, 6, 8). Or Yahweh summons them: e.g. the earth (Ps. 50.1), Moses (Exod. 19.20) or

---

50. Garrett, *Hosea, Joel*, 369, n. 5.

51. Köstenberger and O'Brien, *Salvation*, 35.

52. There does not seem to be a narrative text where 'calling on the name of Yahweh' is predicated of a Gentile or Gentiles.

53. E.g. Isa. 14.2 (13.2 LXX); Ps. 22.27 (22.28 MT; 21.28 LXX).

54. '"Everyone who calls" and the "survivors whom Yahweh will call" are one and the same.' Stuart, *Hosea–Jonah*, 262. See NIV and Wolff, *Joel and Amos*, 68.

55. Wolff, *Joel and Amos*, 68.

Aaron and Miriam (Num. 12.5).[56] The reference here is probably not to election,[57] but to God's gracious invitation or summons to come to Zion in order to escape judgement.[58] While no MT text speaks explicitly of God's calling Gentiles to salvation from judgement, many speak of Gentiles coming to Jerusalem in allegiance to Yahweh.[59] Such coming would be futile, even tragic, if they had not been invited and were not welcome.

5.2.4 *Summary*

With others, Bewer maintains that the seemingly universal expressions in Joel 3.1b, 5a, d MT 'have a universal ring and could later on, when the context was disregarded, be interpreted without much difficulty in a universalistic manner, *cf.* Rom. 10.13. But our authors would have been much astonished over such an interpretation.'[60] The universalism in Joel 3 MT, however, is unavoidable. While the focus is on Judah, the promises must include faithful Jews in the Diaspora (on the one hand) and Gentile slaves and sojourners in Judah (on the other). The expressions 'all flesh', 'everyone who calls on the LORD' and 'everyone the LORD calls' must therefore be read in a universal sense. Gifts of the Spirit and deliverance will be shared by Gentiles who, in the future as in Israel's past, call on the name of Yahweh because they have been called by him. Gentiles are included in the prophecy of Joel.

5.3 *The Expected Spirit*

The gift of the Spirit is 'one of the decisive marks of the new age'.[61] Some see an anticipation of this in Moses' wish (Num. 11.29) 'that all the LORD's people were prophets, that the LORD would put his spirit upon them!' Isaiah envisioned the Spirit resting in a special way on the promised servant-leader (11.2; 42.1 and 61.1, which is cited in Luke 4). Both Isaiah and Ezekiel promised that God would bestow the Spirit on all people (Isa. 32.15; Isa. 44.3; Ezek. 38.29). This gift of the Spirit would be permanent ('shall not depart', Isa. 59.21). Ezekiel foresaw a time when God would 'take out of your flesh the heart of stone', 'put a new spirit within you, and cause you to walk in my statutes and be careful to observe my ordinances' (Ezek. 11.19; 36.26, 27).

---

56. See also Gen. 22.11, 15; Exod. 19.13; Lev. 1.1; 2 Kgs. 3.13; Ps. 50.10; Isa. 22.12; Zech. 7.13.

57. Wolff, *Joel and Amos*, 69.

58. Wolff, curiously, argues that Israelites outside of Jerusalem are not in view. Bewer earlier and more sensibly argued 'that the loyal Jews of the Dispersion are included among the true Yahweh worshippers is obvious. And although it is not directly stated it may be gathered ... that they will all be summoned to Zion.' Bewer, 'Joel', 125; Wolff, *Joel and Amos*, 68–69.

59. Isa. 2.2-4 (‖ Mic. 4.1-3); 25.6-8; 55.5; Jer. 3.17; Zech. 2.10-11; 8.20-23; 14.16; cf. Isa. 45.22.

60. Bewer, 'Joel', 125. So also Chapman, 'Superabundance', 192–93.

61. James D. G. Dunn, *Baptism in the Holy Spirit* (Philadelphia: Westminster Press, 1970), 46; Garrett, *Hosea, Joel*, 368. So also, nearly a century ago, Geerhardus Vos, 'The Eschatological Aspect of the Pauline Conception of the Spirit', in *Redemptive History and Biblical Interpretation: The Shorter Writings of Geerhardus Vos* (ed. Richard B. Gaffin, Jr.; Phillipsburg, NJ: Presbyterian and Reformed, 1980), 95–97.

> The prophets of Israel foretell the coming of the Suffering Servant and of the new age that the outpouring of the Spirit will inaugurate. The Spirit will be pre-eminently concentrated in the Messiah and He will wholly indwell the people of God who shall live in the eschatological period. The abiding presence of the Spirit will be, as Eichrodt has said, 'the central wonder of the new aeon', in which He will no longer appear 'start-wise' but He will exercise 'an enduring influence on men'. Here Incarnation and Pentecost and the new period in the history of redemption that shall be inaugurated by them are adumbrated.[62]

The Spirit was understood as an eschatological gift in the apocryphal/pseudepigraphal and rabbinic literature.

> The prophecy of Joel was taken up in Judaism and understood to refer to an outpouring of the Spirit in the age to come, when prophecy would cease to be confined to a few. Thus *Tanhuma* מקץ § 4 (96b). In this age prophecy has been for one in a thousand but in the age to come prophecy will be for every man; this appears to make prophecy universal, but it should perhaps be understood in the sense of *Tanhuma* בהעלתך § 28 (31a), where the new gift of prophecy is restricted to every Israelite (כל ישראל). Joel 3.1 is quoted in both these passages, but Num 11.29 was no doubt also influential.[63]

In Luke–Acts, the Spirit seems to be everywhere. In the gospel, he is the agent of Jesus' conception (1.35), fills John the Baptist (1.15) and his parents (1.41, 67), and reveals to Simeon that he will not die before seeing the Lord's Christ (2.25-27). John promised that his successor would baptize with the Holy Spirit (3.16). The Spirit descended on Jesus at the time of his baptism (3.22), led him into the desert to be tempted (4.1), and empowered him for his ministry (4.14). Jesus claimed the Spirit's anointing when he cited Isa. 61.1 in his inaugural sermon in Capernaum (4.18),[64] rejoiced in the Spirit (11.21), promised that the Father would give the Spirit to those who ask him (11.13), warned against blaspheming the Spirit (12.10), and promised that the Spirit would supply the words his followers would need to testify to him (12.12). Finally, he promised that his followers would soon be 'clothed with power from on high' (24.49).

In Acts, the risen Jesus instructed his apostles 'through the Holy Spirit' (1.2) and promised the Spirit's power for witness (1.8). He was the one who spoke in the OT scriptures (1.16; 28.25) and is the source of Jesus' power to heal (10.38). The gift of the Spirit at Pentecost, and particularly the praise of God in other languages, prompted the first sermon (2.1-41), which argued from the evident outpouring of the Spirit that God had enthroned Jesus as Lord and Christ (2.33-36). Believers received the Holy Spirit when they believed (2.38; 8.15; 9.31; 10.44-45, 47; 11.15; 13.52; 19.2, 6). Leaders were appointed by the Spirit (20.28), directed by the Spirit (8.29, 39; 10.19; 11.12; 13.2, 4; 16.6-7; 19.21), and filled

---

62. Harry R. Boer, *Pentecost and Missions* (Grand Rapids: Eerdmans, 1961), 69.

63. Barrett, *Acts*, 1.137. See also Bock, *Proclamation*, 346, n. 39; Evans, 'Prophecy and Polemic', 186–87; Vos, 'Eschatological Aspect', 98.

64. Green finds important parallels between Jesus' inaugural sermon in Luke 4 and Peter's speech in Acts 2. Joel B. Green, ' "Proclaiming Repentance and Forgiveness of Sins to All Nations": A Biblical Perspective on the Church's Mission', in *The Mission of the Church in Methodist Perspective: The World Is My Parish* (ed. Alan G. Padgett; Lewiston, NY: Edwin Mellen, 1992), 34. So also Dupont, 'Salvation', 20–24.

with the Spirit for witness (4.8, 31; 7.55; 9.17), service (6.3, 5; 11.24), revelation (11.28; 15.28; 20.22-23; 21.4) and miracles (13.9).

The prevalence of the Spirit, particularly in the prominent accounts of the Spirit's reception by Jesus (Luke 3), the church (Acts 2) and Gentiles (Acts 10), demonstrates how important it was to Luke that God had fulfilled his promise through Joel to 'pour out' his Spirit.

5.4 *Acts 2.17-21*

Acts 2 is familiar as the setting of the first proclamation of the good news following the death and resurrection of Jesus.[65] On the day of Pentecost the Holy Spirit was poured out on the assembled company of believers (2.1-4).[66] The sound[67] drew a diverse crowd which heard the believers 'telling ... the mighty works of God' in their own languages.[68] Some concluded that the believers were drunk (2.13). Taking this accusation as his point of departure, Peter addressed the crowd, explaining that what they were witnessing was what Joel had promised (2.14-21). He argued that scripture demonstrated the necessity of Christ's resurrection from the dead and that the evident gift of the Spirit proved 'that God has made him both Lord and Christ, this Jesus whom you crucified' (2.22-36).[69]

> The benefits of the Spirit, repentance, release of sins, and probably also salvation through the name are viewed as consequences of Jesus' exaltation and enthronement. As the one exalted to God's right hand, Jesus is able to extend the benefits of his ministry to all Israel and the world.[70]

In response to Peter's call to 'repent, and be baptized every one of you in the name of Jesus Christ for the forgiveness of your sins', about 3,000 believed (2.37-42).

65.   Green speaks of 'the central significance of Acts 2.1-41 for the Acts of the Apostles', and argues that it is 'anticipated throughout the Lukan story'. Green, 'Proclaiming Repentance', 33. Tannehill calls it 'one of the most carefully constructed speeches in Acts'. Tannehill, *Narrative Unity*, 2.41.

66.   'It is the unanimous conviction of the New Testament authors that Jesus inaugurated the last days or Messianic age, and that the final proof of this was the outpouring of the Spirit, since this was the Old Testament promise of promises for the end-time.' Stott, *Acts*, 73.

67.   Either of the blowing wind (2.2) or of their speaking in other tongues (2.4). The former view is that of Fitzmyer (*Acts*, 230), the latter that of Bruce (*Acts*, 54).

68.   'Jews, devout men from every nation under heaven' (2.5; see 2.8-11a). Although they come from 'every nation', those present are described only as Jews. 'Nevertheless, by enumerating their geographical places of origin, Luke has symbolized the universal scope of the gospel.' Green, 'Proclaiming Repentance', 36. On the question of whether these were permanent residents or pilgrims, see Marshall, *Acts*, 70; Witherington, *Acts*, 135.

69.   This is 'the key point in the discourse. It is the fact that Jesus is the Lord.' Marshall, *Luke: Historian and Theologian*, 162. See also Fitzmyer, *Acts*, 248. 'The key to the speech is that it presents the imagery of fulfillment for both Davidic and new covenant promise.' Darrell L. Bock, 'Proclamation from Prophecy and Pattern: Luke's Use of the Old Testament for Christology and Mission', in *The Gospels and the Scriptures of Israel* (ed. Craig A. Evans and William Richard Stegner; JSNTSup 104; Sheffield: Sheffield Academic Press, 1994), 297. See also Robert F. O'Toole, 'Acts 2.30 and the Davidic Covenant of Pentecost', *JBL* 102 (1983), 245–58.

70.   Tannehill, *Narrative Unity*, 2.40.

The introductory formula indicates that the prophecy of Joel is being fulfilled:[71] τοῦτό ἐστιν τὸ εἰρημένον διὰ τοῦ προφήτου Ἰωήλ ('this is what was spoken by the prophet Joel').[72] 'The Pentecostal event is the fulfillment of prophecy'.[73] Marshall finds that 'the event is regarded as falling into the pattern of promise and fulfillment, which is central to Luke's theology of history'.[74]

5.4.1 *All Flesh (Acts 2.17c)*
It is 'upon all flesh' that God promises to 'pour out' his Spirit. As in Joel 3, many scholars seek to limit 'all flesh' to Jews; as with Joel 3, there are good reasons to see a broader reference here. In the NT, the expression πᾶσα σάρξ ('all flesh') appears in nine other texts, each time with a universal orientation. In five texts (Matt. 24.22; Mark 13.20; Rom. 3.20; 1 Cor. 1.29; Gal. 2.16), it occurs with a negative, yielding the sense 'no flesh' or 'no one'. The other four texts are Luke 3.6; John 17.2; 1 Cor. 15.39; 1 Pet. 1.24 (cf. also σάρκας πάντων, 'the flesh of all', in Rev. 19.18). In 1 Cor 15.39, the expression refers to the bodily nature of human beings (not just Jews), which is then contrasted with that of animals, birds and fish.[75] 1 Peter 1.24 cites Isa. 40.6, where πᾶσα σάρξ is employed in a contrast between the power of Yahweh and human (not merely Jewish) weakness to guarantee Judah's promised deliverance.[76] In John 17.2, it refers to all human beings, from whom some have been given by the Father to the Son.[77]

The remaining occurrence, in Luke 3.6, is particularly relevant. All three synoptics cite Isaiah 40 as a description and prophecy of the ministry of John. Matthew and Mark cite only 40.3 (Matt. 3.3; Mark 1.3, the latter adding Exod. 23.20). Luke alone continues the citation through the middle clause of Isa. 40.5,

---

71. Fitzmyer, *Acts*, 252; Steyn, *Septuagint Quotations*, 70. Dispensational commentators have claimed that Joel 3 cannot have been fulfilled in Acts 2, because the cosmic signs of Joel 3.3-4 (Acts 2.19-20) did not occur. See the response of Dunn, *Baptism*, 47; Kaiser, 'Promise', 112. For a recent attempt to affirm the fulfilment of Joel 3 in Acts 2, while still allowing for future literal fulfilment of the cosmic signs, see Daniel J. Treier, 'The Fulfillment of Joel 2.28-32: A Multiple-Lens Approach', *JETS* 40 (1997): 13–26. Bock notes 'that the use of the Joel text in Acts 2 is open-ended, that is the fulfilment has begun with the outpouring of God's Spirit but events are still to occur'. Bock, *Proclamation*, 168.

72. Kenneth Litwak has recently argued that these words do not indicate the fulfilment of prophecy, but a 'revisionary reading' of Joel 3 in light of the events at Pentecost. Litwak, *Echoes*, 155–73. While it is certainly true that Jesus' disciples read the OT through a new 'hermeneutical lens', this does not exclude the fulfilment of Joel's prophecy at Pentecost. His assertion that Luke does not attempt to 'prove' anything with this citation is curious. Peter argues that the disciples are not drunk but filled with God's Spirit, and (more importantly) that the outpouring of the Spirit demonstrates that God has enthroned Jesus as 'Lord and Christ'.

73. Barrett, *Acts*, 1.135. Toy asserts, 'Peter finds the fulfillment of this prediction in the disciples of Jesus, as the true Israel'. Toy, *Quotations*, 98.

74. Ian Howard Marshall, 'The Significance of Pentecost', *SJT* 30 (1977): 367.

75. Gordon D. Fee, *The First Epistle to the Corinthians* (NICNT; Grand Rapids: Eerdmans, 1987), 782–83.

76. Edward Gordon Selwyn, *The First Epistle of Peter: The Greek Text with Introduction, Notes and Essays* (2nd edn.; London: Macmillan, 1947), 152. See also Pao, *Acts*, 48.

77. Leon Morris, *The Gospel according to John: The English Text with Introduction, Exposition and Notes* (NICNT; Grand Rapids: Eerdmans, 1971), 718.

reading (as in LXX) καὶ ὄψεται πᾶσα σὰρξ τὸ σωτήριον τοῦ θεοῦ ('and all flesh shall see the salvation of God').[78] While one could conceivably view כָּל־בָּשָׂר as limited to the people of Judah ('Jerusalem'), the expression in 40.6 (cited in 1 Pet. 1.24) refers to human beings generally. The expression in 40.5 is therefore most likely to mean 'all people', including Gentiles.[79] As in Isa. 42.6, 'to see the salvation of God' is not merely to observe it, but to experience it.[80]

> Luke is the only evangelist, therefore, who continues the traditional quotation from Isaiah 40 at this point in his Gospel up to the words, 'And all flesh will see the salvation of God.' Similarly Luke is the only evangelist who continues the Gospel story by going on to narrate the missions of the apostles ... By thus placing Isaiah 40.5 at the beginning of his Gospel story, and also drawing the conclusion of Acts from words that remind us of the same text, Luke betrays his strong interest in the idea that the salvation of God is manifested to all men. It seems reasonable to consider that interest one of the keys to his work: the history Luke wishes to trace is the history of God's salvation for all flesh.[81]

Luke thus introduces an anticipation of the Gentile mission early in the third gospel, using language that will also be evident in the citation of Joel 3.1 in Acts 2.17.

Peter's sermon focused on the gift of the Spirit, not its recipients. His hearers, too, would have paid less attention to 'all flesh' than to 'I will pour out my Spirit'. However, the Gentiles among Luke's readers, who had received the Spirit when they believed in Jesus, could not have helped seeing themselves in 'all flesh'. The use of כָּל־בָּשָׂר in Joel 3 (and the OT), the use of πᾶσα σάρξ in the NT, the evident importance of the Gentile mission to Luke, and the subsequent narrative indicate that 'all flesh' in Acts 2.17c includes Gentiles.[82]

5.4.2 *Everyone Who Calls (Acts 2.21)*

As in the OT, to 'call on the name of the Lord' (ἐπικαλεῖσθαι τὸ ὄνομα κυρίου) is an expression of trust, worship and confession, equivalent to belief in

---

78. Some see an echo of Isa. 40.5 in Luke 2.30, where Simeon's 'eyes have seen thy salvation'. Dupont, 'Salvation', 15.

79. So Craig A. Evans, 'The Prophetic Setting of the Pentecost Sermon', in *Luke and Scripture: The Function of Sacred Tradition in Luke–Acts* (ed. Craig A. Evans and Jack T. Sanders; Minneapolis: Fortress, 1993), 220.

80. 'Seeing' 'need not imply that all flesh will share in its benefits'. W. R. Hanford, 'Deutero-Isaiah and Luke–Acts: Straightforward Universalism?', *CQR* 168 (1967): 147. But see Isa. 9.2; 33.17, 20; 35.2; 52.1 as well as John 3.3, where it is not a matter of merely observing (ἰδεῖν, 3.3) the kingdom, but entering it (εἰσελθεῖν, 3.5; cf. BDAG, s.v. εἶδον, 4.) Motyer speaks of the 'double sense of observing and experiencing'. Motyer, *Prophecy*, 300.

81. Dupont, 'Salvation', 15–16. 'That the Gentiles are the intended objects of God's salvation is announced at the outset by John the Baptist.' Sanders, 'Prophetic Use', 194–95.

82. Green, 'Proclaiming Repentance', 37. Tasker speaks of 'God's Spirit ... poured out not only on Israel, but on "all flesh" '. Randolph V. G. Tasker, *The Old Testament in the New Testament* (2nd rev. edn.; London: SCM Press, 1954), 67. Tannehill sees 'a variation on the promises of worldwide salvation in Luke 2.30-32 and 3.6 ("All flesh will see the salvation of God").' See also Evans, 'Prophetic Setting', 220; Fitzmyer, *Acts*, 252. Bruce and Eckey see Luke 'looking forward' (Bruce) and 'signaling' (Eckey) the coming Gentile mission. Bruce, *Acts* (Greek Text, 3rd edn.), 121; Eckey, *Apostelgeschichte*, 1.83.

Jesus as saviour.[83] (As elsewhere, ὁ κύριος in an OT text is understood to refer to Jesus.[84]) In Acts 9.14, 21, Ananias equates 'all who call upon thy name' with 'the disciples of the Lord' (9.1), 'any belonging to the Way' (9.2) and 'thy saints' (9.13). In 1 Cor. 1.2, it parallels 'those sanctified in Christ Jesus' and 'called to be saints', as 'the church of God which is in Corinth'. In Acts 22.16, 'calling on his name' is connected with baptism in Paul's conversion. Finally, Rom. 10.13 cites Joel 3.5b MT to support the sweeping claim that 'there is no distinction between Jew and Greek; the same Lord is Lord of all and bestows his riches upon all who call upon him'. Yet, as Paul observes, no one can believe unless they hear, nor hear unless someone is sent to them. Paul, at least, understood Joel 3.5a MT to include Gentiles and to require an intentional Gentile mission.

Acts 2.21 thus 'emphasizes the universal character of the gospel and thus anticipates the incorporation of the Gentiles into the Christian community in the dramatic episodes of the remainder of Acts'.[85] The gift of the Spirit and the promised deliverance are for all who call on the name of the Lord Jesus, whether Jews or Gentiles.[86]

5.4.3 *Everyone the Lord Calls (Acts 2.39)*

Although the citation in Acts 2.21 strictly ends with Joel 3.5b MT (omitting the focus of the deliverance on Zion and Jerusalem), words from 3.5d appear in Acts 2.39 ('every one whom the Lord our God will call to him'), οὓς κύριος προσκέκληται.[87] The verb occurs 29 times in the Greek NT, consistently in the sense of 'summon' or 'call'.[88] With the exception of Jas. 5.14 ('let him call for the elders'), it is not used outside the gospels and Acts. It is not used in a theological sense (election) as καλέω is (e.g. Rom. 8.30; 1 Cor. 1.9).

In context, 'the promise' includes 'the forgiveness of your sins' and 'the gift of the Holy Spirit' (2.38). Barrett, however, believes that 'it would be a mistake to confine it … It covers the covenant into which God entered with his people, to which he continues to be faithful.'[89] The noun appears nine times in Luke–Acts.

---

83. Barrett, *Acts*, 1.139. The expression simply refers to believers in and disciples of Jesus. Hans Conzelmann, *Acts of the Apostles* (trans. James A. Limburg et al.; Hermeneia; Philadelphia: Fortress, 1987), 20; Eckey, *Apostelgeschichte*, 1.83–84. The verb may refer to prayer (Acts 7.59 RSV; cf. 2 Tim. 2.22; 1 Pet. 1.17) and is used six times of Paul's appeal to the emperor (Acts 25.11, 12, 21, 25; 26.32; 28.19). The 'name' represents Jesus and becomes almost equivalent to 'the gospel' in Acts 3.16; 4.12; 8.12; 10.43. See Wall, 'Israel', 445–48.

84. 'In Acts 2 all the limits on Christology are broken as Jesus' function is totally equated with that of God.' Bock, 'Proclamation from Prophecy and Pattern', 298.

85. Marion L. Soards, *The Speeches of Acts: Their Content, Context, and Concerns* (Louisville: Westminster John Knox, 1994), 33.

86. 'Luke does not want to limit the quoted words only to the Jews assembled in Jerusalem: all human beings may call on the name of the Lord for salvation.' Fitzmyer, *Acts*, 254.

87. So, e.g. Barrett, *Acts*, 1.139, 156; Conzelmann, *Acts*, 20. Steyn identifies a number of similarities between the Joel quotation and Acts 2.38-41. Steyn, *Septuagint Quotations*, 127.

88. 'To call to or notify in order to secure someone's presence.' BDAG s.v. προσκαλέομαι. It is used twice of calling to service (Acts 13.2; 16.10).

89. Barrett, *Acts*, 1.155.

With the exception of the exodus (Acts 7.17) and the governor's promise to transport Paul for trial (Acts 23.21), the referent is eschatological: the gift of the Spirit (Luke 24.49; Acts 1.4; 2.33); the coming of the Saviour (Acts 13.23, 32 [or perhaps forgiveness of sins, 13.38]); and the resurrection (Acts 26.6; cf. 24.23; 26.8).

'Every one' here is comprehensive. Bruce states that 'the promise is not only to those distant in time, but also to those distant in place, even – as was soon to appear – to Gentiles'.[90] The expression εἰς μακράν refers to distance, as 'children' refers to the future.[91] The adverb μακράν is explicitly employed in LXX texts referring to Gentile nations, as in Mic. 4.3; Joel 4.8; Zech. 10.9; Isa. 5.26. It is likewise employed in relation to the Gentiles in Acts 22.21 ('I will send you far away to the Gentiles') and Eph. 2.13, 17, where the 'far off' Gentiles are explicitly contrasted with the Jews who are 'near'.[92] The 'distance' of the Gentiles may well be spiritual, as Calvin suggests.[93] Kaiser believes '"those who were afar off" was merely a circumlocution for saying "Gentiles"'.[94]

Douglass Stuart rightly observes that, while Jerusalem is 'the dominant subject' of Joel 3.5 MT, there is a larger principle at work. Peter's use of the expressions 'everyone who calls' and 'everyone God calls'

> is faithful to the impact of the verse in its context. Though spoken to encourage Jerusalemites at a time when the holy city was under attack, its real concern is future deliverance for a covenant people. 'Everyone who calls' and the 'survivors whom Yahweh will call' are one and the same – a broad constituency not limited to a single locale, by reason of the spirit and language of the oracle as a whole.[95]

5.4.4 *Peter, Joel and the Gentiles*

The language in Peter's citation from Joel in Acts 2 indicates that the gifts of the Spirit and the eschatological salvation will include Gentiles, as well as Jews, who call on the name of the Lord Jesus. Even if 'all flesh' and 'everyone who calls' did not bring Gentiles into view, εἰς μακράν ('far off') would.

Some have argued that, at this early point in Acts, Peter would not have understood Joel to include the Gentiles, because the narrative portrays the apostles (including Peter, see Acts 10) as slow to grasp the universal scope of their ministry.[96] This reading, however, is not supported by the narrative. While we read

---

90. Bruce, *Acts* (Greek Text, 3rd edn.), 130.

91. Conzelmann, *Acts*, 22. LSJ cites instances where the term refers to distance in space and where it refers to time, although distance predominates. For the view that those 'far off' are Jews living in Gentile lands, see Witherington, *Acts*, 155–56.

92. 'That the same contrast is intended here with ὑμῖν … καὶ τοῖς τέκνοις ὑμῶν is probable, especially in view of Paul's declaration that he was sent εἰς ἔθνη μακράν (Acts 22.21). To be more specific in Acts 2 was not within Luke's plans.' Richard F. Zehnle, *Peter's Pentecost Discourse: Tradition and Lukan Interpretation in Peter's Speeches of Acts 2 and 3* (SBLMS 15; Nashville: Abingdon, 1971), 124. Zehnle also sees the 'near/far' contrast in Isa. 57.19. Others, however, believe that Isa. 57.19 referred originally to Diaspora Jews, e.g. Goppelt, *Typos*, 118.

93. Calvin, *Acts 14–28*, 83.

94. Kaiser, 'Promise', 120.

95. Stuart, *Hosea–Jonah*, 261–62.

96. Haenchen, *Acts*, 179; Witherington, *Acts*, 140–41.

that the Spirit, step by step, directed the church's expanding ministry, there is no rebuke of the apostles on this point.[97] The apostles could not have been ignorant of the eschatological inclusion of Gentiles among the people of God, since this was taught by OT prophecies[98] and reinforced by the teaching of Jesus.[99] It is more likely that the apostles expected the conversion of Jews to be the precursor to and means of Gentile conversion and that, for this reason, they focused first on ministry to ethnic Israel.[100] Paul's reflection on Isa. 49.6 in light of continued Jewish opposition led him (13.46-47), and subsequently the church, to conclude that the time actively to reach out to the Gentiles had come. The account in Acts 10–11 (particularly in light of Acts 15) indicates that Peter's 'problem' was not the fact, but the *means* of Gentile inclusion.

> He [Peter] could never have thought that the Gentiles were excluded from the church or from salvation. There was no such exclusion, even under the restrictive institutions of the old economy. All of the Gentiles in the world might have shared the privileges of the Jews, by complying with the prescribed conditions. Peter's error consisted in believing that these conditions still existed under the gospel, or in other words, that Gentiles must become Jews before they could be Christians. Of this error he was not yet disabused; but there was nothing in it to prevent his applying the expressions here recorded to the Gentiles.[101]

Neither Peter, nor his audience, nor the narrative at this point call attention to Gentiles in the promise of Joel. Yet both volumes of Luke's two-volume work are addressed to a Gentile (Luke 1.1-4; Acts 1.1). From the beginning of his gospel ('light to the nations', 2.32; 'all flesh shall see the salvation of God', 3.5) to its ending ('that repentance and forgiveness of sins should be preached in his name to all nations', 24.47), Luke has had Gentiles in view. Acts begins with the promise of the apostolic witness reaching from Jerusalem 'to the end of the earth' (1.8) and ends with its proclamation in Rome (28.23-31). All these things were already known to Theophilus, whose problem was not ignorance, but a lack of 'certainty' (Luke 1.4).

---

97. Acts 1.8; 2.4; 4.31; 6.10; 8.26, 29, 39, 40; 9.10; 10–11 (esp. 10.3; 11.12); 13.2, 4; 19.21; 21.11; contrast 16.6, 7. While the persecution in 8.1 providentially led to missionary activity (11.19-20; see also later, e.g. 13.50-51; 16.39-40; 17.10, 14), there is no indication in the text that the persecution was punishment for disobedience.

98. E.g. Isa. 2.2; 11.10; 19.16-25; 25.6-8; 45.22-23; Zeph. 3.9; Zech. 2.11; 8.22; 14.16.

99. Jeremias, *Promise*.

100. Munck, *Paul*, 236, 239, 255–59. Chris Wright argues that the apostles inferred from Jesus' identification of himself with the Isaianic servant that the salvation of Gentiles would follow the restoration of Israel, but the rejection of their message by so many Jews (including those in positions of authority) seemed to put the Gentile mission on hold until Israel was restored by its embrace of the gospel. 'But then God surprised them' with the conversion of Cornelius and the events that followed. Christopher J. H. Wright, *Knowing Jesus through the Old Testament* (London: HarperCollins, 1992), 163–70.

101. Alexander, *Acts*, 87. 'At Pentecost ... this *idea* of a universal mission begins to become a reality ... with Pentecost the die had been cast.' Green, 'Proclaiming Repentance', 37. 'From the thrust of the narrative in Acts it becomes clear that Luke is already hinting at the reconstitution of Israel as the people of God, which will incorporate the Gentiles.' Joseph A. Fitzmyer, 'The Use of Explicit Old Testament Quotations in Qumran Literature and in the New Testament', *NTS* 7 (1961): 267.

Although the implications of Joel for the Gentiles are not made explicit in the text of Acts 2, the speeches of Acts have two audiences: *in* the narrative, Peter addresses sermons in Acts 2 and 3 to Jewish audiences in Jerusalem; *through* the narrative, Luke addresses his readers. What may be of little importance to (or even escape the notice of) one audience may be of considerable significance to the other. Luke's readers, who certainly include Gentiles, would have readily seen themselves in the universal language of the Joel citation. In these expressions early in Acts ('all flesh', 'everyone who calls', and 'everyone God calls') Luke anticipates what they already know from 'the rest of the story'. In this way, he uses the Old Testament scriptures to assure Gentile readers like Theophilus of 'the truth concerning the things of which [they have] been informed' (Luke 1.4) and of their place in the promises, programme and people of God.

5.5 *Summary*

The citation of Joel 3 MT in Acts 2 plays a pivotal role in the development of the narrative of Acts. Joel 3 MT resonates throughout the book of Acts. The Spirit is present and active, poured out, even on Gentiles (10.45). Signs and wonders are done by Jesus and his followers (4.16, 22; 5.12; 6.8; 8.6, 13; 14.3; 15.12). Men and women prophesy (19.6; 21.9). Ananias (9.10), Cornelius (10.3), Peter (10.19; 11.5), and Paul (9.12; 16.9-10; 18.9) see visions.[102]

5.5.1 *Text*

Although the form of the citation differs at points from that found in Joel (MT and LXX), there are no substantial differences affecting the portion of the text involved in the present study. The citations of Joel 3.1b, 5a, 5d MT (Acts 2.17c, 21, 39) could equally be based on the MT or the LXX and the argument does not depend on distinctive features in either form of the text.

5.5.2 *Hermeneutic*

Although many have argued that the seemingly universal language of Joel 3.1b, 5a, 5d MT is limited by context to the inhabitants of Judah, we have seen that Gentiles are included in the promises of Joel 3.1–5 MT in their original context and also in the citation in Acts 2. The use of the citation in Acts respects its original context in Joel.[103]

The OT prophecy is understood Christologically, not in the sense of speaking directly about Christ, but as an eschatological promise that is fulfilled only through his agency. Peter argues that the promised outpouring of the Spirit shows that God has raised Jesus and made him 'both Lord and Christ' (2.36). While the promise is initially fulfilled at Pentecost, its complete fulfilment will require (as in Rom. 10.12-17) the proclamation of the gospel to Gentiles, so that they may join many

---

102. Evans, 'Prophetic Setting', 220.

103. It was not necessary to omit Joel 3.5b in order to expand the prophecy to the Gentiles, as contended by Rese, *Alttestamentliche Motive*, 50.

Jews in calling on the name of the Lord Jesus for salvation. The citation thus develops the ecclesiology of Acts and anticipates the Gentile mission.

5.5.3 *Purpose*

Faced with puzzling phenomena and a mocking crowd, Peter cites Joel 3.1-5 MT. The explanation for the events of 2.1-4 is found in the scriptures: 'this [what the crowd has seen and heard] is what was spoken by the prophet Joel'. Adducing additional scriptures, Peter shows that the Christ must suffer and be raised. The outpouring of the Spirit shows that he has been (2.33). The citation is thus employed as 'proof from prophecy', a rhetorical strategy which seeks to persuade Peter's hearers that 'God has made him both Lord and Christ' (2.36).

This early anticipation of the Gentile mission sets the stage for its more explicit treatment in Acts 13 and 15. As a skilful author, Luke has already included earlier indications of what is coming and here continues to prepare for later events. The citation of Joel 3 MT is part of a complex of at least four prophecies that legitimate the early church's Gentile mission. Ultimately, the fulfilment of the prophecy will *require* an intentional and effective mission to Gentiles (as Paul understood, Rom. 10.12-15, where Joel 3.1 MT is also cited).

This anticipation of the Gentile mission would not have been missed by Luke's Gentile readers, given their keen personal interest in its legitimacy. Nor could Luke, a Gentile himself, have failed to see himself included in 'everyone' here. The citation not only explains the events at Pentecost and establishes that Jesus is the Christ, but provides additional assurance for Gentile readers that God had intended their salvation all along. Additional citations and the subsequent narrative will confirm this. Luke's careful crafting of the case for the Gentile mission through anticipation as well as the explicit treatment in Acts 13 and 15 shows the importance of this topic for himself and his readers.

ABRAHAM'S OFFSPRING AND THE FAMILIES OF THE EARTH
(GENESIS 22.18 IN ACTS 3.25)

There is a second anticipation of the Gentile mission in Peter's second programmatic speech, this time in the citation of Gen. 22.18 in Acts 3.25. Again, the
Gentile mission is not explicitly in view. Peter did not draw out the implication
of this citation for the Gentiles and there is no indication in the narrative that
Peter's original audience attended to the implications of these citations for Gentile ministry. However, as noted above, the speeches of Acts have two audiences:
in this narrative, Peter addresses a Jewish audience in Jerusalem; *through* the
narrative, Luke addresses his readers. These readers were, or at least included,
Gentiles who would have been deeply concerned with the legitimacy of the Gentile mission and who would naturally have seen themselves in any apparently
universal references in OT promises.

The first question is which OT text is cited. The promise to Abraham (and the
patriarchs) appears five times in Genesis, none corresponding exactly to the
citation in Acts 3.25.

Acts 3.25	καὶ ἐν τῷ σπέρματί σου [ἐν]ευλογηθήσονται πᾶσαι αἱ πατριαὶ τῆς γῆς.
Gen. 12.3	καὶ ἐνευλογηθήσονται ἐν σοὶ πᾶσαι αἱ φυλαὶ τῆς γῆς
Gen. 18.18	καὶ ἐνευλογηθήσονται ἐν αὐτῷ πάντα τὰ ἔθνη τῆς γῆς
Gen. 22.18	καὶ ἐνευλογηθήσονται ἐν τῷ σπέρματί σου πάντα τὰ ἔθνη τῆς γῆς
Gen. 26.4	καὶ ἐνευλογηθήσονται ἐν τῷ σπέρματί σου πάντα τὰ ἔθνη τῆς γῆς
Gen. 28.14	καὶ ἐνευλογηθήσονται ἐν σοὶ πᾶσαι αἱ φυλαὶ τῆς γῆς καὶ ἐν τῷ σπέρματί σου

As noted by Steyn, the two principal differences between the citation and the
LXX are the transposition of ἐνευλογηθήσονται and the substitution of πᾶσαι
αἱ πατριαὶ τῆς γῆς for πάντα τὰ ἔθνη τῆς γῆς or πᾶσαι αἱ φυλαὶ τῆς
γῆς.[1] No NT MSS support the LXX and no LXX MSS support the reading in Acts.
The differences must be attributed either to Luke or to an otherwise unattested
textual tradition.

The expression πᾶσαι αἱ πατριαὶ τῆς γῆς is unique to Luke. The MT
employs two Hebrew expressions in different occurrences of the promise, כֹּל
מִשְׁפְּחֹת הָאֲדָמָה ('all the families [or 'tribes'] of the earth', LXX πᾶσαι αἱ φυλαὶ
τῆς γῆς) in Gen. 12.3; 28.14 and כֹּל גּוֹיֵי הָאָרֶץ ('all the nations of the earth', LXX
πάντα τὰ ἔθνη τῆς γῆς) in Gen. 18.18; 22.18; 26.4. The expression αἱ

1. Steyn, *Septuagint Quotations*, 154–56.

πατριαὶ τῆς γῆς does not appear in the LXX, where the most common use of πατριαί is for families or tribes within Israel. Some have suggested the influence of Ps. 21.28 LXX (22.28 MT; 22.27 RSV),[2] 'all the ends of the earth (πάντα τὰ πέρατα τῆς γῆς) shall remember and turn to the LORD; and all the families of the nations (πᾶσαι αἱ πατριαὶ τῶν ἐθνῶν, כָּל־מִשְׁפְּחוֹת גּוֹיִם) shall worship before him'. However, Acts 3.25 reads αἱ πατριαὶ τῆς γῆς, not αἱ πατριαὶ τῶν ἐθνῶν or τὰ πέρατα τῆς γῆς, and no satisfactory ground for allusion to this text has been proposed.[3] Most commentators understand Luke's language to be a conscious adaptation, choosing the more neutral πατριαί over ἔθνη (which typically refers to nations other than Jews) to ensure that the promise is understood to include Peter's audience of Jews in Jerusalem.[4]

The presence of ἐν τῷ σπέρματί σου in Acts 3.25 has inclined Steyn and others to conclude that the citation is more similar to Gen. 22.18; 26.4 than to Gen. 12.3; 18.18; 28.14.[5] Genesis 12.3; 18.18 speak of Abraham as the one by or in whom the nations will be blessed; the focus is on Abraham himself (although his descendants may well be included). The σπέρμα does not enter the language of the promise until Gen. 22.18, where it is particularly appropriate given the deliverance of Isaac from impending death and Abraham's own advanced age. The specific mention of Abraham in the introduction to the citation in Acts 3.25 ('the covenant which God gave to your fathers, saying to Abraham') would seem to exclude both Gen. 26.4, which is addressed to Isaac and speaks of Isaac's σπέρμα, and Gen. 28.14, which speaks of Jacob and his σπέρμα. As the only instance of the promise addressed to Abraham which includes his σπέρμα, Gen. 22.18 is the most likely source of the citation.

If, that is, we should seek a specific source at all. Barnabas Lindars has persuasively argued that 'the quotation is thus in a stylized form, and not to be

---

2. See also αἱ πατριαὶ τῶν ἐθνῶν without πᾶσαι in Ps. 95.7 LXX (96.7 MT) ‖ 1 Chr. 16.28.

3. Both πατριά and φυλή translate מִשְׁפָּחָה, the former about two dozen times and the latter about three dozen (out of about 300 instances of מִשְׁפָּחָה). The LXX most often renders מִשְׁפָּחָה by δῆμος (over 100 times), although more than a dozen terms are used. For φυλή (which more often translates מַטֶּה or שֵׁבֶט), see Gen. 10.5, 18, 20, 31, 32; 24.4, 38, 40, 41; 28.14; 36.40; Josh. 21.38; 1 Kgs. 9.21; 10.21; 20.6, 29; Amos 3.1, 2; Mic. 2.3; Nah. 3.4; Zech. 12.12, 13, 14; Ezek. 20.32. For πατριά (which most often translates אָב or בֵּית־אָב), see Lev. 25.10; Deut. 29.18; 2 Chr. 6 (10 times); Ps. 21.27; 95.7; 106.41; Jer. 2.4; 3.14; 25.9. In secular Greek, πατριά refers generally to family (or clan) or lineage (LSJ), as in the only other NT occurrences: Luke 2.4 of the 'lineage' of Joseph and the seemingly universal 'every family in heaven and on earth' (Eph. 3.15).

4. 'If it is accepted that the speech was addressed to *Jews*, and that τὰ ἔθνη means the *Gentiles* in Ac, the change makes sense.' Steyn, *Septuagint Quotations*, 156. 'Luke has replaced the τὰ ἔθνη of the Septuagint with αἱ πατριαί, thus indicating that the Jews are included among those who shall be blessed in the "posterity" of Abraham, i.e. the Christ Jesus.' Dahl, 'Abraham', 149. 'The Greek version of Genesis that Luke was using may have substituted *patriai*, "families", for *ethnē*, "nations", but, more likely, Luke himself has substituted it for the latter term, which he normally uses for "Gentiles."' Fitzmyer, *Acts*, 291.

5. Steyn, *Septuagint Quotations*, 153. See also Barrett, 'Luke/Acts (1988)', 238; Bock, *Proclamation*, 195; van den Eynde, 'Children of the Promise', 472; Fitzmyer, *Acts*, 291. For contrary views, see Dodd, *According to the Scriptures*, 43; Lindars, *New Testament Apologetic*, 208.

interpreted in any single context'.[6] That is, it is the promise itself (more than any particular instance of it) to which appeal is made. As a result, we cannot, on the basis of the citation, reliably draw connections from the context of any particular occurrence of the promise (e.g. from the offering of Isaac in Genesis 22 to the suffering of Christ) and there are no indications that Peter (or Luke) does so.

Gen. 22.18 MT	*Gen. 22.18 LXX*	*Acts 3.25*
		25a ὑμεῖς ἐστε οἱ υἱοὶ τῶν προφητῶν
		b καὶ τῆς διαθήκης ἧς διέθετο ὁ θεὸς πρὸς τοὺς πατέρας ὑμῶν
		c λέγων πρὸς Ἀβραάμ.
וְהִתְבָּרֲכוּ בְזַרְעֲךָ כֹּל גּוֹיֵי 18a הָאָרֶץ	καὶ ἐνευλογηθήσονται ἐν τῷ σπέρματί σου πάντα τὰ ἔθνη τῆς γῆς	d καὶ ἐν τῷ σπέρματί σου ἐνευλογηθήσονται πᾶσαι αἱ πατριαὶ τῆς γῆς.
עֵקֶב אֲשֶׁר שָׁמַעְתָּ בְּקֹלִי	b ἀνθ᾽ ὧν ὑπήκουσας τῆς ἐμῆς φωνῆς.	

6.1 *Text*

The citation may be based on either the MT or LXX.[7] The argument could be made equally well from either. The author has emphasized the 'seed' by bringing the expression ἐν τῷ σπέρματί σου forward in the citation. The apparently more inclusive wording πᾶσαι αἱ πατριαὶ τῆς γῆς appears in place of the LXX πάντα τὰ ἔθνη τῆς γῆς, lest τὰ ἔθνη be understood as a reference to Gentiles only, while Peter presumably wished to include Jews.

6.2 *The Blessing in Genesis*

The promise to Abraham cited in Acts 3 appears with very similar wording five times in the book of Genesis: 12.3; 18.18; 22.18; 26.4; 28.14. The first is the foundational statement and occurs at the beginning of a major section of the book.[8] Its repetition in the subsequent chapters indicates its central role in the narrative. In 18.18, it follows the promise of the imminent birth of Isaac and sets the stage for Abraham's intercession (as a channel of blessing?) for the hypothetical righteous of Sodom. In 22.18, it is reaffirmed following Abraham's demonstration of his willingness to sacrifice Isaac. In 26.4, Yahweh assures Isaac that the promise includes God's care during a time of famine. Finally, the promise is renewed at Bethel as Jacob flees his home and the wrath of his brother Esau (28.14).

---

6. Lindars, *New Testament Apologetic*, 208.
7. Steyn, *Septuagint Quotations*, 156. Bruce believes that 'once again the Gk. of an OT quotation is closer to MT than is LXX'. Bruce, *Acts* (Greek Text, 3rd edn.), 146.
8. Gerhard von Rad, for example, presents this text as the climax of the primeval history and the beginning of the patriarchal narrative. Von Rad, *Genesis*, 154.

The promise in Gen. 12.2-3 has a number of facets: descendants ('a great nation'), fame ('a great name'), protection ('I will bless those who bless you, and him who curses you I will curse'), land, blessing ('I will bless you'), being a blessing to others ('you will be a blessing'), and a central role in God's plan to bless all nations. While these are interconnected and mutually dependent, the last of these is cited in Acts 3.25 and will be the focus here.

This 'blessing' is a familiar *crux interpretum*[9] and a full treatment is beyond the scope of the present study. The issue is the translation of the verb ברך.[10] In 12.3; 18.18; 28.14 the verb occurs in the *nip'al*, while in 22.18; 26.4 it occurs in the *hitpa'el*. Both may be translated as reflexives ('bless oneself'), although the *nip'al* may have a passive sense ('be blessed').[11] The otherwise similar expressions would seem to require a common translation and most scholars have proposed a single translation for all five texts. The LXX renders both forms of the verb with the future passive ἐνευλογηθήσονται. The LXX is followed in this by early versions.[12] More recently, many have argued for a reflexive sense, i.e. that nations would say 'may we be blessed like Abraham'.[13] Delitzsch argues that the existence of 'an unambiguous passive' in the *pu'al* indicates that the *nip'al* (occurring in the MT only in Gen. 12.3; 18.18; 28.14) should be understood as reflexively, like the more common *hitpa'el*.[14] Others still see the passive as the more likely rendering.[15] Gerhard Wehmeier has shown that the context in both Gen. 12.3 and 18.18 militates against a reflexive sense.[16] At the same time, the difference between the *nip'al* and the *hitpa'el* may be smaller than it appears.

9. Westermann writes of 'the long discussion about the translation of נברכו as it continues to sway now one way, now another'. 'This constant change of direction indicates an uncertainty which has not yet been overcome.' Claus Westermann, *Genesis 12–36: A Commentary* (trans. John J. Scullion; Minneapolis: Augsburg, 1985), 151.

10. The central idea of 'blessing' is of God's 'manifesting his favor and grace' toward men, resulting in 'well-being, prosperity'. J. Y. Campbell, *IDB*, 'Blessedness', 1.445–46. The term appears five times in Gen. 12.2-3. Von Rad, *Genesis*, 159.

11. GKC, §39f.

12. The Vg, *Tg. Onk.*, Sir 44:21 and Gal. 3:8. Wenham, *Genesis*, 1.277.

13. *HALOT* proposes 'to wish on oneself a blessing like that of (cf. Gn 48:20), with ב of the person compared' for the *nip'al* and '1. to wish a blessing on oneself (on one another?) to be blessed ... with ב ... 2. to bless oneself.'

14. Franz Delitzsch, *New Commentary on Genesis* (trans. Sophia Taylor; 2 vols.; Clark's Foreign Theological Library 36–37; Edinburgh: T&T Clark, 1899), 1.379. So also Bruce Vawter, *On Genesis: A New Reading* (New York: Doubleday, 1977), 177.

15. 'The translation "be blessed" is preferable because it sets forward the idea of "to be a blessing." It also corresponds more closely with the original declaration, "I will bless."' Gerhard Ch. Aalders, *Genesis* (2 vols.; BSC; Grand Rapids: Zondervan, 1981), 1.269–70. See also Oswald T. Allis, 'The Blessing of Abraham', *PTR* 25 (1927): 263–98; Christopher Wright Mitchell, *The Meaning of* BRK *'To Bless' in the Old Testament* (SBLDS 95; Atlanta: Scholars Press, 1987), 31–35; von Rad, *Genesis*, 155–56.

16. Wehmeier notes the contrast in number in 12.3 ('I will bless *those*' vs. 'I will curse *him*') and argues that 'what is expected to be the normal action is expressed by the plural, that others bless Israel and consequently receive blessings themselves ... . Hence the context does not favor the reflexive understanding of the Nif'al.' He argues that, in 18.18, 'a statement that the nations *wished* to participate in Abraham's blessing would be quite out of place here. It is only because they *receive* blessing

> God will bless those whom Abraham blesses, and it shall come to pass that at last all the
> families of the earth shall wish and seek to participate in the blessing of which he is the
> vehicle, which is the same as to say that they shall be actually blessed in him.[17]

Wenham believes that in 12.3 the *nip'al* is best understood as a middle ('find blessing').

> Already it has been stated that Abram will be a blessing, which presupposes both the
> passive sense, 'Abram has been blessed,' and the reflexive sense, men will use his name
> in blessing one another. Then it was stated that all individuals who bless Abram will
> themselves be blessed. Finally, this clause brings the passage to a triumphant and uni-
> versal conclusion: 'all the families of the earth will find blessing in you.' … Finally it
> should be noted that even if a reflexive 'bless themselves' is preferred here, it would also
> carry the implications of a middle or passive. For if those who bless Abram are blessed,
> and all families of the earth bless Abram, then it follows that 'all families will be blessed/
> find blessing in him.'[18]

Waltke concludes simply that 'in either case, God mediates his blessing to the nations through Abraham'.[19] Kaiser concludes that Abraham 'was the medium and agency through whom the divine blessing would come'.[20]

In a recent paper, Benjamin J. Noonan has offered additional light on the meaning of the promise.[21] Noonan characterizes the debate as one between 'bless-ing mediation or blessing utterance'. After a detailed examination of the linguistic issues, Noonan concludes that the *nip'al* should be understood as a medio-passive and the *hitpa'el* as a reflexive 'make/declare/consider oneself blessed', thus under-standing both as referring to 'blessing mediation'. Then he conducts an examina-tion of the patriarchal narratives, pursuing questions posed by Grüneberg about which understanding of the promise the narratives support.[22] Noonan finds that, while there is no indication that anyone invokes the name of Abraham as a for-mula in blessing, others are repeatedly blessed through their association with Abraham and his descendants, particularly in the three stories of the 'endangered ancestress' (12.10-20; 20.1-18; 26.6-11) and in the Joseph story (Potiphar, the

---

through Abraham that the patriarch's role is so important.' Gerhard Wehmeier, 'The Theme "Blessing for the Nations" in the Promises to the Patriarchs and in Prophetical Literature', *Bangalore Theologi-cal Forum* 6 (1974): 5–6.

17. Delitzsch, *Genesis*, 1.379.

18. Gordon J. Wenham, *Genesis* (2 vols.; WBC 1–2; Waco: Word, 1987–94), 1.277–78. Another recent advocate for a middle sense for both *nip'al* and *hitpa'el* is Keith N. Grüneberg, *Abraham, Blessing and the Nations: A Philological and Exegetical Study of Genesis 12.3 in Its Narrative Context* (BZAW 332; Berlin: Walter de Gruyter, 2003), 242.

19. Bruce K. Waltke and Cathi J. Fredricks, *Genesis: A Commentary* (Grand Rapids: Zondervan, 2001), 206. Westermann terms the controversy 'otiose'. He concludes that 'the reflexive translation is saying no less than the passive or receptive' and 'there is no opposition between the passive and reflexive'. Westermann, *Genesis 12–36: A Commentary*, 152. 'It is, however, hermeneutically wrong to limit such a programmatic saying, circulating in such exalted style, to only *one* meaning (restric-tively).' Von Rad, *Genesis*, 160.

20. Kaiser, *Messiah*, 48.

21. Benjamin J. Noonan, 'Abraham, Blessing, and the Nations: A Proposed Paradigm', paper pre-sented at the November 2007 annual meeting of the Evangelical Theological Society, San Diego.

22. Grüneberg, *Abraham*.

jailer, the cupbearer, the people of Egypt and the other nations that secure food from Egypt). Noonan thus concludes, on the basis of both linguistic and narrative arguments, that the promise is one of blessing mediation, conveying blessing to others.

Although כֹּל מִשְׁפְּחֹת הָאֲדָמָה (12.3; 28.14) could conceivably be translated 'all the tribes of the land' (i.e. all of Israel),[23] the parallel כֹּל גּוֹיֵי הָאָרֶץ (18.18; 22.18; 26.4) more likely refers to Gentiles, in contrast to Abraham's 'seed' (בְזַרְעֶךָ). The promise is thus a universal one.[24] This was apparently the view of Nachmanides.[25] Von Rad states that 'Abraham is assigned the role of a mediator of blessing in God's saving plan, for "all the families of the earth"'.[26]

> In one of the oldest strata of the O.T. we find a concept which rightly can be termed uni-versalistic. The Yahwist clearly indicates that from the very beginning God is interested in mankind as a whole, and not only concerned about Israel. The choosing of Israel serves the purpose that God's plan with the world might be carried out. ... the line of thinking which has been opened by the Yahwist, has never completely ceased to be effective in Israel.[27]

The thought of a 'plan' that 'might be carried out' hints at a second question about the promise to Abraham. Did the promise to Abraham include an obliga-tion actively to communicate blessing to the nations? Did the OT envision a 'Gentile mission'? Kidner writes:

> Blessing for the world was a vision fitfully seen at first (it disappears between the patriarchs and the kings, apart from a reminder of Israel's priestly role in Ex. 19.5, 6). Later, it reappeared in the psalms and prophets, and perhaps even at its faintest it always imparted some sense of mission to Israel; yet it never became a programme of concerted action until the ascension.[28]

Was there supposed to have been 'a programme of concerted action' by Abraham's descendants? Some have argued that there was.[29] Grüneberg, however, argues that Abraham was given a promise, not a commission, and that he (and his descen-dants) would bless the nations as models or pioneers of the way of blessing.[30]

---

23. Alexis Léonas, 'A Note on Acts 3,25-26: The Meaning of Peter's Genesis Quotation', *ETL* 77 (2000): 159. Haenchen suggests the presence of an echo of Ezek. 30.5 (וּבְנֵי אֶרֶץ, lit. 'sons of the land', LXX τῶν υἱῶν τῆς διαθήκης μου), but this seems highly unlikely.

24. 'Not every individual is promised blessing in Abram but every major group in the world will be blessed.' Wenham, *Genesis*, 278.

25. 'Not only the families of Canaan, but the families of all the earth shall be blessed through thee.' Abraham Cohen, *The Soncino Chumash: The Five Books of Moses with Haphtaroth* (Soncino Books of the Bible; London: Soncino, 1947), 60.

26. Von Rad, *Genesis*, 156.

27. Wehmeier, 'Blessing for the Nations', 12.

28. Derek Kidner, *Genesis: An Introduction and Commentary* (TOTC; Downers Grove, Ill.: Inter-Varsity, 1967), 114.

29. So Kaiser, *Mission*, 9, 62–63, 74; David Filbeck, *Yes, God of the Gentiles, Too* (Wheaton, Ill.: Billy Graham Center, Wheaton College, 1994), 65, 130–32; Robert Martin-Achard, *A Light to the Nations: A Study of the Old Testament Conception of Israel's Mission to the World* (trans. John Penney Smith; Edinburgh: Oliver & Boyd, 1962), 23.

30. Grüneberg, *Abraham*, 244. Similarities between the promise to Abraham and the language of

Brueggemann believes the idea is 'not that Israel has a direct responsibility to do something for others, but that the life of Israel under the promise will energize and model a way for other nations to receive a blessing from this God'.[31] Matthew 23.15 appears to indicate that there was some deliberate missionary activity by the time of Jesus,[32] yet in Acts 22.21-22, it appears that the idea of an intentional mission to Gentiles was offensive to at least some Jews. Either way, the citation of Isa. 49.6 in Acts 13.47 makes it clear that Luke believed an active and intentional Gentile mission had now been commanded by God.

The repetition of the promise to Abraham five times in Genesis indicates its importance. Yahweh promised not only that Abraham will be blessed, but that he and his 'seed' will be a blessing to all peoples. At the heart of OT particularism is the promise that God's choice of Abraham and his descendants was for the purpose of blessing the world.

6.3 *The Expected Blessing*

Yahweh's covenant with Abraham is the basis of his subsequent acts on behalf of Israel and the guarantee of his continued mercy.[33] In Genesis, the promise to Abraham provides repeated assurance to his descendants (26.3, 24; 28.4, 13; 21.42; 31.42; 35.12; 48.15-16; 50.24). It is because 'God remembered his covenant with Abraham, with Isaac, and with Jacob' that he rescued Israel from Egypt (Exod. 2.24). The land of Canaan is 'the land which he swore to your fathers, to Abraham, to Isaac, and to Jacob, to give you' (Exod. 6.8; 33.1; Num. 32.11; Deut. 1.8; 6.10; 9.5; 30.20; 34.4). Yahweh is known as the God of Abraham, Isaac and Jacob (Exod. 3.6, 15, 16; 4.5; 1 Kgs. 18.36). Nevertheless, the promise to Abraham does not appear to be explicitly connected with the prophets' expectation of eschatological blessing for the Gentiles.[34]

A mixed picture of the promise to Abraham regarding the nations appears in available intertestamental materials.

Isaiah 42 lead Goldingay to conclude that neither Abraham nor Israel was called to preach to Gentiles. Goldingay, *Isaiah*, 241.

31. Walter Brueggemann, *Genesis* (IBC; Atlanta: John Knox, 1982), 120. Similarly Köstenberger and O'Brien, *Salvation*, 28–36; Christopher J. H. Wright, *The Mission of God: Unlocking the Bible's Grand Narrative* (Downers Grove, Ill.: InterVarsity Press, 2006), 501–05.

32. A substantial recent study of Jewish universalism concludes that, while 'there is little evidence of an active mission designed to create interest where it did not already exist ... many Jews were eager to instruct and encourage those who were attracted to Judaism and who took the initiative to seek them out'. It is in this sense that Matt. 23.15 should probably be understood. Terence L. Donaldson, *Judaism and the Gentiles: Jewish Patterns of Universalism (to 135 CE)* (Waco: Baylor University Press, 2007), 492.

33. Exod. 2.24; 6.3; 32.13; Lev. 26.42; Deut. 9.27; 29.13; Josh. 24.2, 3; 2 Kgs. 13.23; Isa. 29.22; 41.8; 51.2; Mic. 7.20; cf. Isa. 63.16; Ezek. 33.24.

34. Unless the בְּרָכָה ('blessing') on Egypt and Assyria in Isa. 19.24-25 is meant to evoke Gen. 12.2.

The blessing of the nations through Abraham's offspring is also explicitly mentioned in early Judaism but plays a less significant role, probably due to the political and social situation of most Jews in the first century C.E., in Palestine and in the Diaspora.[35]

The promise is cited in Sirach, but without elaboration of its meaning or application.

Therefore the Lord assured him by an oath that the nations would be blessed [ἐνευλογ-ηθῆναι ἔθνη] through his posterity; that he would multiply him like the dust of the earth, and exalt his posterity like the stars, and cause them to inherit from sea to sea and from the River to the ends of the earth. (Sir. 44.21)

While some texts positively enumerate intellectual and spiritual blessings that come to the nations through Abraham, others see the blessing as wrested from Israel by Gentile exploitation.[36] Other studies have found that second temple traditions regarding Abraham vary between exclusivism and universalism.[37]

Abraham figures prominently in Luke–Acts, being mentioned 22 times. As in the exodus, the promise to Abraham is the basis for God's mercy to his people (Luke 1.55, 73).[38] The promise figures as well in Stephen's speech (Acts 7.17; cf. 'our fathers', Acts 13.17, 32;[39] 26.6). God is identified as the God of Abraham, Isaac and Jacob (Luke 20.37; Acts 3.13; 7.32; cf. 'God of our fathers', Acts 5.30; 22.14). When Jesus comes bringing healing and restoration, it is specifically to an unnamed 'daughter of Abraham', who is released from her sickness (Luke 13.16) and to a 'son of Abraham', the chief tax collector, Zacchaeus (Luke 19.9). 'Abraham's bosom' is the place of eternal blessing (Luke 16.22, 23, 24, 25, 29, 30; cf. the presence of Abraham, Isaac and Jacob 'in the kingdom', 13.28). Apart from Acts 3.25, there appears to be no other explicit reference to blessing of the nations through Abraham.[40] Jeffrey P. Siker has argued that in Abraham texts in the gospel, Luke consistently downplays physical descent and highlights God's mercy to the outcasts who repent, while in Acts those who receive the promise are those who worship God (7.7) from all nations (3.25; 13.47).[41] Thus, although Abraham figures somewhat more prominently in the gospel than in Acts, Siker correctly notes that in the work as a whole

35. Jeffrey S. Siker, *Disinheriting the Jews: Abraham in Early Christian Controversy* (Louisville: Westminster John Knox, 1991), 20.

36. At least some of this material is later and may have been shaped in response to Christian appropriation of this promise. Evans, 'Prophecy and Polemic', 192; Witherington, *Acts*, 188.

37. Brawley cites an unpublished 1997 Fuller Seminary Ph.D. dissertation that was not available to me: P. Choi, 'Abraham Our Father: Paul's Voice in the Covenant Debate of the Second Temple Period'. Robert L. Brawley, 'Abrahamic Traditions and the Characterization of God in Luke–Acts', in *The Unity of Luke–Acts* (ed. Jozef Verheyden; BETL 142; Leuven: Leuven University Press, 1999).

38. Litwak has argued for recognition of repeated echoes of the Abraham narrative in Luke 1 as an important part of the author's framing of the entire narrative. Litwak, *Echoes*, 82–89.

39. 'What God promised to the fathers' in Acts 13.32 'cannot refer exclusively to God's promise to the patriarchs, but must include both the promise given to David and later prophecies', but these later promises 'reiterate and unfold' the foundational promise to Abraham. Dahl, 'Abraham', 148.

40. This remains true even when texts such as those referring to 'the fathers' are taken into account.

41. Siker, *Disinheriting the Jews*, 103–27.

Luke–Acts uses Abraham in order to show that Gentile Christians have a legitimate claim
to Abraham as their father, on the same terms as Jews, and thus they have a share in the
promise to Abraham along with the Jews.[42]

6.4 *Acts 3.25*

Acts 3 records the first miracle in Acts and the beginning of conflict between the
church and the religious leaders in Jerusalem.[43] On their way into the temple,
Peter and John met an apparently well-known cripple who regularly begged alms
from those passing by (3.1-10). When healed through the name of Jesus, the
cripple responded with joy and followed Peter and John into the temple, 'walking
and leaping and praising God' (3.8, 9). His actions drew the attention of some
who recognized him as the former cripple (3.10). The man's exuberance, together
with the 'wonder and amazement' of those who recognized him, attracted a crowd
(3.11). Provided another opportunity to address an uncomprehending crowd (cf.
2.14), Peter began to speak. His address was apparently terminated by the arrival
of temple officials (4.1),[44] who arrested Peter and John (4.3). Nevertheless, many
responded favourably to the message and believed (4.4). Following an abbrevi-
ated hearing the next day before a frustrated tribunal (before whom Peter again
preached), Peter and John were instructed 'not to speak or teach at all in the name
of Jesus' (4.18), an admonition they declined (4.19-20, 31, 33). Upon their
release, they rejoined the church, which responded by praying for boldness and
power (4.24-30).

As in his Pentecost sermon, Peter began with the (mis)perception of the crowd.
It was not Peter or John who had healed the cripple, but Jesus, the Jesus whom
they had handed to the Romans to be killed and whom God had raised and
glorified (3.11-16). In vv. 17-26, Peter three times calls for repentance, each time
identifying Jesus as the fulfilment of OT expectation. In 17-21, Jesus is the Messiah, who suffered as God had 'foretold by the mouth of all the prophets' (18).
Peter's hearers must repent of their complicity (if only in ignorance) in his death
(17), so that (εἰς τό + infinitive) their sins might be taken away and they may
share in the promised messianic blessings, i.e. 'that times of refreshing[45] may
come from the presence of the Lord, and that he may send the Christ appointed
for you, Jesus' (3.19-20) to restore all things as 'God spoke by the mouth of his
holy prophets from of old' (21). Second, in 22-23, Peter identifies Jesus as the
prophet like Moses, warning that 'every soul that does not listen to that prophet

---

42. Siker, *Disinheriting the Jews*, 103.
43. Fitzmyer, *Acts*, 275–76; Marshall, *Acts*, 86. Both see this conflict section continuing through
chapter 5. It may also be seen as continuing through the scattering of the church in Acts 8.1.
44. Barrett finds that 'the speech ends abruptly', but does not believe it 'is unfinished'. Barrett,
Acts, 1.214.
45. 'The expression as such occurs only here, and its specific meaning is not clear.' Johnson, *Acts*,
69. Nevertheless, 'the healing of the lame man brackets the reference to the Abrahamic covenant in
3,25 in such a fashion that it is a concrete instance of the times of refreshing and the blessing of all
the families of the earth (3,19-20, 25)'. Brawley, 'Abrahamic Traditions', 126.

shall be destroyed from the people' (quoting Deut. 18.15, 19 and possibly Lev. 23.29; the former is also cited in 7.37).[46] Finally, after asserting that 'all the prophets who have spoken, from Samuel and those who came afterwards, also proclaimed these days' (3.24) and that his hearers are 'the sons of the prophets and of the covenant which God gave to your fathers', Peter cites the promise to Abraham, 'in your posterity shall all the families of the earth be blessed' (3.25), but again urges repentance as he warns that God sent Jesus to 'bless you in turning every one of you from your wickedness' (3.26).[47]

The two distinctive changes in the citation indicate something of its significance. First, ἐν τῷ σπέρματί σου ('in your posterity' [lit. 'seed']) has been brought forward. Steyn attributes the transposition to the desire to emphasize ἐν τῷ σπέρματί σου.[48] In Genesis the 'seed' is generally understood as a collective noun encompassing Abraham's (or Isaac's or Jacob's) offspring.[49] Some interpreters understand the term in Acts 3 in the same way, as a collective noun referring to Israel.[50] In this case, the 'sons ... of the covenant' and Abraham's 'seed' would be one and the same.[51] Others see a singular noun, referring to Christ,[52] believing that Luke follows Paul's reading of the promise in Gal. 3.16, where he famously argues that the promise 'does not say, "And to offsprings," referring to many; but, referring to one, "And to your offspring," which is Christ'.[53] (Such reasoning is not made explicit, however, in the text of Acts.) A few see a double reference to both Israel and Christ.[54]

Since Christ has been the focus of the entire sermon,[55] it is most natural to see

46. Max Turner argues that 'Luke combines ... Davidic Christology with a prophet-like-Moses motif.' Turner, *Power*, 267, 279–89 and elsewhere.

47. Steyn observes that in Luke 20.37-44, Luke also joins references to Abraham, Moses and the Davidic Messiah. Steyn, *Septuagint Quotations*, 156. In Luke 20, however, only David and the Messiah appear in connection with a predictive prophecy.

48. Steyn, *Septuagint Quotations*, 154–55. So also Bock, *Acts*, 180. On the earlier position as emphatic, see BDF, §472.

49. Wenham, *Genesis*, 2.113.

50. Bock, *Acts*, 180–81; Johnson, *Acts*, 70. Other instances of σπέρμα in Luke–Acts appear to be collective (Luke 1.55; Acts 7.5, 6; 13.23; and probably Luke 20.28).

51. Jervell, 'Divided People', 58–60; Turner, *Power*, 310. Thus Jervell concludes, 'God sent Christ first to Jews with the intention of reaching Gentiles through them.' Jervell, 'Divided People', 60.

52. Bruce, *Acts (Greek Text, 3d ed.)*, 146; van den Eynde, 'Children of the Promise', 472; Foakes Jackson and Lake, eds., *Beginnings*, 4.39; Marshall, *Acts*, 96; Rese, *Alttestamentliche Motive;* Roloff, *Apostelgeschichte*, 78.

53. See the survey of hermeneutical proposals for this passage in Clifford John Collins, 'Galatians 3.16: What Kind of Exegete Is Paul?', *TynBul* 54 (2003): 76–79. See also Frederick F. Bruce, *The Epistle to the Galatians: A Commentary on the Greek Text* (NIGTC; Grand Rapids: Eerdmans, 1982); Ernest De Witt Burton, *A Critical and Exegetical Commentary on the Epistle to the Galatians* (ICC; Edinburgh: T&T Clark, 1921).

54. The term here would then function in a 'twofold way: not just generically of all the Jewish people, but more specifically as a reference to an individual descendant of Abraham, the risen Christ.' Fitzmyer, *Acts*, 291. So also Siker, *Disinheriting the Jews*, 119–20. A specifically typological understanding of the relationship between the corporate and individual seed would be an attractive possibility (see ch. 3 of the present work).

55. Hans F. Bayer, 'Christ-Centered Eschatology in Acts 3.17–26', in *Jesus of Nazareth: Lord*

the 'seed' as one more reference to him. He has already been described as 'the Holy and Righteous One' (3.14), 'the Author of life' (3.15), 'his Christ' (3.18, 20), the prophet like Moses (3.22), and the divine 'servant' (3.13, 26). It is this individual who brings life (3.15); health (3.16), forgiveness of sins (3.19), 'times of refreshing' (3.19) – in short, all that 'God spoke by the mouth of his holy prophets from of old' (3.21). Peter distinguishes the 'seed' from his hearers. His hearers are not the means of this blessing, but its first recipients. The promise is for all nations, but comes 'first' to Israel, as God's servant is 'raised up' and sent 'to you first, to bless you in turning every one of you from your wickedness'. The 'servant' who first brings blessing to Israel is the 'seed' who will also bring blessing to all the nations. Thus Bock writes that 'in verse 21, Peter particularizes the means of blessing and the seed (v. 25) through whom the promise comes. Blessing comes through the servant (v. 13) God raised up (v. 22) to turn (v. 19) each one of them from their acts of wickedness. This ties the speech together and makes the point that one descendant in particular is fundamental to the plan'.[56] The 'raising up' of the servant in 3.26 (echoing that of the prophet like Moses in 3.22) may evoke the promise to 'raise up seed' in Yahweh's promise to David (ἀναστήσω τὸ σπέρμα σου μετὰ σέ in 2 Sam 7.11 ‖ 1 Chr. 17.11),[57] a seed that is clearly understood as an individual. While the 'seed' in Genesis is best understood as a collective noun, this understanding does not prevent one of those descendants from assuming a primary role in its fulfillment. (There is perhaps an imperfect analogy in the way we attribute to an entire people the actions of its leader, such as its foreign policy.) Historically, Jews are the means by which the blessing of the 'seed' is initially communicated to the nations, but this was neither in view in Acts 3 nor of particular concern to Luke and his audience. The focus in Acts 3 is on the individual servant/seed as the one through whom the blessing is to come.

The second distinctive reading in the citation is πᾶσαι αἱ πατριαὶ τῆς γῆς ('all the families of the earth') where the LXX has πάντα τὰ ἔθνη τῆς γῆς ('all the nations of the earth', 22.18; 26.4; 18.18) or αἱ φυλαὶ τῆς γῆς ('all the families of the earth', 12.3; 28.14). As noted earlier, the expression πᾶσαι αἱ πατριαὶ τῆς γῆς ('all the families of the earth') appears to reflect adaptation of the citation to include Peter's Jewish audience by substituting the more neutral πατριαί for ἔθνη (lest the latter be understood as a reference only to Gentiles). The focus in Peter's speech is on fulfilment of the promise to Israel.

The following verse (3.26) applies the promise and concludes the speech: 'God, having raised up his servant, sent him to you first, to bless you in turning every one of you from your wickedness.' 'His servant' (τὸν παῖδα αὐτοῦ) echoes 3.13 ('his servant, Jesus'). Since Moses and David are commonly referred

---

and Christ: Essays on the Historical Jesus and New Testament Christology (ed. Joel B. Green and Max Turner; Grand Rapids: Eerdmans, 1994), 236–50.

56. Bock, *Acts*, 181.

57. Cf. the only other instance of this expression in the description of the levirate custom in Gen. 38.8. The OT never speaks of the 'raising up' of a servant in this sense.

to as Yahweh's servant, the term may also allude to the prophet like Moses (3.22-23) and the Davidic Messiah (3.18-21; cf. 4.27, 30).[58]

God 'raised up' (ἀναστήσας) his servant, not in the sense of resurrection,[59] but as God promised to 'raise up' (ἀναστήσει) the prophet like Moses (3.22), i.e. 'provide, cause to appear'.[60] God raised up his servant to 'bless' (εὐλογοῦντα) Peter's audience, by 'turning every one of you from your wickedness' (ἐν τῷ ἀποστρέφειν ἕκαστον ἀπὸ τῶν πονηριῶν ὑμῶν).[61] This blessing of repentance (3.26) is not the promised blessing for 'all the families of the earth'. As in 3.19-21, repentance is the prerequisite to the experience of promised blessing (God's provision of what is needed to obtain the blessing is itself a blessing.)

'First' (πρῶτον) again brings the Gentiles into view. God has not sent his servant only to ὑμῖν ('you') Jews,[62] but to ὑμῖν πρῶτον ('you first').[63] 'First' suggests 'second',[64] a subsequent stage in the work of the servant, that the promise to Abraham 'will be realized for others at a later stage'.[65] Steyn concludes that 'the πρῶτον in v. 26 clearly suggests that the circle is wider than Jews alone'.[66] Barrett's careful discussion touches on so many matters of importance that it is worth quoting at length:

> πρῶτον implies that the offer of messianic salvation made to the Jews as heirs of the prophets and inheritors of the covenant (see above, v. 25) will be followed by another – to the Gentiles. Other ways of taking it, such as that Jesus was the first to be raised from the dead (cf. 1 Cor. 15.20), or that he was raised before the parousia took place, have little to commend them. ... πρῶτον must then be taken closely with ὑμῖν: It was

58. Barrett characterizes the term as a title that 'grows out of wide-spreading roots. In the OT many are spoken of as God's servant: kings, priests, prophets, and others (e.g. Abraham).' Barrett, *Acts*, 1.214. See section 3.2.1 above.

59. As contended by Fitzmyer, *Acts*, 291; Tannehill, *Narrative Unity*, 2.56. Nor does it refer to the servant's 'appointment' as suggested by Léonas, 'Acts 3,25-26', 160.

60. L. T. Johnson finds that 'the Mosaic imagery is obvious'. Johnson, *Acts*, 70–71. The verb already occurs in 3.22 (LXX of Deut. 18.18). It is used in the sense of 'cause to appear for a role or function', BDAG, s.v. ἀνίστημι, 4 (although BDAG assigns 3.26 to def. 2, 'to raise up by bringing back to life', with def. 4 present only as wordplay). Similarly (of coming 'on to the stage of history', or of 'raising up' a leader), see Barrett, *Acts*, 1.213; Bruce, *Acts* (Greek Text, 3rd edn.), 88. The *hifʿil* of קום is commonly translated by ἵστημι (or one of its compounds) or ἐγείρω. Also 'raised up' (LXX ἀνίστημι) are a priest (to replace Eli, 1 Sam. 2.35), David's throne (2 Sam. 3.10), David's 'seed' (2 Sam. 7.12), the king (Deut. 28.36, καθίστημι), the judges (e.g. Judg. 2.16, ἐγείρω), and evil (2 Sam. 12.11, ἐξεγείρω).

61. Barrett understands the infinitive in an active transitive sense: God (or the servant) 'turns you from your wickedness'. Barrett, *Acts*, 1.214. If so, it is part of the promise; if not, it reinforces the command to repent (3.19).

62. That Jews are in view is evident from the beginning of 3.25: 'You [emphatic, ὑμεῖς ἐστε] are the sons of the prophets and of the covenant which God gave to your fathers, saying to Abraham ... '

63. The word πρῶτον here may anticipate its occurrence in 13.46: 'It was necessary that the word of God should be spoken first to you' before turning to the Gentiles.

64. Van den Eynde, 'Children of the Promise', 472.

65. Dupont, 'Salvation', 23. Similarly, Fitzmyer speaks of a 'note of universalism' provided by the citation and indicates that 'this quotation in Peter's speech foreshadows the spread of the Christian message to non-Jewish families as well'. Fitzmyer, *Acts*, 291.

66. Steyn, *Septuagint Quotations*, 156.

initially but not exclusively for your benefit that God sent his Servant; that is, the first sending will turn out not in the first instance but eventually to be of benefit not only to Jews but to Gentiles also: to the Jew first and also to the Greek (Rom. 1.16). ... The relation between Judaism and the Christian church is a question that is frequently raised in Acts and one that cannot be adequately considered on the basis of one passage. The present passage does however suggest that for Luke the question was not a difficult one. It is God's intention to have a newly constituted people of which the original heirs of the covenant and Gentiles, newly called through the Gospel, may be members. For both there is only one way into the inheritance: Jesus the Messiah.[67]

In Isa. 49.6, Yahweh's servant has a calling 'first' to Israel, but this is so that 'my salvation may reach to the end of the earth'. Acts 3.26 displays the same pattern: the servant is sent first to 'you' Jews, but the blessing is intended for 'all the families of the earth'. 'To the Jew first, and also to the Greek' (Rom. 1.16) remains the pattern of ministry throughout the book of Acts, both in the overall narrative of Acts as it follows 1.8 ('in Jerusalem and in all Judea and Samaria and to the end of the earth') and as Paul at every stop in his travels first seeks out the local synagogue in order to preach there.

The promise to bless 'the families of the earth' through Abraham, then, is a promise of salvation through Jesus for both Jews and Gentiles. 'Peter's point is that the messianic blessing, though destined first for the Jews (3.26), must extend to all nations: the risen Christ is a principle of salvation for the Gentiles, too.'[68] 'It is generally agreed that there is a reference to the future Gentile mission in the phrase πᾶσαι αἱ πατριαὶ τῆς γῆς and allusion to it implied in the use of ὑμῖν πρῶτον (v. 26).'[69]

This is not to say that this assertion was explicitly intended by Peter[70] or understood by his hearers. Marshall believes 'the reference to the Gentiles is at this stage a quiet hint (contrast 13.46)'.[71] Witherington finds that 'here and in v. 26 the blessing of the Gentiles is clearly alluded to, but only in connection with Jews or following blessing given to Jews. Luke is masterfully preparing for later developments in his narrative.'[72] Nevertheless, in light of the later progress of the narrative and the way in which Luke elsewhere appeals to the OT to legitimate the Gentile mission, it is impossible to imagine that Luke or his readers would have missed the implication of the language here. As a Gentile believer, Theophilus would have welcomed this early indication in the narrative of Acts that, because Jesus came in fulfilment of God's promise to Abraham, the promised

---

67. Barrett, *Acts*, 1.213. Eckey likewise sees the redemptive-historical priority of Israel set forth here (and also references Rom. 1.16). Eckey, *Apostelgeschichte*, 1.110. See also 13.46: 'it was necessary that the word of God should be spoken first to you'.

68. Dupont, 'Apologetic', 135.

69. Wilson, *Gentile Mission*, 219.

70. 'It may have taken the apostles some time to fully realize the implications of the missionary imperative, but there it is. Peter was primarily concerned with the Jews. The gospel was preached to them first. Soon it would reach far beyond the boundaries of Judaism "to all the peoples on earth".' Polhill, *Acts*, 137.

71. Marshall, *Acts*, 96.

72. Witherington, *Acts*, 188.

blessing is not only for Jews, but for Gentiles (like him) as well. Further, the fulfilment of God's promise and purpose requires that Gentiles receive the blessing promised. If the blessing comes by faith (16), knowledge (17), repentance (19, 26) and hearing (22-23), then the Gentiles must be told about Jesus. There must be a Gentile mission.

6.5 *Summary*

6.5.1 *Text*
The form of the promise to Abraham in Acts 3.25 differs from any extant form of the promise in any of its expressions in either the MT or LXX, although the language of Gen. 22.18 comes closest. It may be that the appeal is to the promise itself, more than to any particular instance of it. Neither the form of the citation nor the argument based on it depends particularly on either the LXX or the MT.

6.5.2 *Hermeneutic*
Acts 3 understands the promise to Abraham as a promise that God would bring blessing to all nations through an individual descendant of Abraham. There has been disagreement over the interpretation of the promise in Genesis: whether Gentiles are included, whether Israel was given a mission to Gentiles, and whether the seed who brings blessing would be an individual. The present study has shown good reason to understand the promise in Genesis as in Acts 3, i.e., that the Gentiles are included in the blessing and that the seed through whom the blessing comes is ultimately an individual. (The question of a mission to Gentiles by Israel before the coming of the 'seed' is not addressed.) The interpretation of the promise to Abraham in Acts 3.25 is therefore consistent with a proper understanding of the promise in its original context.

The citation is employed with respect for its original contexts. God promised Abraham 'seed' through whom all nations would be blessed. In his sermon in the temple, Peter announced that the time of blessing promised to Abraham had begun. The eventual inclusion of the Gentiles among God's people can legitimately be seen in the OT original. The fulfilment of the promise requires the proclamation of the gospel to the nations. While these implications are not explicit at this point in the narrative, the subsequent narrative and Luke's evident interest in Gentile mission support the assertion that an intentional Gentile mission is anticipated in these citations.

The citation is interpreted by a Christocentric hermeneutic. In Acts 3, Peter associates the expected Messiah (Christ), the prophet like Moses, the servant, and the 'seed' of Abraham with the risen Jesus who had restored the lame man in token of the restoration of all things (3.21, cf. 3.19). This hermeneutic is applied (in principle) to texts from all of 'the law of Moses and the prophets and the psalms'. The coming of Jesus in fulfilment of these promises requires the inclusion of the Gentiles for their intended consummation, just as the coming of the servant demands an intentional Gentile mission, the restoration of the kingdom in Jesus necessitates accommodations to ensure the unhindered extension of God's name over Gentiles, and the outpouring of the Spirit on all flesh demands the proclamation of the gospel to the nations. The citation thus develops the ecclesiology of Acts. Although it is sent to Jews 'first', the promise of blessing through Abraham is for 'all the families of the earth'.

6.5.3 *Purpose*

The argument in Acts 3 is based on the promise to Abraham as the foundation of all the promises God made 'to our fathers' (Luke 1.55, 72) 'by the mouth of his holy prophets from of old' (Luke 1.70). To support this claim, Peter appeals to the foundational promise of the OT, the promise to Abraham. Luke views promises made to Moses as part of the promise to Abraham[73] and connects the promises to David to the promise to Abraham.[74] The promise to Abraham is the basis of God's subsequent redemptive work. In his influential study of 'The Story of Abraham in Luke–Acts', Dahl has observed that, unlike Paul or the author of Hebrews, Luke does not point to Abraham's faith. Instead 'God's word to Abraham is seen as the beginning of a history in which partial realizations are interconnected with new promises, until the coming of the Righteous One, of whom all the prophets spoke (cf. [Acts] 7.52).' Two conclusions of Dahl's study are particularly worth noting. First, Dahl finds the use of Abraham in Luke–Acts to be 'a confirmation of Paul Schubert's thesis that "proof-from-prophecy" is a main theological and literary device of the work'. Second,

> Salvation of Gentiles was from the beginning envisaged by God and included as part of his promises to Israel. Luke does not claim that the church has replaced Israel as the people of God, nor does he call Gentile believers Abraham's children. Gentiles are saved as Gentiles. Luke takes care to adduce prophecies that really spoke of them. This 'proof-from-prophecy' has a double function: to prove the legitimacy of the Gentile mission and Gentile churches, and to prove that Jesus is the Anointed One of whom the prophets spoke.[75]

As in Acts 2, Luke here cites the OT to demonstrate that 'the things which have been accomplished among us' (τῶν πεπληροφορημένων ἐν ἡμῖν πραγμάτων, Luke 1.1) have happened just as God had foretold. Gentiles are included in the promises of God that were made to the fathers and that have been fulfilled in Jesus. Both the narrative of Acts as a whole and the particular accounts of each of Paul's missionary visits follow the pattern inherent in the promise to Abraham – 'to the Jew first and also to the Greek'. This 'proof from prophecy' assures Theophilus, and Luke's other readers, of the truth of the message they have

---

73. In Acts 7.7, for example, the promise that Israel will serve God in the land (λατρεύσουσιν) owes more to Exod. 3.12 than Gen. 15.13-14. Van den Eynde, 'Children of the Promise', 473.

74. Thus, although the announcement to Mary is made in terms of the promise to David (1.30-33), the Magnificat speaks of God's mercy to Abraham (1.55, cf. 37). Zachariah also moves from David (1.69) to Abraham (1.73). 'Not only the Davidic Messiah, but also the prophet like Moses is a particular way God moves the Abrahamic covenant toward its term.' Brawley, 'Abrahamic Traditions', 112–13, 125.

75. Dahl, 'Abraham', 144, 152, 151.

believed, particularly that by fulfilling the promise to Abraham in Jesus, God extended his blessing to all the families of the earth.

The citation is a deliberate rhetorical strategy that advances the author's purpose. Peter (and Luke) connects the covenant with Abraham and other promises to announce that 'all the prophets ... proclaimed these days' of blessing through the name of Jesus and to secure the hearers' repentance (3.19).

7

CONCLUSION

This study has underscored the importance of the OT in the development of key themes in Luke–Acts. Appeals to the OT play a prominent role in the narrative and the development of central themes.

Chapter 2 surveyed Luke's appeals to the OT. There are 14 statements which summarize OT teachings and 78 explicit OT citations (identified in the text of NA^{27} and/or UBS^4), 48 of which are marked by an introductory formula. The summaries claim that prophecy has been (or is about to be) fulfilled in relation to the coming of Christ. Over half of the citations (42 of the 78 texts and 29 of the 48 with introductory formulas) are employed in prophecy-fulfilment contexts. (The remaining citations refer to provisions of the law, historical events or doctrinal teachings.) The scripture summaries and the explicit citations focus on five themes: the suffering, death, resurrection and exaltation of the Messiah; the consequent coming of eschatological blessings; God's judgement; the rejection of Christ by many Jews; and the offer of forgiveness to all (Jew or Gentile) through Jesus. This analysis of Luke's approach to the OT is one of the contributions of the present study.

In his work on OT citations in Paul, Christopher Stanley has observed that authors appeal to authority in regard to issues that are in dispute. These five themes offer a window into the concerns of Luke and his readers, and particularly into the areas in which Theophilus was in need of greater 'certainty' (ἀσφάλεια). It is clear elsewhere in the NT that Jesus' suffering and death raised questions concerning his Messiahship and that his resurrection was widely doubted. The NT also indicates that the rejection of Jesus by many Jews raised questions: if Jesus was indeed the awaited Messiah, why had so many Jews rejected him? Finally, Acts indicates that the Gentile mission and the Gentiles' place in the church were matters of controversy, both between Jewish and Gentile believers, and between the church and synagogue. All of these would have been matters of substantial concern to Theophilus as a Gentile believer: whether Jesus was indeed the Lord's Messiah, and whether Theophilus as a Gentile was entitled to participate in the people and promises of God. Both the summaries and the explicit citations seek to show from the OT that these things – the suffering, death and resurrection of Christ; the rejection of Christ by many Jews; and the inclusion of the Gentiles – are part of God's plan, long foreseen and announced in the law, the prophets and the psalms. Through these appeals to the OT, along with other aspects of his narrative, Luke offers Theophilus assurance regarding the things he has been taught.

Christology and ecclesiology have been recognized as central concerns for Luke, but the use of appeals to the OT as a means of identifying the author's concerns is another contribution of this study.

The survey of explicit citations (Chapter 2) identified four texts that are relevant to the Gentile mission and the inclusion of Gentiles among the people of God. Two are introduced explicitly in connection with disputes over the Gentile mission: the citation of Isa. 49.6 in Acts 13.47 and the citation of Amos 9.11-12 in Acts 15.16-18. Two other citations are introduced in programmatic texts earlier in Acts to address other questions, but they also anticipate the Gentile mission: the citation of Joel 3.1-5 MT in Acts 2.16-21 and the citation of Gen. 22.18 in Acts 3.25. The diverse sources of these four OT texts (Genesis, Isaiah, Joel and Amos), the central prophetic themes they invoke (the promise to Abraham, the Servant, the Spirit and the kingdom), and the centrality of the characters who cite them (Peter, Paul and James) indicate the importance of the Gentile mission to the author.

7.1 *Text*

It is generally agreed that the texts of Luke's citations most often come from the LXX, although occasional differences suggest that he may sometimes quote from memory or somewhat freely. The four citations examined here are generally closer in form to the LXX than the MT.

Bock has argued that there are two senses in which we may talk about an author's 'use' of the OT: the form of the text cited and the use (or argument) that is made of it. The first is the question of whether a citation appears closer to the LXX or MT. The second is whether the argument is based on a distinctive form of the text. In other words, has the author cited the LXX simply because it was familiar or ready to hand, or because the argument he wishes to make depends on it? In the case of the four citations examined here, the argument nowhere depends on distinctive readings of the LXX form of the text. In every case the MT would serve just as well.

In Acts 13.47, the citation of Isa. 49.6 exactly reproduces the LXX, but omits the LXX text where the latter apparently adds to the MT. Whether the form of the citation in Acts 13 represents a fresh rendering of the MT, or an LXX MS closer to the MT than most extant LXX MSS, the form of the text actually cited in the NT does not significantly diverge from the MT or LXX.

The MT and LXX of Amos 9.11-12 differ significantly and the citation in Acts 15.16-18 differs from both. The NT citation seems to be based upon, if adapted from, the LXX. Nevertheless, neither the LXX nor the citation distort the sense of the original words of Amos. Despite frequent assertions to the contrary, there is no substantial evidence that the citation contains allusions to other OT texts or that the argument in Acts 15 depends particularly on the LXX form of the text.

The lengthy quotation from Joel in Acts 2 appears at points to be cited somewhat freely, but neither the NT nor LXX differs significantly from the MT in the portions of Joel examined here. The citation of the promise to Abraham in Acts 3 does not exactly match any of its occurrences in the LXX, but the substance of the promise is repeated closely enough. In neither does the argument in any way depend on the LXX more than the MT.

7.2 Hermeneutic

These four citations are each used in a way that is congruent with the meaning in their original contexts. Luke did not disregard or distort the original sense of the Hebrew text (even when the words of the citation appear to come from the LXX). There is no evidence that meanings were based on wordplay or linguistic ambiguities, or that texts were linked merely on the basis of catchwords. These findings are important because these texts have so often been seen as examples of an imaginative and arbitrary hermeneutic. If this is not the case here, it may be worth reexamining other citations where similar claims have been made.

Luke consistently employs the Christocentric hermeneutic expressed in Luke 24.44: 'everything written about me in the law of Moses and the prophets and the psalms must be fulfilled'. The varied sources of the citations and the central prophetic themes they evoke illustrate how Luke understands all of the OT to be about Christ and how broadly the OT supports the Gentile mission.

In Acts 13.47, Isa. 49.6 is applied to Paul and Barnabas. The same text is applied to Jesus on at least two other occasions (Luke 2.30; Acts 26.23). The application of Isa. 49.6 in Acts 13.47 to Paul and Barnabas is not an alternative to its fulfilment in Christ, but an extension of it. Several rationales have been used to explain this relationship in Acts 13, but Richard Davidson's understanding of appropriated/ecclesiological typology offers an attractive conceptual framework for understanding how this apparently Christological text might also be applied to Christ's apostolic messengers on behalf of the church.

In Acts 15, the citation of Amos 9.11-12 is also used in a manner consistent with its original contextual meaning. A Christocentric hermeneutic is again evident. The reestablishment of the Davidic kingdom lies at the centre of God's eschatological work. James argues from Amos 9 that the reestablishment of the kingdom in Christ necessarily implies the inclusion of the Gentiles among the people of God – as Gentiles, not as converts to Judaism. Although God's acceptance of the Gentiles was first apparent through God's directing Peter to the house of Cornelius, James finds it confirmed in the words of Amos. This then becomes the basis on which to settle, once and for all, whether Gentile believers in Jesus must be circumcised and keep the law of Moses.

Joel 3 and Genesis 22.18 are also employed in ways that are congruent with and respectful of their original contexts. Both citations are applied to present circumstances by means of a Christ-centred hermeneutic. In Peter's speech, the observed outpouring of the Spirit (as promised by Joel) provides evidence that Jesus has been enthroned as 'Lord and Christ'. However, the larger narrative of Acts indicates that the outpouring of the Spirit on 'all flesh' will also include Gentiles, as it does in Joel. Similarly, the promised blessing to Abraham will be shared by all who call on the name of Jesus, even by Gentiles. The extension of eschatological blessing to the Gentiles is evident in both of these citations in their original contexts.

7.3 *Purpose*

Luke uses these four citations to legitimate the church's Gentile mission. Although the episode at Cornelius' house had demonstrated God's acceptance of Gentiles, Paul's appeal to Isa. 49.6 initiated an intentional programme of Gentile mission. James's appeal to Amos 9.11-12 settled the question of the conditions under which Gentiles were to be admitted to the people of God. The Gentile mission was not merely the result of rejection of the gospel by many Jews, but was a necessary consequence of the coming of the Messiah, Jesus. The ministry of the servant, the restoration of the kingdom, the fulfilment of the promised gift of the Spirit, and the promised blessing to Abraham all required the inclusion of Gentiles among the people of God.

These four citations are employed as 'proof from prophecy'. The characters in Luke's narrative encounter find themselves in uncharted territory. The citations are employed to explain the dramatic new developments in the fulfilment of God's purposes. The speakers (and the narrator) argue that these events are simply what God had promised long ago. What Paul and Barnabas do in turning to the Gentiles (Acts 13.47) is simply what God had announced through Isaiah (49.6). What Peter and Paul reported of Gentiles coming to faith (Acts 15.7-12) was confirmed in the prophecy of Amos (9.11-12). The outpouring of the Spirit at Pentecost was 'what was spoken by the prophet Joel' (Acts 2.16). And the extension of the blessing through Jesus to 'all the families of the earth' (Acts 3.26) is what God had promised long before to Abraham (Gen. 22.18). 'This is that', i.e. this is what God promised long before and those who accept the authority of the scriptures are expected to share this conclusion.

Luke's appeal to the OT is one of his narrative strategies. He legitimates the Gentile mission by finding divine sanction for it in the OT. The Gentile mission was a matter of some controversy and one about which his Gentile readers needed assurance. The survey of scripture summaries and explicit citations (Chapter 2) indicated that Gentiles and the Gentile mission are of considerable concern to Luke and his readers.

At the same time, Luke's argument does not rest upon appeal to scripture alone. The narrative of God's pouring out the Spirit on the household of Cornelius, the divinely directed (and successful) ministry of Paul to Gentiles, and the remarkable unity of the council in Jerusalem indicate God's blessing on the Gentile mission demanded by the OT. The use of appeals to the OT alongside other rhetorical strategies may be a fruitful avenue to pursue in the study of other OT citations in Luke–Acts and elsewhere in the NT.

The citation of Isa. 49.6 in Acts 13.47 marks a turning-point in the book of Acts. The chapter begins with the commissioning of Paul and Barnabas for a then unspecified 'work to which [God] called them' (13.2). The narrative subsequently confirms that this work is a mission to Gentiles. They initially preach in synagogues to Jews and 'Gentiles who worship God' (13.16), but when they encounter opposition there, they declare their intention to 'turn to the Gentiles' (13.46), appealing to Isa. 49.6 as a divine command addressed to them. The Isaianic servant experienced frustration and futility in his ministry to Israel, just as Paul and Barnabas now do; just as God gave the servant a broader ministry as light to the nations, so Paul and Barnabas have been sent by God to the Gentiles. Their subsequent ministry will be described chiefly in terms of response among Gentiles (God's having 'opened a door of faith to the Gentiles', 14.27), even as it continues to be 'to the Jew first' in every town Paul will visit. What Paul and Barnabas do in turning to the Gentiles is simply what God had announced through Isaiah. The appeal to Isa. 49.6 is thus an appeal to 'proof from prophecy'.

Although the mission of Acts 13–14 is not the direct cause of the controversy that led to the Jerusalem council in Acts 15, it is the narrative precursor to the council, and the account of the council three times mentions the success of that mission among the Gentiles (15.3, 4, 12). The citation of Isa. 49.6 in Acts 13.47 thus plays a pivotal role, not only demonstrating the necessity of an intentional mission to Gentiles, but in setting the stage for the final decision of the church regarding the way in which the Gentiles are to be included among the people of God. These three chapters (13–15) at the centre of Acts provide the definitive justification for the Gentile mission and the means of Gentile inclusion among the people of God.

The council in Acts 15 determined the conditions under which Gentiles are to be included among the people of God, i.e. by faith in Jesus alone (without circumcision or obedience to the ceremonial provisions of the law). The citation of Amos 9 by James appears to have played a decisive role in the council's decision. God's providential directing of Peter to the house of Cornelius, supplemented by accounts of 'what God had done through' Barnabas and Paul 'among the Gentiles' (15.12), is confirmed by James's appeal to the words of Amos. This is what God had said would happen – 'proof from prophecy'. At the same time, the citation is embedded in the narrative of the council, whose decision appears to have been endorsed by the Holy Spirit, and the larger narrative of Acts, which repeatedly underscores the divinely enabled success of the Gentile mission.

Likewise, Peter's citations of Joel 3 and Gen. 22.18 are both instances of 'proof from prophecy'. Neither is introduced explicitly for the purpose of legitimating the Gentile mission, but the language of both texts ('all flesh', 'everyone who calls', 'everyone God calls', 'all the families of the earth') in their original contexts and in the larger narrative of Acts anticipates that mission. While the implications of these citations for the Gentile mission are not developed at these early points in the narrative, Luke is writing (at least in part) for Gentile readers who could not help but read these in light of 'the rest of the story'. Their cumulative effect is to assure Gentile readers like Theophilus of their place in the promises, programme and people of God.

7.4 *Excursus: Jews, Gentiles and the People of God*

The important questions of God's 'rejection' of Jews and of the 'supersession' of Israel by the church[1] (understood as a Gentile entity) are beyond the scope of this study, but it is difficult to avoid reflecting briefly on them.

In Acts 13, a deliberate Gentile mission begins, following opposition from many Jews. Its justification, however, is not Jewish opposition but the mission given by God to his servant (Isa. 49.6). The servant's ministry as 'a light to the nations' was based on God's desire to honour his servant, not on rejection of Jews by God. In fact, the servant's mission explicitly includes the calling to 'raise up the tribes of Jacob and to restore the preserved of Israel'. The servant's calling to be 'a light to the nations' is an addition, not a substitution. The succeeding narrative makes clear that neither Paul nor Luke understood the Gentile mission as a rejection of the Jews. In city after city, Paul first seeks out the synagogue and preaches there. As in Pisidian Antioch (13.43), many believe, but many also oppose the message. When they do, Paul focuses his ministry on Gentiles. It is again and again 'to the Jew first and also to the Greek' (Rom. 1.16).

Likewise, the citation of Amos 9.11-12 does not support 'rejectionist' or 'supersessionist' readings. The centrepiece of God's eschatological work is the restoration of the Davidic kingdom, a kingdom in which Jews who believe in Jesus as the Messiah play the initial, foundational and central role. The church is 'built upon the foundation of the apostles and prophets' (Eph. 2.20), the former all Jews and the latter (the NT prophets) principally Jews. God restores his kingdom, however, so that the nations will seek the Lord and be called by his name. In the MT of Amos 9, the kingdom 'possesses' or conquers the Gentiles; they are not destroyed but are brought into the sphere of the blessings God pours out through his Messiah. In the Greek (LXX and NT), the kingdom is restored so that Gentiles may seek the Lord. In either case the Gentiles are described in terms normally applied to pious Israelites. The citation thus indicates that believing Gentiles are to be included among the people of God, not distinguished from them.[2] The church is not the home of a Gentile religion, but of all those who, through the promised Davidic Messiah, belong to the God of Israel, the creator of all.

This reading of the citation is supported by the larger context. Peter argues that God has now 'made no distinction between us [Jews] and them [Gentiles]' (15.9). God treats believing Gentiles just as he does Jews who believe in Jesus – he has 'cleansed their hearts by faith', making the ceremonial cleansing of circumcision unnecessary (15.9). Acts 15 applies to Gentiles language reminiscent of God's initial election and redemption of Israel ('signs and wonders', 15.12; 'take out of them a people for his name', 15.14). These are not indicators that God has rejected his people and started over (cf. Exod. 32.9-10), but that he has

---

1. Its very name, ἐκκλησία, is itself rich with OT associations. Edmund P. Clowney, *The Church* (Downers Grove, Ill.: InterVarsity, 2000), 30–32.

2. Craig A. Evans argues that the incorporation of the Gentiles 'is not at Israel's expense but to its glory (Luke 2.32)'. Evans, 'Prophecy and Polemic', 207.

extended Israel's election and blessing to believing Gentiles.[3] Just as the servant's mission in Isa. 49.6 is expanded, Israel's blessing is expanded, not revoked. Acts 15 does not describe the establishment of a rival people of God, but addresses the means of incorporation of believing Gentiles into the one people of God. The church does not replace Israel. In Acts, there remains one people of God.[4]

The earlier citations (Acts 2.17-21; 3.25) support this as well. The prophecy of Joel focused on Judah, but overflowed to 'all flesh'. God promised Abraham that he would bless him and his descendants, but again the blessing overflows as Abraham's blessing includes being the means by which God would bless the nations. In neither case are Jews 'left out'. The inclusion of Gentiles in these promises does not mean Israel's elimination. As Paul argues in Rom. 11.28, 'the gifts and the call of God are irrevocable'.

Yet for Luke, as for Paul, participation in the promised blessings requires faith in Jesus. This is not the mark of a Gentile religion. It is the gospel of God's Messiah, for Jews and Gentiles. God sent his servant to Jews 'first', even as he fulfilled the promise to Abraham to bless 'all the families of the earth' (Acts 3.25-26).[5] The church is still called to preach 'repentance and forgiveness of sins ... in his name to all nations' (Luke 24.47). And the promise remains that 'whoever calls on the name of the Lord shall be saved' (Acts 2.21). All who do, Jew or Gentile, belong by faith to the one people of God that extends throughout time and reaches to the ends of the earth.

---

3. Franklin, *Christ the Lord*, 125; Goppelt, *Typos*, 118.

4. 'Luke does not consider the Gentile Christians as the new Israel, disqualifying the historical people of God.' Sandt, 'Explanation', 92.

5. If Acts sadly records that many Jews rejected the good news about Jesus, it also relates that many Gentiles did as well (e.g. 16.20-24; 17.32; 19.23-41; 24.25-26). The preachers of Acts warn both Jews and Gentiles of the danger of unbelief (e.g. 13.40-41; 24.23-25). In judgement, as well as blessing, 'God shows no partiality' (10.46).

Appendix 1

Scripture Summaries in Luke–Acts

Underlined text indicates the general reference to the Old Testament. ***Bold italic*** text marks the content of the Old Testament teaching. References given in **bold** type indicate texts of particular clarity and importance.

Reference	RSV	Theme
Luke 1.68-75	Blessed be the Lord God of Israel, for he has visited and redeemed his people, and has raised up a horn of salvation for us in the house of his servant David, <u>as he spoke by the mouth of his holy prophets from of old,</u> that we should be saved from our enemies, and from the hand of all who hate us; <u>to perform the mercy promised to our fathers, and to remember his holy covenant, the oath which he swore to our father Abraham,</u> to grant us that we, being delivered from the hand of our enemies, might serve him without fear, in holiness and righteousness before him all the days of our life.	Eschatological blessing
Luke 18.31-33	And taking the twelve, he said to them, 'Behold, we are going up to Jerusalem, and <u>everything that is written of the Son of man by the prophets will be accomplished.</u> ***For he will be delivered to the Gentiles, and will be mocked and shamefully treated and spit upon; they will scourge him and kill him, and on the third day he will rise.***'	Christology (suffering, death, resurrection) Rejection
Luke 21.20-24	But when you see ***Jerusalem surrounded by armies***, then know that ***its desolation has come near***. Then let those who are in Judea flee to the mountains, and let those who are inside the city depart, and let not those who are out in the country enter it; for these are ***days of vengeance***, <u>to fulfil all that is written.</u> Alas for those who are with child and for those who give suck in those days! For ***great distress shall be upon the earth and wrath upon this people; they will fall by the edge of the sword, and be led captive among all nations; and Jerusalem will be trodden down by the Gentiles, until the times of the Gentiles are fulfilled.***	Judgement
Luke 24.25-27	And he said to them, 'O foolish men, and slow of heart to believe <u>all that the prophets have spoken!</u> Was it not ***necessary that the Christ should suffer these things and enter into his glory***?' And <u>beginning with Moses and all the prophets, he interpreted to them in all the scriptures the things concerning himself.</u>	Christology (suffering, glorification)
Luke 24.44-49	Then he said to them, 'These are my words which I spoke to you, while I was still with you, that <u>everything written about me in the law of Moses and the prophets and the psalms must be fulfilled.</u>' Then he opened their minds to understand the scriptures, and said to them, '<u>Thus it is written,</u> that ***the Christ should suffer and on the third day rise from the dead, and that repentance and forgiveness of sins should be preached in his name to all nations, beginning from Jerusalem. You are witnesses of these things. And behold, I send the promise of my Father upon you; but stay in the city, until you are clothed with power from on high.***'	Christology (suffering, death, resurrection) Proclamation

Reference	RSV	Theme
Acts 3.18-26	But <u>what God foretold by the mouth of all the prophets</u>, that his ***Christ should suffer***, <u>he thus fulfilled</u>. Repent therefore, and turn again, that your sins may be blotted out, that times of refreshing may come from the presence of the Lord, and that he may send the Christ appointed for you, Jesus, whom heaven must receive until the time for establishing <u>all that God spoke by the mouth of his holy prophets from of old</u>. Moses said, '***The Lord God will raise up for you a prophet from your brethren as he raised me up. You shall listen to him in whatever he tells you. And it shall be that every soul that does not listen to that prophet shall be destroyed from the people*****.' And <u>all the prophets who have spoken, from Samuel and those who came afterwards</u>, also proclaimed *these days*. You are the sons of the prophets and of the covenant which God gave to your fathers, saying to Abraham, 'And in your posterity shall all the families of the earth be blessed.' *God, having raised up his servant, sent him to you first, to bless you in turning every one of you from your wickedness.*	Christology (suffering) Eschatological blessing Judgement
Acts 7.52	Which of <u>the prophets</u> did not your fathers persecute? And they killed <u>those who announced beforehand</u> *the coming of the Righteous One*, whom you have now betrayed and murdered.	Rejection Christology (the Righteous One)
Acts 10.43	To him <u>all the prophets bear witness</u> that every one who believes in him receives forgiveness of sins through his name.	Proclamation
Acts 13.27-29	For those who live in Jerusalem and their rulers, because they did not recognize him nor understand <u>the utterances of the prophets which are read every sabbath</u>, fulfilled these by *condemning him*. Though they could charge him with nothing deserving death, yet they asked Pilate to *have him killed*. And when they had fulfilled <u>all that was written of him</u>, they took him down from the tree, and laid him in a tomb.	Christology (death) Rejection
Acts 17.2-3	And Paul went in, as was his custom, and for three weeks he argued with them from <u>the scriptures</u>, explaining and proving that *it was necessary for the Christ to suffer and to rise from the dead*, and saying, '*This Jesus*, whom I proclaim to you, *is the Christ*.'	Christology (suffering, resurrection, the Christ)
Acts 18.28	for he [Apollos] powerfully confuted the Jews in public, showing by <u>the scriptures</u> that *the Christ was Jesus*.	Christology (the Christ)
Acts 24.14-15	But this I admit to you, that according to the Way, which they call a sect, I worship the God of our fathers, believing <u>everything laid down by the law or written in the prophets</u>, having *a hope in God* which these themselves accept, that *there will be a resurrection of both the just and the unjust.*	Eschatological blessing
Acts 26.22-23	To this day I have had the help that comes from God, and so I stand here testifying both to small and great, saying nothing but <u>what the prophets and Moses said would come to pass</u>: that *the Christ must suffer, and that, by being the first to rise from the dead, he would proclaim light both to the people and to the Gentiles*.	Christology (suffering, death, resurrection) Proclamation
Acts 28.23	When they had appointed a day for him, they came to him at his lodging in great numbers. And he expounded the matter to them from morning till evening, testifying to *the kingdom of God* and trying to convince them *about Jesus* <u>both from the law of Moses and from the prophets</u>.	Eschatological blessing Christology

Appendix 2

EXPLICIT OLD TESTAMENT CITATIONS IN LUKE–ACTS

Bold italics indicates the text cited from the Old Testament. <u>Underlining</u> indicates the use of an introductory formula.

* indicates a text marked as a citation only in NA[27]; ° indicates a text marked as a citation only in UBS[4].

Key to Prophetic texts: C = Christological, J = Judgement, R = Rejection, S = Soteriological, U = Universal.

Luke–Acts	Source	RSV	Use
Luke 1.15*	Num. 6.3; Lev. 10.9	for he will be great before the Lord, and *he shall drink no wine nor strong drink*, and he will be filled with the Holy Spirit, even from his mother's womb.	Legal
<u>Luke 2.23</u>	Exod. 13.2, 12, 15	(<u>as it is written in the law of the Lord,</u> '*Every male that opens the womb shall be called holy to the Lord*')	Legal
<u>Luke 2.24</u>	Lev. 5.11*; 12.8	and to offer a sacrifice <u>according to what is said in the law of the Lord,</u> '*a pair of turtledoves, or two young pigeons.*'	Legal
<u>Luke 3.4-6</u>	Isa. 40.3-5	<u>As it is written in the book of the words of Isaiah the prophet,</u> '*The voice of one crying in the wilderness: Prepare the way of the Lord, make his paths straight. Every valley shall be filled, and every mountain and hill shall be brought low, and the crooked shall be made straight, and the rough ways shall be made smooth; and all flesh shall see the salvation of God.*'	Prophetic (S) Prophetic (J) Prophetic (U)
<u>Luke 4.4</u>	Deut. 8.3	And Jesus answered him, '<u>It is written,</u> "*Man shall not live by bread alone.*"'	Legal
<u>Luke 4.8</u>	Deut. 6.13; 10.20*	And Jesus answered him, '<u>It is written,</u> "*You shall worship the Lord your God, and him only shall you serve.*"'	Legal
<u>Luke 4.10-11</u>	Ps. 91.11-12	for <u>it is written,</u> '*He will give his angels charge of you, to guard you,*' and '*On their hands they will bear you up, lest you strike your foot against a stone.*''	Other
<u>Luke 4.12</u>	Deut. 6.16	And Jesus answered him, '<u>It is said,</u> "*You shall not tempt the Lord your God.*"'	Legal
<u>Luke 4.17-19</u>	Isa. 61.1-2; Isa. 58.6	and there was given to him <u>the book of the prophet Isaiah.</u> He opened the book and found the place where <u>it was written,</u> '*The Spirit of the Lord is upon me, because he has anointed me to preach good news to the poor. He has sent me to proclaim release to the captives and recovering of sight to the blind, to set at liberty those who are oppressed, to proclaim the acceptable year of the Lord.*'	Prophetic (C) Prophetic (S)
Luke 7.22*	Isa. 29.18*; 35.5*; 42.18*; 26.19*	And he answered them, 'Go and tell John what you have seen and heard: *the blind receive their sight*, the lame walk, lepers are cleansed, and *the deaf hear, the dead are raised up*, the poor have good news preached to them.'	Prophetic (S)

Luke–Acts	Source	RSV	Use
<u>Luke 7.27</u>	Mal. 3.1; cf. Exod. 23.20	<u>This is he of whom it is written</u>, '***Behold, I send my messenger before thy face, who shall prepare thy way*** before thee.'	Prophetic (S)
Luke 8.10°	Isa. 6.9	he said, 'To you it has been given to know the secrets of the kingdom of God; but for others they are in parables, so that ***seeing they may not see, and hearing they may not understand.'***	Prophetic (J) Prophetic (R)
Luke 9.54•	2 Kgs. 1.10, 12	And when his disciples James and John saw it, they said, 'Lord, do you want us to ***bid fire come down from heaven and consume them?'***	Other
<u>Luke 10.26-27</u>	Deut. 6.5	He said to him, '<u>What is written in the law?</u> How do you read?' And he answered, '***You shall love the Lord your God with all your heart, and with all your soul, and with all your strength, and with all your mind.'***	Legal
<u>Luke 10.27</u>	Lev. 19.18	'and ***your neighbor as yourself.'***	Legal
Luke 12.35•	Exod. 12.11	'***Let your loins be girded*** and your lamps burning.'	Legal
Luke 12.53•	Mic. 7.6	they will be divided, father against son and ***son*** against ***father***, mother against daughter and ***daughter against her mother***, mother-in-law against her daughter-in-law and ***daughter-in-law against her mother-in-law.***	Prophetic (J) Prophetic (R)
Luke 13.19•	Ps. 104.12 [103.12 LXX]	It is like a grain of mustard seed which a man took and sowed in his garden; and it grew and became a tree, and ***the birds of the air made nests in its branches.***	Other or Prophetic (S)
Luke 13.27•	Ps. 6.8 [6.9 MT, LXX]	But he will say, 'I tell you, I do not know where you come from; ***depart from me, all you workers of iniquity!'***	Prophetic (J) Prophetic (R)
Luke 13.35	Ps. 118.26	Behold, your house is forsaken. And I tell you, you will not see me until you say, '***Blessed is he who comes in the name of the Lord!'***	Prophetic (C)
<u>Luke 18.20</u>	Exod. 20.12-16; Deut. 5.16-20	You know <u>the commandments</u>: '***Do not commit adultery, Do not kill, Do not steal, Do not bear false witness, Honor your father and mother.'***	Legal
Luke 19.38	Ps. 118.26	saying, '***Blessed is*** the King ***who comes in the name of the Lord!*** Peace in heaven and glory in the highest!'	Prophetic (C)
<u>Luke 19.46</u>	Isa. 56.7	saying to them, '<u>It is written</u>, "***My house shall be a house of prayer*** ".'	Prophetic (S)
<u>Luke 19.46</u>•	Jer. 7.11	'but you have made it a ***den of robbers.'***	Prophetic (J)
<u>Luke 20.17</u>	Ps. 118.22	But he looked at them and said, '<u>What then is this that is written</u>: "***The very stone which the builders rejected has become the head of the corner***"?'	Prophetic (C)
<u>Luke 20.28</u>	Deut. 25.5	and they asked him a question, saying, 'Teacher, <u>Moses wrote for us that</u> ***if a man's brother dies***, having a wife but ***no children, the man must take the wife and raise up children for his brother.'***	Legal
<u>Luke 20.37</u>	Exod. 3.6	But that the dead are raised, even <u>Moses</u> showed, <u>in the passage about the bush</u>, where he <u>calls</u> ***the Lord the God of Abraham and the God of Isaac and the God of Jacob.***	Doctrinal
<u>Luke 20.42-43</u>	Ps. 110.1	For <u>David himself says in the Book of Psalms</u>, '***The Lord said to my Lord, Sit at my right hand, till I make thy enemies a stool for thy feet.'***	Prophetic (C) Prophetic (J)

Luke–Acts	Source	RSV	Use
Luke 21.26*	Isa. 34.4	men fainting with fear and with foreboding of what is coming on the world; for *the powers of the heavens* will be shaken.	Prophetic (J)
Luke 21.27	Dan 7.13, 14*	And then they will see *the Son of man coming in a cloud* with power and great glory.	Prophetic (C)
Luke 22.37	Isa. 53.12	For I tell you that this <u>scripture must be fulfilled</u> in me, '*And he was reckoned with transgressors*'; for what is written about me has its fulfilment.	Prophetic (C)
Luke 22.69°	Ps. 110.1	But from now on *the Son of man shall be seated at the right hand of the power of God.*	Prophetic (C)
Luke 23.30	Hos. 10.8	Then they will begin *to say to the mountains, 'Fall on us'; and to the hills, 'Cover us.'*	Prophetic (J)
			Prophetic (R)
Luke 23.34*	Ps. 22.19	And Jesus said, 'Father, forgive them; for they know not what they do.' *And they cast lots to divide his garments.*	Prophetic (C)
Luke 23.46	Ps. 31.5 [31.6 MT; 30.6 LXX]	Then Jesus, crying with a loud voice, said, 'Father, *into thy hands I commit my spirit!*' And having said this he breathed his last.	Prophetic (C)
Acts 1.20	Ps. 69.25 [69.26 MT; 68.26 LXX]	For <u>it is written in the book of Psalms</u>, '*Let his habitation become desolate, and let there be no one to live in it*';	Prophetic (J)
Acts 1.20	Ps. 109.8	and '*His office let another take.*'	Prophetic (J)
Acts 2.16-21	Joel 3.1-5 MT [Engl. 2.28-32]	but <u>this is what was spoken by the prophet Joel</u>: 'And in the last days *it shall be*, God declares, that *I will pour out my Spirit upon all flesh, and your sons and your daughters shall prophesy, and your young men shall see visions, and your old men shall dream dreams; yea, and on my menservants and my maidservants in those days I will pour out my Spirit; and they shall prophesy. And I will show wonders in the heaven above and signs on the earth beneath, blood, and fire, and vapor of smoke; the sun shall be turned into darkness and the moon into blood, before the day of the Lord comes, the great and manifest day. And it shall be that whoever calls on the name of the Lord shall be saved.*'	Prophetic (S) Prophetic (J) Prophetic (U)
Acts 2.25-28	Ps. 16.8-11 [15.8-11 LXX]	For <u>David says</u> concerning him, '*I saw the Lord always before me, for he is at my right hand that I may not be shaken; therefore my heart was glad, and my tongue rejoiced; moreover my flesh will dwell in hope. For thou wilt not abandon my soul to Hades, nor let thy Holy One see corruption. Thou hast made known to me the ways of life; thou wilt make me full of gladness with thy presence.*'	Prophetic (C)
Acts 2.30°	Ps. 132.11	Being therefore a prophet, and knowing that God *had sworn* with an oath *to him that he would set one of his descendants upon his throne.*	Prophetic (C)
Acts 2.31°	Ps. 16.10	<u>he foresaw and spoke</u> of the resurrection of the Christ, that *he was not abandoned to Hades, nor did* his flesh *see corruption.*	Prophetic (C)
Acts 2.34-35	Ps. 110.1 [109.1 LXX]	For <u>David</u> did not ascend into the heavens; but <u>he himself says</u>, '*The Lord said to my Lord, Sit at my right hand, till I make thy enemies a stool for thy feet.*'	Prophetic (C)

Luke–Acts	Source	RSV	Use
Acts 3.13	Exod. 3.6	*The God of Abraham and of Isaac and of Jacob, the God of our fathers*, glorified his servant Jesus, whom you delivered up and denied in the presence of Pilate, when he had decided to release him.	Doctrinal
Acts 3.22	Deut. 18.15-16	Moses said, '*The Lord God will raise up for you a prophet from your brethren as he raised me up. You shall listen to him in whatever he tells* you.'	Prophetic (C)
Acts 3.23	Deut. 18.19	*And it shall be that every soul that does not listen to that prophet*	Prophetic (J)
Acts 3.23	Lev. 23.29	*shall be destroyed from the people.*	Prophetic (J)
			Prophetic (R)
Acts 3.25	Gen. 22.18; 26.4	You are the sons of the prophets and of the covenant which God gave to your fathers, saying to Abraham, '*And in your posterity shall all the families of the earth be blessed.*'	Prophetic (S)
			Prophetic (U)
Acts 4.11°	Ps. 118.22	This is *the stone which was rejected by* you *builders, but which has become the head of the corner.*	Prophetic (C)
			Prophetic (R)
Acts 4.24•	Exod. 20.11; Ps. 146.6; see also 2 Kgs. 19.15 ‖ Isa. 37.16; Neh. 9.6	And when they heard it, they lifted their voices together to God and said, 'Sovereign Lord, *who didst make the heaven and the earth and the sea and everything in them*'	Doctrinal
Acts 4.25-26	Ps. 2.1–2	'who by the mouth of our father David, thy servant, didst say by the Holy Spirit, "*Why did the Gentiles rage, and the peoples imagine vain things? The kings of the earth set themselves in array, and the rulers were gathered together, against the Lord and against his Anointed*"'	Prophetic (J)
			Prophetic (R)
Acts 7.3	Gen. 12.1	and said to him, '*Depart from your land and from your kindred and go into the land which I will show you.*'	Historical
Acts 7.5	Gen. 17.8; 48.4	yet he gave him no inheritance in it, not even a foot's length, but promised *to give it to him in possession and to his posterity after him*, though he had no child.	Historical
Acts 7.6-7	Gen. 15.13-14; Exod. 2.22•	And God spoke to this effect, that *his posterity would be aliens in a land belonging to others, who would enslave them and ill-treat them four hundred years. 'But I will judge the nation which they serve,*' said God, '*and after that they shall come out*'	Historical
Acts 7.7°	Exod. 3.12	'and *worship me in this place.*'	Historical
Acts 7.18	Exod. 1.8	till *there arose over Egypt another king who had not known Joseph.*	Historical
Acts 7.27-28	Exod. 2.14	But the man who was wronging his neighbor thrust him aside, saying, '*Who made you a ruler and a judge over us? Do you want to kill me as you killed the Egyptian yesterday?*'	Historical
Acts 7.30°	Exod. 3.2	Now when forty years had passed, *an angel appeared to him* in the wilderness of Mount Sinai, *in a flame of fire in a bush.*	Historical
Acts 7.31-32	Exod. 3.6	When Moses saw it he wondered at the sight; and as he drew near to look, the voice of the Lord came, '*I am the God of your fathers, the God of Abraham and of Isaac and of Jacob.*' And Moses trembled and did not dare to look.	Historical

Luke–Acts	Source	RSV	Use
Acts 7.33	Exod. 3.5	And the Lord said to him, '*Take off the shoes from your feet, for the place where you are standing is holy ground.*'	Historical
Acts 7.34	Exod. 3.7-8, 10	*I have surely seen the ill-treatment of my people that are in Egypt and heard their groaning, and I have come down to deliver them. And now come, I will send you to Egypt.*	Historical
Acts 7.35	Exod. 2.14	This Moses whom they refused, saying, '*Who made you a ruler and a judge?*' God sent as both ruler and deliverer by the hand of the angel that appeared to him in the bush.	Historical
Acts 7.37	Deut. 18.15	This is the Moses who said to the Israelites, '*God will raise up for you a prophet from your brethren as he raised me up.*'	Historical
Acts 7.40	Exod. 32.1, 23	saying to Aaron, '*Make for us gods to go before us; as for this Moses who led us out from the land of Egypt, we do not know what has become of him.*'	Historical
Acts 7.42-43	Amos 5.25-27	But God turned and gave them over to worship the host of heaven, as it is written in the book of the prophets: '*Did you offer to me slain beasts and sacrifices, forty years in the wilderness, O house of Israel? And you took up the tent of Moloch, and the star of the god Rephan, the figures which you made to worship; and I will remove you beyond Babylon.*'	Historical
Acts 7.49-50	Isa. 66.1-2	Yet the Most High does not dwell in houses made with hands; as the prophet says, '*Heaven is my throne, and earth my footstool. What house will you build for me, says the Lord, or what is the place of my rest? Did not my hand make all these things?*'	Historical
Acts 8.32-33	Isa. 53.7-8	Now the passage of the scripture which he was reading was this: '*As a sheep led to the slaughter or a lamb before its shearer is dumb, so he opens not his mouth. In his humiliation justice was denied him. Who can describe his generation? For his life is taken up from the earth.*'	Prophetic (C)
Acts 13.22°	Ps. 89.20	And when he had removed him, he raised up David to be their king; of whom he testified and said, '*I have found in David the son of Jesse*'	Historical
Acts 13.22°	1 Sam 13.14	'*a man after my heart*, who will do all my will.'	Historical
Acts 13.33	Ps. 2.7	this he has fulfilled to us their children by raising Jesus; as also it is written in the second psalm, '*Thou art my Son, today I have begotten thee.*'	Prophetic (C)
Acts 13.34	Isa. 55.3	And as for the fact that he raised him from the dead, no more to return to corruption, he spoke in this way, 'I will give *you the holy and sure blessings of David.*'	Prophetic (C)
Acts 13.35	Ps. 16.10	Therefore he says also in another psalm, '*Thou wilt not let thy Holy One see corruption.*'	Prophetic (C)
Acts 13.40-41	Hab. 1.5	Beware, therefore, lest there come upon you what is said in the prophets: '*Behold, you scoffers, and wonder, and perish; for I do a deed in your days, a deed you will never believe, if one declares it to you.*'	Prophetic (J) Prophetic (R)
Acts 13.47	Isa. 49.6	For so the Lord has commanded us, saying, '*I have set you to be a light for the Gentiles, that you may bring salvation to the uttermost parts of the earth.*'	Prophetic (U)

Luke–Acts	Source	RSV	Use
Acts 14.15*	Exod. 20.11; Ps. 146.6	Men, why are you doing this? We also are men, of like nature with you, and bring you good news, that you should turn from these vain things to a living God *who made the heaven and the earth and the sea and all that is in them.*	Doctrinal
Acts 15.15-17	Amos 9.11-12	And with this <u>the words of the prophets agree, as it is written,</u> '*After this I will return, and I will rebuild the dwelling of David, which has fallen; I will rebuild its ruins, and I will set it up, that the rest of men may seek the Lord, and all the Gentiles who are called by my name, says the Lord, who has made these things.*'	Prophetic (S) Prophetic (U)
Acts 15.18*	Isa. 45.21	*known from of old.*	Prophetic (S)
Acts 23.5	Exod. 22.28 [22.27 MT, LXX]	And Paul said, 'I did not know, brethren, that he was the high priest; for <u>it is written,</u> "*You shall not speak evil of a ruler of your people.*"'	Legal
Acts 28.25-27	Isa. 6.9–10	So, as they disagreed among themselves, they departed, after Paul had made one statement: 'The <u>Holy Spirit was right in saying to your fathers through Isaiah the prophet</u>: "*Go to this people, and say, You shall indeed hear but never understand, and you shall indeed see but never perceive. For this people's heart has grown dull, and their ears are heavy of hearing, and their eyes they have closed; lest they should perceive with their eyes, and hear with their ears, and understand with their heart, and turn for me to heal them.*" Let it be known to you then that this salvation of God has been sent to the Gentiles; they will listen.'	Prophetic (J) Prophetic (R)

BIBLIOGRAPHY

Aalders, Gerhard Ch. *Genesis*. 2 vols. Bible Student's Commentary. Grand Rapids: Zondervan, 1981.

Abegg, Martin, Jr., et al. *The Dead Sea Scrolls Bible*. New York: HarperCollins, 1999.

Accordance, version 6.9.2. Altamonte Springs, Fla.: Oak Tree Software, 2006.

Achtemeier, Elizabeth. 'The Book of Joel: Introduction, Commentary, and Reflections'. Pages 299–336 in vol. 7 of *The New Interpreter's Bible*. Nashville: Abingdon, 1996.

Ådna, Jostein. 'Die Heilige Schrift als Zeuge der Heidenmission: Die Rezeption von Amos 9,11-12 in Apg 15,16-18'. Pages 1–23 in *Evangelium, Schriftauslegung, Kirche*. Edited by Jostein Ådna, Scott J. Hafemann and Otfried Hofius. Göttingen: Vandenhoeck & Ruprecht, 1997.

——. 'James' Position at the Summit Meeting of the Apostles and Elders in Jerusalem (Acts 15)'. Pages 125–61 in *The Mission of the Early Church to Jews and Gentiles*. Edited by Jostein Ådna and Hans Kvalbein. Tübingen: Mohr Siebeck, 2000.

Aland, Barbara, et al., eds. *The Greek New Testament*. 4th rev. edn. Stuttgart: Deutsche Bibelgesellschaft, 1993.

——, eds. *Novum Testamentum Graece*. 27th rev. edn. Stuttgart: Deutsche Bibelgesellschaft, 1993.

Aldrich, Willard M. 'The Interpretation of Acts 15:13-18'. *BSac* 111 (1954): 317–23.

Alexander, Desmond. 'Further Observations on the "Seed" in Genesis'. *TynBul* 48 (1997): 363–67.

Alexander, Joseph Addison. *Commentary on the Acts of the Apostles*. 3rd edn. New York: Scribner, Armstrong & Co., 1875. Reprint, Grand Rapids: Zondervan, 1956.

——. *Commentary on the Prophecies of Isaiah*. New and rev. edn. 2 vols. New York: Charles Scribner's Sons, 1865.

Alexander, Loveday. *The Preface to Luke's Gospel: Literary Convention and Social Context in Luke 1.1-4 and Acts 1.1*. Society for New Testament Studies Monograph Series. Cambridge: Cambridge University Press, 1993.

Allen, Leslie C. *The Books of Joel, Obadiah, Jonah, and Micah*. New International Commentary on the Old Testament. Grand Rapids: Eerdmans, 1976.

Allis, Oswald T. 'The Blessing of Abraham'. *PTR* 25 (1927): 263–98.

——. *The Unity of Isaiah: A Study in Prophecy*. Philadelphia: Presbyterian and Reformed, 1950.

Amsler, Samuel. *L'Ancien Testament dans l'Eglise: Essai d'herméneutique chrétienne*. Neuchâtel: Delachaux & Niestlé, 1960.

——. *David, Roi et Messie: La tradition davidique dans l'Ancien Testament*. Cahier Théologiques 49. Neuchâtel: Delachaux & Niestlé, 1963.

Andersen, Francis I. and David Noel Freedman. *Amos: A New Translation with Introduction and Commentary*. Anchor Bible 24A. New York: Doubleday, 1989.

Archer, Gleason L. and Gregory Chirichingo. *Old Testament Quotations in the New Testament*. Chicago: Moody, 1983.

Aune, David E. *The New Testament in Its Literary Environment*. Edited by Wayne A. Meeks. Library of Early Christianity. Philadelphia: Westminster, 1987.

Baldwin, Joyce. *Haggai, Zechariah, Malachi: An Introduction and Commentary*. Tyndale Old Testament Commentaries. Downers Grove, Ill.: Inter-Varsity, 1972.

Baltzer, Klaus. *Deutero-Isaiah: A Commentary on Isaiah 40–55*. Translated by Margaret Kohl. Hermeneia. Minneapolis: Fortress Press, 2001.

Barrett, Charles K. *A Critical and Exegetical Commentary on the Acts of the Apostles*. 2 vols. International Critical Commentary. Edinburgh: T&T Clark, 1994–98.

——. 'The Gentile Mission as an Eschatological Phenomenon'. Pages 65–75 in *Eschatology and the New Testament: Essays in Honor of George Raymond Beasley-Murray*. Edited by W. Hulitt Gloer. Peabody, Mass.: Hendrickson, 1988.

——. 'Luke/Acts'. Pages 231–44 in *It Is Written: Scripture Citing Scripture*. Edited by Donald A. Carson and Hugh G. M. Williamson. Cambridge: Cambridge University Press, 1988.

Barstad, Hans M. 'The Future of the "Servant Songs": Some Reflections on the Relationship of Biblical Scholarship to Its Own Tradition'. Pages 261–70 in *Language, Theology, and the Bible: Essays in Honour of James Barr*. Edited by Samuel E. Balentine and John Barton. Oxford: Clarendon, 1994.

Barth, Markus. *Ephesians: A New Translation with Introduction and Commentary*. 2 vols. Anchor Bible 34–34A. New York: Doubleday, 1974.

Bassler, Jouette M. 'A Man for All Seasons: David in Rabbinic and New Testament Literature'. *Int* 40 (1986): 156–69.

Bauckham, Richard. 'James and the Gentiles (Acts 15.13-21)'. Pages 154–84 in *History, Literature, and Society in the Book of Acts*. Edited by Ben Witherington III. Cambridge: Cambridge University Press, 1996.

——. 'James and the Jerusalem Church'. Pages 415–80 in *The Book of Acts in Its Palestinian Setting*. Edited by Richard Bauckham. Grand Rapids: Eerdmans, 1995.

Bayer, Hans F. 'Christ-Centered Eschatology in Acts 3:17-26'. Pages 236–50 in *Jesus of Nazareth: Lord and Christ. Essays on the Historical Jesus and New Testament Christology*. Edited by Joel B. Green and Max Turner. Grand Rapids: Eerdmans, 1994.

——. 'The Preaching of Peter in Acts'. Pages 257–74 in *Witness to the Gospel: The Theology of Acts*. Edited by Ian Howard Marshall and David Peterson. Grand Rapids: Eerdmans, 1998.

Beale, Gregg K. and D. A. Carson, eds. *Commentary on the New Testament Use of the Old Testament*. Grand Rapids: Baker Academic, 2007.

Benoît, Pierre, et al. *Les grottes de Murabba'at*. 2 vols. Discoveries in the Judean Desert II. Oxford: Clarendon, 1961.

Benson, Alphonsus. '"… From the Mouth of the Lion": The Messianism of Amos'. *CBQ* 19 (1957): 199–212.

Bewer, Julius A. 'Commentary on Joel'. Pages 47–144 (part 2) in *A Critical and Exegetical Commentary on Micah, Zephaniah, Nahum, Habakkuk, Obadiah and Joel*. International Critical Commentary. Edinburgh: T&T Clark, 1911.

Blass, Friedrich, et al. *A Greek Grammar of the New Testament and Other Early Christian Literature*. Chicago: University of Chicago Press, 1961.

Blocher, Henri. *Songs of the Servant*. Downers Grove, Ill.: Inter-Varsity, 1975.

Bock, Darrell L. *Acts*. Baker Exegetical Commentary on the New Testament. Grand Rapids: Baker Academic, 2007.

——. 'Evangelicals and the Use of the Old Testament in the New: Parts 1 and 2'. *BSac* 142 (1985): 209–23, 306–19.

——. *Luke*. 2 vols. Baker Exegetical Commentary on the New Testament 3. Grand Rapids: Baker, 1994–96.

——. *Proclamation from Prophecy and Pattern: Lucan Old Testament Christology*. Journal for the Study of the New Testament Supplement Series 12. Sheffield: Sheffield Academic Press, 1987.

——. 'Proclamation from Prophecy and Pattern: Luke's Use of the Old Testament for Christology and Mission'. Pages 280–307 in *The Gospels and the Scriptures of Israel*. Edited by Craig A. Evans and William Richard Stegner. Journal for the Study of the New Testament Supplement Series 104. Sheffield: Sheffield Academic Press, 1994.

——. 'Scripture and the Realization of God's Promises'. Pages 41–62 in *Witness to the Gospel*. Edited by Ian Howard Marshall and David Peterson. Grand Rapids: Eerdmans, 1998.

——. 'The Use of the Old Testament in Luke–Acts: Christology and Mission'. Pages 494–511 in *Society of Biblical Literature Seminar Papers, 1990*. Edited by Edward J. Lull. Atlanta: Scholars Press, 1990.

——. 'Use of the Old Testament in the New'. Pages 97–114 in *Foundations for Biblical Interpretation*. Edited by David S. Dockery, K. A. Mathews and Robert Bryan Sloan. Nashville: Broadman & Holman, 1994.

Boer, Harry R. *Pentecost and Missions*. Grand Rapids: Eerdmans, 1961.

Bolt, Peter G. 'Mission and Witness'. Pages 191–214 in *Witness to the Gospel: The Theology of Acts*. Edited by Ian Howard Marshall and David Peterson. Grand Rapids: Eerdmans, 1998.

Botterweck, G. Johannes and Helmer Ringgren, eds. *Theological Dictionary of the Old Testament*. Translated by John T. Willis, Geoffrey W. Bromiley, David E. Green and Douglas W. Stott. 15 vols. Grand Rapids: Eerdmans, 1974–.

Bovon, François. *Luke the Theologian: Thirty-Three Years of Research (1950–1983)*. Translated by Ken McKinney. Allison Park, Pa.: Pickwick Publications, 1987.

Bowker, J. W. 'Speeches in Acts: A Study in Proem and Yelammedenu Form'. *NTS* 14 (1967): 96–111.

Bratcher, Robert G. *Old Testament Quotations in the New Testament*. 3rd rev. edn. Helps for Translators 3. London: United Bible Societies, 1987.

Braun, Michael A. 'James' Use of Amos at the Jerusalem Council: Steps toward a Possible Solution of the Textual and Theological Problems'. *JETS* 20 (1977): 113–21.

Brawley, Robert L. 'Abrahamic Traditions and the Characterization of God in Luke–Acts'. Pages 109–32 in *The Unity of Luke–Acts*. Edited by Jozef Verheyden. Bibliotheca Ephemeridum theologicarum Lovaniensium 142. Leuven: Leuven University Press, 1999.

——. *Luke–Acts and the Jews*. Society of Biblical Literature Monograph Series 33. Atlanta: Scholars Press, 1987.

——. *Text to Text Pours Forth Speech: Voices of Scripture in Luke–Acts*. Edited by Herbert Marks and Robert Polzin. Indiana Studies in Biblical Literature. Bloomington: Indiana University Press, 1995.

Bright, John. *A History of Israel*. Philadelphia: Westminster, 1972.

——. 'Isaiah—I'. Pages 489–515 in *Peake's Commentary on the Bible*. Edited by Matthew Black. Sunbury-on-Thames: Thomas Nelson, 1962.

——. *The Kingdom of God: The Biblical Concept and Its Meaning for the Church*. Nashville: Abingdon, 1953.

Brooke, Alan E. and Norman McLean, eds. *Genesis*. Vol. 1:1. *The Old Testament in Greek according to the Text of Codex Vaticanus, Supplemented from Other Uncial Manuscripts, with a Critical Apparatus Containing the Variants of the Chief Ancient Authorities for the Text of the Septuagint*. Cambridge: Cambridge University Press, 1906.

Brooke, George J. *Exegesis at Qumran: 4QFlorilegium in Its Jewish Context*. Journal for the Study of the Old Testament Supplement Series 29. Sheffield: JSOT Press, 1985.

Brown, Colin, ed. *The New International Dictionary of New Testament Theology*. 4 vols. Grand Rapids: Zondervan, 1975–85.

Brown, Francis, et al. *A Hebrew and English Lexicon of the Old Testament*. Corrected edn. Oxford: Clarendon, 1972.

Brown, Raymond E. *The Birth of the Messiah: A Commentary on the Infancy Narratives in the Gospels of Matthew and Luke*. New updated edn. New York: Doubleday, 1993.

Bruce, Frederick F. *The Acts of the Apostles: The Greek Text with Introduction and Commentary*. 3rd rev. and enl. edn. Grand Rapids: Eerdmans, 1990.

——. *The Book of the Acts*. Rev. edn. New International Commentary on the New Testament. Grand Rapids: Eerdmans, 1988.

——. *Commentary on the Book of the Acts: The English Text with Introduction, Exposition and Notes*. New International Commentary on the New Testament. Grand Rapids: Eerdmans, 1954.

——. *The Defense of the Gospel in the New Testament*. Grand Rapids: Eerdmans, 1977.

——. *The Epistle to the Galatians: A Commentary on the Greek Text*. New International Greek Testament Commentary. Grand Rapids: Eerdmans, 1982.

——. 'Eschatology in Acts'. Pages 51–63 in *Eschatology and the New Testament: Essays in Honor of George Raymond Beasley-Murray*. Edited by W. Hulitt Gloer. Peabody, Mass.: Hendrickson, 1988.

——. *Paul: Apostle of the Heart Set Free*. Grand Rapids: Eerdmans, 1977.

——. 'Paul's Use of the Old Testament in Acts'. Pages 71–79 in *Tradition and Interpretation in the New Testament*. Edited by Gerald F. Hawthorne and Otto Betz. Grand Rapids: Eerdmans, 1987.

——. *Peter, Stephen, James and John: Studies in Early Non-Pauline Christianity*. Grand Rapids: Eerdmans, 1979.

——. 'Prophetic Interpretation in the Septuagint'. *BIOSCS* 12 (1979): 17–26.

——. *The Speeches in the Acts of the Apostles*. London: Tyndale Press, 1942.

Brueggemann, Walter. *Genesis*. Interpretation: A Bible Commentary for Teaching and Preaching. Atlanta: John Knox, 1982.

——. *Isaiah*. 2 vols. Westminster Bible Companion. Louisville: Westminster John Knox, 1998.

Burnside, Walter F. *The Acts of the Apostles: The Greek Edited with Introduction and Notes for the Use of Schools*. Cambridge: Cambridge University Press, 1916.

Burrows, Millar, ed. *The Dead Sea Scrolls of St. Mark's Monastery*. 2 vols. New Haven: American Schools of Oriental Research, 1951.

Burton, Ernest De Witt. *A Critical and Exegetical Commentary on the Epistle to the Galatians*. International Critical Commentary. Edinburgh: T&T Clark, 1921.

Buttrick, George A. *The Interpreter's Bible: The Holy Scriptures in the King James and Revised Standard Versions with General Articles and Introduction, Exegesis, Exposition for Each Book of the Bible*. 12 vols. New York: Abingdon, 1951–58.

——, ed. *Interpreter's Dictionary of the Bible*. 4 vols. Nashville: Abingdon, 1962.

Cadbury, Henry J. *The Making of Luke–Acts*. 2nd edn. London: SPCK, 1958.

——. 'The Speeches in Acts'. Pages 402–27 in vol. 5 of *The Beginnings of Christianity. Part I: The Acts of the Apostles*. Edited by Frederick J. Foakes Jackson and Kirsopp Lake. London: Macmillan, 1920–33. Reprint, Grand Rapids: Baker, 1979.

Calvin, John. *Acts 1–13*. Translated by John W. Fraser and W. J. G. McDonald. Edited by David W. Torrance and Thomas F. Torrance. Calvin's New Testament Commentaries. Grand Rapids: Eerdmans, 1995.

——. *Acts 14–28*. Translated by John W. Fraser. Edited by David W. Torrance and Thomas F. Torrance. Calvin's New Testament Commentaries. Grand Rapids: Eerdmans, 1995.

——. *Commentaries on the Twelve Minor Prophets*. Calvin's Commentaries 14. Grand Rapids: Baker, 1979. Reprint of Calvin Translation Society edn., Edinburgh, 1845–56.

——. *Commentary on the Book of the Prophet Isaiah*. Calvin's Commentaries 8. Grand Rapids: Baker, 1979. Reprint of Calvin Translation Society edn., Edinburgh, 1845–56.

Carroll, John T. 'The Uses of Scripture in Luke–Acts'. Pages 512–28 in *Society of Biblical Literature Seminar Papers, 1990*. Edited by David J. Lull. Atlanta: Scholars Press, 1990.

Cashdan, Eli. 'Malachi'. Pages 335–56 in *The Twelve Prophets: Hebrew Text, English Translation and Commentary*. Edited by Abraham Cohen. Soncino Books of the Bible. Bournemouth: Soncino, 1948.

Chance, J. Bradley. *Jerusalem, the Temple and the New Age in Luke–Acts*. Macon, Ga.: Mercer University Press, 1988.

Chapman, David W. 'A Superabundance of Blessing: The Discourse Intent of Joel 3:1-5 and Its Canonical Implications'. M.A. thesis, Trinity Evangelical Divinity School, 1996.

Charlesworth, James H. *The Old Testament Pseudepigrapha*. 2 vols. New York: Doubleday, 1983–85.

Chester, Andrew. 'Citing the Old Testament'. Pages 141–69 in *It Is Written: Scripture Citing Scripture*. Edited by Donald A. Carson and Hugh G. M. Williamson. Cambridge: Cambridge University Press, 1988.

Childs, Brevard S. *Isaiah: A Commentary*. Old Testament Library. Louisville: Westminster John Knox, 2001.

Clarke, William Kemp Lowther. 'The Use of the Septuagint in Acts'. Pages 66–105 in vol. 2 of *The Beginnings of Christianity. Part I: The Acts of the Apostles*. Edited by Frederick J. Foakes Jackson and Kirsopp Lake. London: Macmillan, 1920–33. Reprint, Grand Rapids: Baker, 1979.

Clements, Ronald E. *Abraham and David: Genesis XV and Its Meaning in Israelite Tradition*. Studies in Biblical Theology, Second Series 5. London: SCM Press, 1967.

———. *Isaiah 1–39*. New Century Bible. Grand Rapids: Eerdmans, 1980.

———. *Prophecy and Covenant*. Studies in Biblical Theology 43. London: SCM Press, 1965.

Clowney, Edmund P. *The Church*. Contours of Christian Theology. Downers Grove, Ill.: Inter-Varsity, 2000.

Cohen, Abraham. *The Soncino Chumash: The Five Books of Moses with Haphtaroth*. Soncino Books of the Bible. London: Soncino, 1947.

———.. ed. *The Twelve Prophets: Hebrew Text, English Translation and Commentary*. Soncino Books of the Bible. Bournemouth: Soncino, 1948.

Cole, Alan. *The New Temple: A Study in the Origins of the Catechetical 'Form' of the Church in the New Testament*. London: Tyndale Press, 1950.

Collins, Clifford John. 'Galatians 3:16: What Kind of Exegete Is Paul?' *TynBul* 54 (2003): 75–86.

———. 'A Syntactical Note (Genesis 3:15): Is the Woman's Seed Singular or Plural?' *TynBul* 48 (1997): 141–48.

Collins, John J. *The Scepter and the Star: The Messiahs of the Dead Sea Scrolls and Other Ancient Literature*. Anchor Bible Reference Library. New York: Doubleday, 1995.

Conzelmann, Hans. *Acts of the Apostles*. Translated by James A. Limburg, Thomas Kraabel, and Donald Juel. Hermeneia. Philadelphia: Fortress, 1987.

———. *Theology of St. Luke*. Translated by Geoffrey Buswell. New York: Harper & Row, 1961.

Creed, John Martin. *The Gospel according to St. Luke: The Greek Text with Introduction, Notes, and Indices*. London: Macmillan, 1965.

Crenshaw, James L. *Joel: A New Translation with Introduction and Commentary*. Anchor Bible 24C. New York: Doubleday, 1995.

Crim, Keith D. *The Interpreter's Dictionary of the Bible. Supplementary Volume*. Nashville: Abingdon, 1976.

Cripps, Richard S. *A Critical & Exegetical Commentary on the Book of Amos*. New York: SPCK, 1929.

Dahl, Nils A. 'A People for His Name (Acts XV.14)'. *NTS* 4 (1958): 324–25.

———. 'The Purpose of Luke–Acts'. Pages 87–98 in *Jesus in the Memory of the Early Church*. Minneapolis: Augsburg, 1976.

———. 'The Story of Abraham in Luke–Acts'. Pages 139–58 in *Studies in Luke–Acts*. Edited by Leander E. Keck and J. Louis Martyn. Nashville: Abingdon, 1966. Reprint, Mifflintown, Pa.: Siglar Press, 1999.

Danby, Herbert. *The Mishnah: Translated from the Hebrew with Introduction and Brief Explanatory Notes*. Oxford: Oxford University Press, 1937.

Danker, Frederick William. *A Greek–English Lexicon of the New Testament and Other Early Christian Literature*. 3rd edn. Chicago: University of Chicago Press, 2000.

Davids, Peter H. *The Epistle of James: A Commentary on the Greek Text*. New International Greek Text Commentary. Grand Rapids: Eerdmans, 1982.

Davidson, Richard M. 'The Eschatological Structure of Biblical Typology'. Paper presented at the annual meeting of the Evangelical Theological Society, 19 November 1999.

——. 'Is Biblical Typology Really Predictive? Some Possible Indicators of the Existence and Predictive Quality of OT Types'. Paper presented at the midwestern regional meeting of the Evangelical Theological Society, St Paul, Minn., 26–27 February 1999.

——. 'Israel Typology'. Paper presented at the annual meeting of the Evangelical Theological Society, 16 November 2000.

——. *Typology in Scripture: A Study of Hermeneutical τυπος Structures*. Andrews University Seminary Doctoral Dissertation Series 2. Berrien Springs, Mich.: Andrews University Press, 1981.

Delitzsch, Franz. *Isaiah*. Edited by C. F. Keil and Franz Delitzsch. Commentary on the Old Testament. Grand Rapids: Eerdmans, 1975.

——. *New Commentary on Genesis*. Translated by Sophia Taylor. 2 vols. Clark's Foreign Theological Library 36–37. Edinburgh: T&T Clark, 1888–89.

Denova, Rebecca. *The Things Accomplished Among Us: Prophetic Tradition and the Structural Pattern of Luke–Acts*. Edited by Stanley E. Porter. Journal for the Study of the New Testament Supplement Series 141. Sheffield: Sheffield Academic Press, 1997.

deSilva, David A. 'Paul's Sermon in Antioch of Pisidia'. *BSac* 151 (1994): 32–49.

de Waard, Jan. *A Comparative Study of the Old Testament Text in the Dead Sea Scrolls and in the New Testament*. Studies on the Texts of the Desert of Judah 4. Leiden: Brill, 1965.

de Waard, Jan and William A. Smalley. *A Translator's Handbook on the Book of Amos*. Helps for Translators. Stuttgart: United Bible Societies, 1979.

Dibelius, Martin. *Studies in the Acts of the Apostles*. Edited by Heinrich Greeven. New York: Charles Scribner's Sons, 1956.

Dillard, Raymond Bryan. 'Joel'. Pages 239–313 in *The Minor Prophets: An Exegetical and Expositional Commentary*. Edited by Thomas Edward McComiskey. 3 vols. Grand Rapids: Baker, 1992.

Dodd, Charles H. *According to the Scriptures*. London: Fontana Books, 1952.

Doeve, Jan W. *Jewish Hermeneutics in the Synoptic Gospels and Acts*. Assen: Van Gorcum, 1953.

Donaldson, Terence L. *Judaism and the Gentiles: Jewish Patterns of Universalism (to 135 CE)*. Waco: Baylor University Press, 2007.

Donfried, Karl P. 'Attempts at Understanding the Purpose of Luke–Acts: Christology and the Salvation of the Gentiles'. Pages 112–22 in *Christological Perspectives: Essays in Honor of Harvey K. McArthur*. Edited by Robert F. Berkey and Sarah A. Edwards. New York: Pilgrim Press, 1982.

Dormeyer, Detlev and Florenzio Galindo. *Die Apostelgeschichte. Ein Kommentar für die Praxis*. Stuttgart: Verlag Katholisches Bibelwerk, 2003.

Driver, Samuel R. *The Book of Genesis with Introduction and Notes*. 3rd edn. London: Methuen, 1904.

——. *An Introduction to the Literature of the Old Testament*. 11th rev. and enl. edn. New York: Charles Scribner's Sons, 1905.

Duling, Dennis C. 'The Promises to David and Their Entrance into Christianity: Nailing Down a Likely Hypothesis'. *NTS* 20 (1973): 55–77.

Dunn, James D. G. *The Acts of the Apostles*. Valley Forge: Trinity Press International, 1996.

——. *Baptism in the Holy Spirit*. Philadelphia: Westminster Press, 1970.

Dupont, Jacques. 'Apologetic Use of the Old Testament in the Speeches of Acts'. Pages 129–59 in *The Salvation of the Gentiles: Essays on the Acts of the Apostles*. Translated by John R. Keating. New York: Paulist, 1979.

——. *Etudes sur les Actes des Apôtres*. Paris: Cerf, 1967.

——. ' "Je rabâtirai la cabane de David qui est tombée" (Ac 15,16 = Am 9,11)'. Pages 19–32 in *Glaube und Eschatologie*. Edited by Erich Grässer and Otto Merk. Tübingen: J. C. B. Mohr, 1985.

——. 'Je t'ai établi lumière des nations (Ac 13, 14, 43-52)'. Pages 343–49 in *Nouvelles Etudes sur les Actes des Apôtres*. Paris: Cerf, 1984.

——. 'La portée christologique de l'evangélisation des nations'. Pages 37–57 in *Nouvelles Etudes sur les Actes des Apôtres*. Paris: Cerf, 1984.

——. 'ΛΑΟΣ ῈΞ ἘΘΝΩΝ (Act. xv. 14)'. *NTS* 3 (1956): 47–50. Reprint, pages 361–65 in *Etudes sur les Actes des Apôtres*. Paris: Cerf, 1967.

——. *Nouvelles Etudes sur les Actes des Apôtres*. Lectio Divina 118. Paris: Cerf, 1984.

——. 'Un peuple d'entre les nations (Actes 15.14)'. *NTS* 31 (1985): 321–35.

——. 'The Salvation of the Gentiles and the Theological Significance of the Book of Acts'. Pages 11–33 in *The Salvation of the Gentiles: Essays on the Acts of the Apostles*. Translated by John R. Keating. New York: Paulist, 1979.

——. *The Salvation of the Gentiles: Essays on the Acts of the Apostles*. Translated by John R. Keating. New York: Paulist, 1979.

Easton, Burton Scott. *The Purpose of Acts*. 'Theology' Occasional Papers 6. London: SPCK, 1936.

Eckey, Wilfried. *Die Apostelgeschichte: Der Weg des Evangeliums von Jerusalem nach Rom*. 2 vols. Neukirchen-Vluyn: Neukirchener, 2000.

Eissfeld, Otto. *The Old Testament: An Introduction*. Translated by Peter J. Ackroyd. New York: Harper & Row, 1965.

Ekblad, Eugene Robert, Jr. *Isaiah's Servant Poems according to the Septuagint*. Leuven: Peters, 1999.

Elliger, Karl and Wilhelm Rudolph. *Biblia Hebraica Stuttgartensia*. 4th corrected edn. Stuttgart: Deutsche Bibelgesellschaft, 1990.

Ellis, Edward Earle. 'Biblical Interpretation in the New Testament Church'. Pages 691–725 in *Mikra: Text, Translation, Reading and Interpretation of the Hebrew Bible in Ancient Judaism and Early Christianity*. Edited by Martin Jan Mulder. Compendia rerum Iudaicarum ad Novum Testamentum 2.1. Assen: Van Gorcum, 1988.

——. 'Isaiah and the Eschatological Temple'. Pages 52–61 in *Christ and the Future in New Testament History*. Edited by Edward Earle Ellis. Supplements to Novum Testamentum 97. Leiden: Brill, 2000.

——. 'Λέγει Κύριος Quotations in the New Testament'. Pages 182–87 in *Prophecy and Hermeneutic in Early Christianity*. Grand Rapids: Eerdmans, 1978.

——. 'Midrashic Features in the Speeches of Acts'. Pages 198–208 in *Prophecy and Hermeneutic in Early Christianity*. Grand Rapids: Eerdmans, 1978.

——. 'Midrash, Targum and New Testament Quotations'. Pages 61–69 in *Neotestamentica et Semitica*. Edited by Edward Earle Ellis and Max Wilcox. Edinburgh: T&T Clark, 1969.

——. *Paul's Use of the Old Testament*. Grand Rapids: Eerdmans, 1957.

Epp, Eldon Jay. *The Theological Tendency of Codex Bezae Cantabrigiensis in Acts*. Society for New Testament Studies Monograph Series 3. Cambridge: Cambridge University Press, 1966.

Evans, Craig A. 'The Function of the Elijah/Elisha Narratives in Luke's Ethic of Election'. Pages 70–83 in *Luke and Scripture: The Function of Sacred Tradition in Luke–Acts*. Edited by Craig A. Evans and Jack T. Sanders. Minneapolis: Fortress, 1993.

——. 'Prophecy and Polemic: Jews in Luke's Scriptural Apologetic'. Pages 171–211 in *Luke*

and Scripture: The Function of Sacred Tradition in Luke–Acts. Edited by Craig A. Evans
    and James A. Sanders. Minneapolis: Fortress, 1993.
——. 'The Prophetic Setting of the Pentecost Sermon'. Pages 212–24 in Luke and Scripture:
    The Function of Sacred Tradition in Luke–Acts. Edited by Craig A. Evans and Jack T.
    Sanders. Minneapolis: Fortress, 1993.
——. 'The Twelve Thrones of Israel: Scripture and Politics in Luke 22:24-30'. Pages 154–70
    in Luke and Scripture: The Function of Sacred Tradition in Luke–Acts. Edited by Craig
    A. Evans and James A. Sanders. Minneapolis: Fortress, 1993.
Evans, Craig A. and Jack T. Sanders. Early Christian Interpretation of the Scriptures of Israel.
    Journal for the Study of the New Testament Supplement Series 148. Sheffield: Sheffield
    Academic Press, 1997.
Evans, Craig A. and James A. Sanders. Luke and Scripture: The Function of Sacred Tradition
    in Luke–Acts. Minneapolis: Fortress, 1993.
Fee, Gordon D. The First Epistle to the Corinthians. New International Commentary on the
    New Testament. Grand Rapids: Eerdmans, 1987.
Filbeck, David. Yes, God of the Gentiles, Too. Wheaton, Ill.: Billy Graham Center, Wheaton
    College, 1994.
Fischer, Bonifatio, et al., eds. Biblia Sacra Iuxta Vulgatam Versionem. 4th edn. Stuttgart:
    Deutsche Bibelgesellschaft, 1994.
Fishbane, Michael. 'Use, Authority and Interpretation of Mikra at Qumran'. Pages 339–77 in
    Mikra: Text, Translation, Reading and Interpretation of the Hebrew Bible in Ancient
    Judaism and Early Christianity. Edited by Martin Jan Mulder. Compendia rerum
    Iudaicarum ad Novum Testamentum 2.1. Assen: Van Gorcum, 1988.
Fitzmyer, Joseph A. The Acts of the Apostles. Anchor Bible 31. New York: Doubleday, 1998.
——. The Gospel according to Luke. 2 vols. Anchor Bible 28–28A. Garden City, NY: Double-
    day, 1981–85.
——. 'Index of Biblical Passages'. Pages 152–71 in The Dead Sea Scrolls: Major Publications
    and Tools for Study. Sources for Biblical Study 8. Missoula, Mont.: Scholars Press, 1975.
——. 'The Use of Explicit Old Testament Quotations in Qumran Literature and in the New
    Testament'. NTS 7 (1961): 297–333.
Foakes Jackson, Frederick J. and Kirsopp Lake, eds. The Beginnings of Christianity. Part I:
    The Acts of the Apostles. 5 vols. London: Macmillan, 1920–33. Reprint, Grand Rapids:
    Baker, 1979.
Franklin, Eric. Christ the Lord: A Study in the Purpose and Theology of Luke–Acts. Philadel-
    phia: Westminster, 1975.
Frein, Brigid Curtin. 'Narrative Predictions, Old Testament Prophecies and Luke's Sense of
    Fulfillment'. NTS 40 (1994): 23–37.
Gallagher, Robert L. and Paul Hertog. Mission in Acts: Ancient Narratives in Contemporary
    Context. American Society of Missiology Series 34. Maryknoll, NY: Orbis, 2004.
Galling, Kurt. 'Die Ausrufung des Namens als Rechtsakt in Israel'. TLZ 81 (1956): 66–68.
García Martinéz, Florentino and Eiblert J. C. Tigchelor. The Dead Sea Scrolls Study Edition. 2
    vols. Grand Rapids: Eerdmans, 1997–98.
Garrett, Duane A. Hosea, Joel. New American Commentary 19A. Nashville: Broadman &
    Holman, 1997.
Gasque, W. Ward. 'The Speeches of Acts: Dibelius Reconsidered'. Pages 222–50 in New
    Dimensions in New Testament Study. Edited by Richard N. Longenecker and Merrill C.
    Tenney. Grand Rapids: Zondervan, 1974.
Gempf, Conrad. 'Public Speaking and Published Accounts'. Pages 259–303 in The Book of
    Acts in Its Ancient Literary Setting. Edited by Bruce W. Winter and Andrew D. Clarke.
    Grand Rapids: Eerdmans, 1993.

Gerstmyer, Robert Henry Madison. 'The Gentiles in Luke–Acts'. Ph.D. diss., Duke University, 1995.

Gesenius, Friedrich H. W. *Gesenius' Hebrew Grammar*. Translated by Arthur E. Cowley. Edited by Emil Kautzsch. 2nd English edn. Oxford: Clarendon, 1910.

Gibbs, Jeffrey A. 'Israel Standing with Israel: The Baptism of Jesus in Matthew's Gospel (Matt 3:13-17)'. *CBQ* 64 (2002): 511–26.

Godet, Frédéric. *A Commentary on the Gospel of St. Luke*. Translated by E. W. Shalders and M. D. Cusin. 5th edn. 2 vols. Clark's Foreign Theological Library. Edinburgh: T&T Clark, 1957.

Goldingay, John. *Isaiah*. New International Biblical Commentary on the Old Testament 13. Peabody, Mass.: Hendrickson, 2001.

——. *The Message of Isaiah 40–55: A Literary-Theological Commentary*. London: T&T Clark, 2005.

Goldingay, John and David Payne. *A Critical and Exegetical Commentary on Isaiah 40–55*. International Critical Commentary. London: T&T Clark, 2006.

Gooding, David. *According to Luke: A New Exposition of the Third Gospel*. Grand Rapids: Eerdmans, 1987.

Goppelt, Leonhard. *Typos: The Typological Interpretation of the Old Testament in the New*. Translated by Donald H. Madvig. Grand Rapids: Eerdmans, 1982.

Green, Joel B. *The Gospel of Luke*. New International Commentary on the New Testament. Grand Rapids: Eerdmans, 1997.

——. '"Proclaiming Repentance and Forgiveness of Sins to All Nations": A Biblical Perspective on the Church's Mission'. Pages 13–43 in *The Mission of the Church in Methodist Perspective: The World Is My Parish*. Edited by Alan G. Padgett. Studies in the History of Mission 10. Lewiston, NY: Edwin Mellen, 1992.

Green, Joel B. and Michael D. McKeever. *Luke–Acts and New Testament Historiography*. IBR Bibliographies 8. Grand Rapids: Baker, 1994.

Grelot, Pierre. 'Note sur Actes, XIII, 47'. *RB* 88 (1981): 368–72.

Grüneberg, Keith N. *Abraham, Blessing and the Nations: A Philological and Exegetical Study of Genesis 12:3 in Its Narrative Context*. Beihefte zur Zeitschrift für die alttestamentliche Wissenschaft 332. Berlin: Walter de Gruyter, 2003.

Guthrie, Donald. *New Testament Introduction*. 3rd rev. edn. Downers Grove, Ill.: Inter-Varsity, 1970.

Haenchen, Ernst. *The Acts of the Apostles: A Commentary*. Translated by R. McL. Williams. Philadelphia: Westminster, 1971.

Hamilton, Victor P. *The Book of Genesis*. 2 vols. New International Commentary on the Old Testament. Grand Rapids: Eerdmans, 1990–95.

Hammershaimb, Erling. *The Book of Amos: A Commentary*. Translated by John Sturdy. Oxford: Basil Blackwell, 1970.

Hanford, W. R. 'Deutero-Isaiah and Luke–Acts: Straightforward Universalism?' *CQR* 168 (1967): 142–52.

Hanson, Paul D. *Isaiah 40–66*. Interpretation: A Bible Commentary for Teaching and Preaching. Louisville: John Knox, 1995.

Harper, William Rainey. *A Critical and Exegetical Commentary on Amos and Hosea*. International Critical Commentary. Edinburgh: T&T Clark, 1905.

Harris, Robert Laird, et al. *Theological Wordbook of the Old Testament*. 2 vols. Chicago: Moody, 1980.

Harrison, Roland K. *Introduction to the Old Testament*. Grand Rapids: Eerdmans, 1969.

Hasel, Gerhard F. *The Remnant: The History and Theology of the Remnant Idea from Genesis to Isaiah*. Berrien Springs, Mich.: Andrews University Press, 1972.

——. *Understanding the Book of Amos: Basic Issues in Current Interpretations*. Grand Rapids: Baker, 1991.

Hatch, Edwin and Henry A. Redpath. *A Concordance to the Septuagint and the Other Greek Versions of the Old Testament (including the Apocryphal Books)*. 3 vols. Oxford: Clarendon, 1897. Reprint, 3 vols. in 2, Grand Rapids: Baker, 1983.

Hays, Richard B. *Echoes of Scripture in the Letters of Paul*. New Haven: Yale University Press, 1989.

Hayward, Claude E. 'A Study in Acts XV. 16-18'. *EvQ* 8 (1936): 163–66.

Henderson, Ebenezer. *The Book of the Twelve Minor Prophets*. Boston: Draper, 1859.

Henderson, Suzanne Watts. 'The Messianic Community: The Mission of Jesus as Collective Christology'. Paper presented at the AAR/SBL Annual Meeting, San Diego, 2007.

Hengel, Martin and Daniel P. Bailey. 'The Effective History of Isaiah 53 in the Pre-Christian Period'. Pages 75–146 in *The Suffering Servant: Isaiah 53 in Jewish and Christian Sources*. Edited by Bernd Janowski and Peter Stuhlmacher. Translated by Daniel P. Bailey. Grand Rapids: Eerdmans, 2004.

Herbert, Arthur S. *The Book of the Prophet Isaiah: Chapters 40–66*. Cambridge Bible Commentary. Cambridge: Cambridge University Press, 1975.

Herrick, Gregory C. 'Isaiah 55:3 in Acts 13:34: Luke's Polemic for Equality of Gentile Participation in Davidic Promise'. Ph.D. diss., Dallas Theological Seminary, 1999.

Holtz, Traugott. *Untersuchungen über die alttestamentlichen Zitate bei Lukas*. Texte und Untersuchungen zur Geschichte der altchristlichen Literatur 104. Berlin: Akademie Verlag, 1968.

Hooker, Morna D. *Jesus and the Servant: The Influence of the Servant Concept of Deutero-Isaiah in the New Testament*. London: SPCK, 1959.

Hornblower, Simon and Antony Spawforth. *Oxford Classical Dictionary*. 3rd edn. Oxford: Oxford University Press, 1996.

Hubbard, David Allan. *Joel and Amos: An Introduction and Commentary*. Tyndale Old Testament Commentaries. Downers Grove, Ill.: Inter-Varsity, 1989.

Hummel, Horace D. *The Word Becoming Flesh: An Introduction to the Origin, Purpose and Meaning of the Old Testament*. St Louis: Concordia, 1959.

Janowski, Bernd and Peter Stuhlmacher, eds. *The Suffering Servant: Isaiah 53 in Jewish and Christian Sources*. Translated by Daniel P. Bailey. Grand Rapids: Eerdmans, 2004.

Jeremias, Joachim. *Jesus' Promise to the Nations*. Translated by S. H. Hooke. Studies in Biblical Theology 24. Naperville, Ill.: Allenson, 1958.

Jeremias, Jörg. *The Book of Amos: A Commentary*. Translated by Douglas W. Stott. Old Testament Library. Louisville: Westminster John Knox, 1998.

Jervell, Jacob. *Die Apostelgeschichte*. Kritisch-exegetischer Kommentar über das Neue Testament. Göttingen: Vandenhoeck & Ruprecht, 1998.

——. 'The Center of Scripture in Luke'. Pages 122–37 in *The Unknown Paul: Essays on Luke–Acts and Early Christian History*. Translated by Roy A. Harrisville. Minneapolis: Augsburg, 1984.

——. 'The Divided People of God: The Restoration of Israel and the Salvation of the Gentiles'. Pages 41–74 in *Luke and the People of God: A New Look at Luke–Acts*. Minneapolis: Augsburg, 1972.

——. 'James: The Defender of Paul'. Pages 185–207 in *Luke and the People of God: A New Look at Luke–Acts*. Minneapolis: Augsburg, 1972.

——. *Luke and the People of God: A New Look at Luke–Acts*. Minneapolis: Augsburg, 1972.

——. *The Theology of the Acts of the Apostles*. New Testament Theology. Cambridge: Cambridge University Press, 1996.

——. 'The Twelve on Israel's Thrones: Understanding the Apostolate'. Pages 75–112 in *Luke and the People of God: A New Look at Luke–Acts*. Minneapolis: Augsburg, 1972.

Jobes, Karen H. and Moisés Silva. *Invitation to the Septuagint*. Grand Rapids: Baker, 2000.

Johnson, Dennis E. 'Jesus Against the Idols: The Use of Isaianic Servant Songs in the Missiology of Acts'. *WTJ* 52 (1990): 343–53.

——. *The Message of Acts in the History of Redemption*. Phillipsburg, NJ: P & R, 1997.

Johnson, Franklin. *The Quotations of the New Testament from the Old Considered in the Light of General Literature*. Philadelphia: American Baptist Publication Society, 1896.

Johnson, Luke Timothy. *The Acts of the Apostles*. Sacra Pagina 5. Collegeville, Minn.: Liturgical Press, 1992.

——. *The Gospel of Luke*. Sacra Pagina 3. Collegeville, Minn.: Liturgical Press, 1991.

——. *The Letter of James: A New Translation with Introduction and Commentary*. Anchor Bible 37A. New York: Doubleday, 1994.

——. *Septuagintal Midrash in the Speeches of Acts*. The Père Marquette Lecture in Theology. Milwaukee: Marquette University Press, 2002.

Jones, Donald L. 'The Title "Servant" in Luke–Acts'. Pages 148–65 in *Luke–Acts: New Perspectives from the Society of Biblical Literature Seminar*. Edited by Charles H. Talbert. New York: Crossroad, 1984.

Joüon, Paul. *A Grammar of Biblical Hebrew*. Translated by T. Muraoka. Subsidia Biblica 14. Rome: Pontifical Biblical Institute, 1991.

Just, Arthur A., Jr. *Luke*. Edited by Jonathan F. Grothe. 2 vols. Concordia Commentary. St Louis: Concordia, 1997.

Kaiser, Walter C., Jr. 'The Blessing of David: The Charter for Humanity'. Pages 298–318 in *The Law and the Prophets*. Edited by John H. Skilton. Nutley, NJ: Presbyterian and Reformed, 1974.

——. 'The Davidic Promise and the Inclusion of the Gentiles (Amos 9:9-15 and Acts 15:13-18): A Test Passage for Theological Systems'. *JETS* 20 (1977): 97–111. Reprint, pages 177–94 (with revisions) in *The Uses of the Old Testament in the New*. Chicago: Moody, 1985.

——. *The Messiah in the Old Testament*. Studies in Old Testament Biblical Theology. Grand Rapids: Zondervan, 1995.

——. *Mission in the Old Testament: Israel as a Light to the Nations*. Grand Rapids: Baker, 2000.

——. 'The Promise of God and the Outpouring of the Holy Spirit'. Pages 109–22 in *The Living and Active Word of God: Studies in Honor of Samuel J. Schulz*. Edited by Morris Inch and Ronald Youngblood. Winona Lake, Ind.: Eisenbrauns, 1983. Reprint, pages 89–100 (with revisions) in *The Uses of the Old Testament in the New*. Chicago: Moody, 1985.

——. *The Uses of the Old Testament in the New*. Chicago: Moody, 1985.

Kapelrud, Arvid S. *Central Ideas in Amos*. Oslo: Oslo University Press, 1961.

Keck, Leander E. and James Louis Martyn, eds. *Studies in Luke–Acts*. Nashville: Abingdon, 1966. Reprint, Mifflintown, Pa.: Sigler Press, 1999.

Keil, Carl F. *Minor Prophets*. Translated by James Martin. Commentary on the Old Testament. Grand Rapids: Eerdmans, 1973.

Kidner, Derek. *Genesis: An Introduction and Commentary*. Tyndale Old Testament Commentaries. Downers Grove, Ill.: Inter-Varsity, 1967.

Kilpatrick, George D. 'Some Quotations in Acts'. Pages 81–97 in *Les Actes des Apôtres: Traditions, rédaction, théologie*. Edited by J. Kremer. Bibliotheca Ephemeridum theologicarum Lovaniensium 48. Leuven: J. Duculot, 1979.

Kimball, Charles A. *Jesus' Exposition of the Old Testament in Luke's Gospel*. Edited by Stanley E. Porter. Journal for the Study of the New Testament Supplement Series 94. Sheffield: Sheffield Academic Press, 1994.

Kittel, Gerhard and Gerhard Friedrich, eds. *Theological Dictionary of the New Testament*. Translated by Geoffrey W. Bromiley. 10 vols. Grand Rapids: Eerdmans, 1964–76.

Knight, George A. F. *Servant Theology: A Commentary on the Book of Isaiah 40–55*. Rev. edn. International Theological Commentary. Grand Rapids: Eerdmans, 1984.

Koehler, Ludwig and Walter Baumgartner. *The Hebrew and Aramaic Lexicon of the Old Testament*. Translated by Mervyn E. J. Richardson. Study edn. 2 vols. Leiden: Brill, 2001.

Koole, Jan L. *Isaiah, Part 3*. Translated by Anthony P. Runia. 3 vols. Historical Commentary on the Old Testament. Kampen: Kok Pharos, 1997–2001.

Köstenberger, Andreas J. and Peter T. O'Brien. *Salvation to the Ends of the Earth: A Biblical Theology of Mission*. New Studies in Biblical Theology 11. Downers Grove, Ill.: Inter-Varsity, 2001.

Krodel, Gerhard A. *Acts*. Augsburg Commentary on the New Testament. Minneapolis: Augsburg, 1986.

Kummel, Werner Georg. *Introduction to the New Testament*. Translated by Howard Clark Kee. Nashville: Abingdon, 1975.

Ladd, George Eldon. *A Theology of the New Testament*. Grand Rapids: Eerdmans, 1974.

Lake, Kirsopp. 'The Apostolic Council of Jerusalem'. Pages 195–212 in *Additional Notes to the Commentary*. Edited by Kirsopp Lake and Henry J. Cadbury. Vol. 5 of *The Beginnings of Christianity. Part I: The Acts of the Apostles*. Edited by Frederick J. Foakes Jackson and Kirsopp Lake. London: Macmillan, 1933. Reprint, Grand Rapids: Baker, 1979.

——. *The Apostolic Fathers*. 2 vols. Loeb Classical Library. Cambridge, Mass.: Harvard University Press, 1912–13.

Lane, Thomas J. *Luke and the Gentile Mission: Gospel Anticipates Acts*. European University Studies, Series XXIII 571. Frankfurt am Main: Peter Lang, 1996.

Langford, Norman F. 'The Book of Joel: Exposition'. Pages 727–60 in vol. 6 of *The Interpreter's Bible*. Edited by George A. Buttrick et al. New York: Abingdon, 1956.

Larkin, William J. *Acts*. IVP New Testament Commentary Series 5. Downers Grove, Ill.: Inter-Varsity, 1995.

——. 'Toward a Holistic Description of Luke's Use of the Old Testament: A Method Described and Illustrated from Luke 23:33-38, 44-49'. In *Evangelical Theological Society Papers*. Portland, Ore.: Theological Research Exchange Network, 1987.

LaSor, William Sanford, et al. *Old Testament Survey*. Grand Rapids: Eerdmans, 1982.

Lehrman, Simon M. 'Amos'. Pages 80–124 in *The Twelve Prophets: Hebrew Text, English Translation and Commentary*. Edited by Abraham Cohen. Soncino Books of the Bible. Bournemouth: Soncino, 1948.

——. 'Joel'. Pages 56–79 in *The Twelve Prophets: Hebrew Text, English Translation and Commentary*. Edited by Abraham Cohen. Soncino Books of the Bible. Bournemouth: Soncino, 1948.

Léonas, Alexis. 'A Note on Acts 3,25-26: The Meaning of Peter's Genesis Quotation'. *ETL* 77 (2000): 149–61.

Liddell, Henry G., et al. *A Greek–English Lexicon*. 9th edn. Oxford: Clarendon, 1996.

Lindars, Barnabas. *New Testament Apologetic*. Philadelphia: Fortress, 1961.

Lindblom, Johannes. *The Servant Songs in Deutero-Isaiah*. Lund: Gleerup, 1951.

Lindsey, Franklin Duane. *The Servant Songs*. Chicago: Moody, 1985.

Litwak, Kenneth D. *Echoes of Scripture in Luke–Acts: Telling the History of God's People Intertextually*. Journal for the Study of the New Testament: Supplement Series 282. London: T&T Clark, 2005.

Longenecker, Richard N. 'Acts'. Pages 205–573 in vol. 9 of *The Expositor's Bible Commentary*. Edited by Frank E. Gaebelein. Grand Rapids: Zondervan, 1981.

——. *Biblical Exegesis in the Apostolic Period*. 2nd edn. Grand Rapids: Eerdmans, 1999.

Louw, Johannes P. and Eugene Albert Nida. *Greek–English Lexicon of the New Testament: Based on Semantic Domains*. 2 vols. New York: United Bible Societies, 1989.

MacNaughton, Gail Thomas. 'An Examination of the Servant Songs of Isaiah with Particular Reference to the Servant's Role in the Promise to the Nations'. M.A. thesis, Covenant Theological Seminary, 1984.

MacRae, Allan A. 'The Scientific Approach to the Old Testament'. *BSac* 110 (1953): 309–20.

Maddox, Robert. *The Purpose of Luke–Acts*. Edinburgh: T&T Clark, 1982.

Marshall, Ian Howard. *The Acts of the Apostles: An Introduction and Commentary*. Tyndale New Testament Commentaries. Grand Rapids: Eerdmans, 1980.

———. *The Gospel of Luke: A Commentary on the Greek Text*. New International Greek Testament Commentary. Grand Rapids: Eerdmans, 1978.

———. *Luke: Historian and Theologian*. 3rd edn. Downers Grove, Ill.: InterVarsity, 1988.

———. 'The Significance of Pentecost'. *SJT* 30 (1977): 347–69.

Marshall, Ian Howard and David Peterson, eds. *Witness to the Gospel: The Theology of Acts*. Grand Rapids: Eerdmans, 1998.

Martin, Ralph P. *Colossians and Philemon*. Edited by Ronald E. Clements and Matthew Black. New Century Bible. London: Oliphants, 1974.

Martin-Achard, Robert. *A Light to the Nations: A Study of the Old Testament Conception of Israel's Mission to the World*. Translated by John Penney Smith. Edinburgh: Oliver & Boyd, 1962.

Mauchline, John. 'Implicit Signs of a Persistent Belief in the Davidic Empire'. *VT* 20 (1970): 287–303.

Mauro, Philip. 'Building the Tabernacle of David'. *EvQ* 9 (1937): 398–413.

Mayor, Joseph B. *The Epistle of St. James*. 3rd edn. New York: Macmillan, 1912.

Mays, James Luther. *Amos: A Commentary*. Old Testament Library. Philadelphia: Westminster, 1969.

McLay, R. Timothy. *The Use of the Septuagint in New Testament Research*. Grand Rapids: Eerdmans, 2003.

McLean, John A. 'Did Jesus Correct the Disciples' View of the Kingdom?' *BSac* 151 (1994): 215–27.

McNeill, Alan Hugh. *The Gospel according to St. Matthew: The Greek Text with Introduction, Notes, and Indices*. New York: Macmillan, 1915. Reprint, Grand Rapids: Baker, 1980.

McNicol, Allan J. 'Rebuilding the House of David: The Function of the Benedictus in Luke–Acts'. *ResQ* 40 (1998): 25–38.

Menzies, Robert P. *Empowered for Witness: The Spirit in Luke–Acts*. London: T&T Clark, 2004.

Metzger, Bruce M. 'The Formulas Introducing Quotations of Scripture in the NT and the Mishnah'. *JBL* 70 (1951): 297–307.

———. *A Textual Commentary on the Greek New Testament*. 2nd edn. Stuttgart: Deutsche Bibelgesellschaft, 2002.

Mitchell, Christopher Wright. *The Meaning of BRK 'To Bless' in the Old Testament*. Society of Biblical Literature Dissertation Series 95. Atlanta: Scholars Press, 1987.

Moessner, David P. 'The Ironic Fulfillment of Israel's Glory'. Pages 35–50 in *Luke–Acts and the Jewish People*. Edited by Joseph B. Tyson. Minneapolis: Augsburg, 1988.

———. *Lord of the Banquet: The Literary and Theological Significance of the Lukan Travel Narrative*. Minneapolis: Fortress, 1989.

———, ed. *Jesus and the Heritage of Israel: Luke's Narrative Claim upon Israel's Legacy*. Harrisburg, Pa.: Trinity Press International, 1999.

Moore, Thomas S. 'Luke's Use of Isaiah for the Gentile Mission and Jewish Rejection Theme in the Third Gospel'. Ph.D. diss., Dallas Theological Seminary, 1995.

———. '"To the End of the Earth": The Geographical and Ethnic Universalism of Acts 1:8 in Light of Isaianic Influence on Luke'. *JETS* 40 (1997): 389–99.

Morgenstern, Julian. 'The Rest of the Nations'. *JSS* 2 (1957): 225–31.

Morris, Leon. *The Gospel according to John: The English Text with Introduction, Exposition and Notes.* New International Commentary on the New Testament. Grand Rapids: Eerdmans, 1971.

———. *The Gospel according to St. Luke: An Introduction and Commentary.* Tyndale New Testament Commentaries. Grand Rapids: Eerdmans, 1974.

Motyer, J. Alec. *The Day of the Lion.* Downers Grove, Ill.: Inter-Varsity, 1975.

———. *Isaiah: An Introduction and Commentary.* Edited by D. J. Wiseman. Tyndale Old Testament Commentaries. Downers Grove, Ill.: InterVarsity, 1999.

———. *The Prophecy of Isaiah.* Downers Grove, Ill.: InterVarsity, 1993.

Moule, Charles F. D. *The Epistles to the Colossians and to Philemon.* Edited by Charles F. D. Moule. Cambridge Greek Testament Commentary. Cambridge: Cambridge University Press, 1957.

Moulton, James Hope, et al. *A Grammar of New Testament Greek.* 4 vols. Edinburgh: T&T Clark, 1906–76.

Muilenberg, James. 'The Book of Isaiah: Chapters 40–66'. Pages 381–733 in vol. 5 of *The Interpreter's Bible.* Edited by George A. Buttrick et al. New York: Abingdon, 1956.

Müller, Mogens. 'The Reception of the Old Testament in Matthew and Luke–Acts: From Interpretation to Proof from Scripture'. *NovT* 43 (2001): 315–30.

Munck, Johannes. *The Acts of the Apostles.* Anchor Bible 31. Garden City, NY: Doubleday, 1967.

———. *Paul and the Salvation of Mankind.* Translated by Frank Clarke. London: SCM Press, 1959.

Muraoka, Takamitsu. *Emphatic Words and Structures in Biblical Hebrew.* Jerusalem: Magnes Press, 1985.

Nägele, Sabine. *Laubhütte Davids und Wolkensohn: Eine auslegungsgeschichtliche Studie zu Amos 9,11 in der jüdischen und christlichen Exegese.* Arbeiten zur Geschichte des antiken Judentums und des Urchristentums 24. Leiden: Brill, 1995.

Neusner, Jacob. *What Is Midrash?* Guides to Biblical Scholarship. Philadelphia: Fortress, 1987.

The New Interpreter's Bible: General Articles & Introduction, Commentary, & Reflections for Each Book of the Bible, Including the Apocryphal/Deuterocanonical Books. 12 vols. Nashville: Abingdon, 1994–2004.

Niehaus, Jeffery. 'Amos'. Pages 315–494 in *The Minor Prophets: An Exegetical and Expositional Commentary.* Edited by Thomas Edward McComiskey. 3 vols. Grand Rapids: Baker, 1992.

Nogalski, James D. 'The Problematic Suffixes of Amos IX 11'. *VT* 43 (1993): 411–18.

Noonan, Benjamin J. 'Abraham, Blessing, and the Nations: A Proposed Paradigm'. Paper presented at the annual meeting of the Evangelical Theological Society, San Diego, 2007.

North, Christopher R. *The Suffering Servant in Deutero-Isaiah: An Historical and Critical Study.* 2nd edn. London: Oxford University Press, 1956.

Odendaal, Dirk H. *The Eschatological Expectation of Isaiah 40–66 with Special Reference to Israel and the Nations.* Nutley, NJ: Presbyterian and Reformed, 1970.

Oesterley, William O. E. *Studies in the Greek and Latin Versions of the Book of Amos.* Cambridge: Cambridge University Press, 1902.

Orlinsky, Harry M. 'The So-Called "Servant of the Lord" and "Suffering Servant" in Second Isaiah'. Pages 1–133 in *Studies on the Second Part of the Book of Isaiah.* Supplements to Vetus Testamentum 14. Leiden: Brill, 1967.

Oswalt, John. *The Book of Isaiah: Chapters 1–39.* New International Commentary on the Old Testament. Grand Rapids: Eerdmans, 1986.

O'Toole, Robert F. 'Acts 2:30 and the Davidic Covenant of Pentecost'. *JBL* 102 (1983): 245–58.

———. *The Christological Climax of Paul's Defense.* Analecta Biblica 78. Rome: Biblical Institute Press, 1978.

——. *The Unity of Luke's Theology: An Analysis of Luke–Acts*. Edited by Robert J. Karris. Good News Studies 9. Wilmington, Del.: Michael Glazier, 1984.

Ottley, Richard R. *The Book of Isaiah according to the Septuagint (Codex Alexandrinus)*. Cambridge: Cambridge University Press, 1906.

Pao, David W. *Acts and the Isaianic New Exodus*. Wissenschaftliche Untersuchungen zum Neuen Testament. 2 Reihe 130. Tübingen: Mohr, 2000. Reprint, Grand Rapids: Baker, 2002.

Paul, Shalom M. *Amos: A Commentary on the Book of Amos*. Hermeneia. Minneapolis: Fortress, 1991.

Pesch, Rudolf. *Die Apostelgeschichte*. 2 vols. Evangelisch-katholischer Kommentar zum Neuen Testament. Neukirchen-Vluyn: Neukirchener Verlag, 1986.

Pfeiffer, Robert H. *Introduction to the Old Testament*. New York: Harper & Brothers, 1941.

Pieper, August. *Isaiah II: An Exposition of Isaiah 40–66*. Translated by Erwin E. Kowalke. Milwaukee: Northwestern, 1979.

Plummer, Alfred. *A Critical and Exegetical Commentary on the Gospel according to S. Luke*. 5th edn. International Critical Commentary. Edinburgh: T&T Clark, 1922.

Polhill, John B. *Acts*. New American Commentary 26. Nashville: Broadman, 1992.

Polley, Max E. *Amos and the Davidic Kingdom: A Socio-Historical Approach*. New York: Oxford University Press, 1989.

Raabe, Paul R. *Obadiah: A New Translation with Introduction and Commentary*. Anchor Bible 24D. New York: Doubleday, 1995.

——. 'The Particularizing of Universal Judgment in Prophetic Discourse'. *CBQ* 64 (2002): 652–74.

Rabin, Chaim. *The Zadokite Documents*. 2nd rev. edn. Oxford: Clarendon, 1958.

Rackham, Richard B. *The Acts of the Apostles*. Westminster Commentaries. Grand Rapids: Baker, 1978.

Rahlfs, Alfred. *Septuaginta*. Stuttgart: Deutsche Bibelgesellschaft, 1935.

Ravens, David. *Luke and the Restoration of Israel*. Edited by Stanley E. Porter. Journal for the Study of the New Testament Supplement Series 119. Sheffield: Sheffield Academic Press, 1995.

Rese, Martin. *Alttestamentliche Motive in der Christologie des Lukas*. Studien zum Neuen Testament 1. Gütersloh: Gerd Mohn, 1969.

——. 'Die Funktion der alttestamentlichen Zitate und Anspielungen in den Reden der Apostelgeschichte'. Pages 61–79 in *Les Actes des Apôtres: Traditions, rédaction, théologie*. Edited by Jacob Kremer. Bibliotheca Ephemeridium theologicarum Lovaniensium 48. Leuven: Leuven University Press, 1979.

Revised Standard Version. New York: Division of Christian Education of the National Council of the Churches of Christ in the United States of America, 1973.

Richard, Earl. 'The Creative Use of Amos by the Author of Acts'. *NovT* 24 (1982): 37–53.

——. 'The Divine Purpose: The Jews and the Gentile Mission (Acts 15)'. Pages 188–209 in *Luke–Acts: New Perspectives from the Society of Biblical Literature Seminar*. Edited by Charles H. Talbert. New York: Crossroad, 1984.

Richardson, H. Neil. '*SKT* (Amos 9:11): "Booth" or "Succoth"'. *JBL* 92 (1973): 375–81.

Ridderbos, Herman N. *The Speeches of Peter in the Acts of the Apostles*. London: Tyndale Press, 1962.

Ridderbos, Jan. *Isaiah*. Translated by John Vriend. The Bible Student's Commentary. Grand Rapids: Zondervan, 1984.

Riesner, Rainer. 'James's Speech, Simeon's Hymn, and Luke's Sources'. Pages 263–78 in *Jesus of Nazareth: Lord and Christ*. Edited by Joel B. Green and Max Turner. Grand Rapids: Eerdmans, 1994.

Ringgren, Helmer. 'Luke's Use of the Old Testament'. *HTR* 79 (1986): 227–35.

——. *The Messiah in the Old Testament*. Studies in Biblical Theology 18. London: SCM Press, 1956.

Roberts, Jimmy J. M. 'The Old Testament's Contribution to Messianic Expectation'. Pages 39–51 in *The Messiah: Developments in Earliest Judaism and Christianity*. Edited by James H. Charlesworth. Minneapolis: Fortress, 1992.

Robertson, O. Palmer. 'Hermeneutics of Continuity'. Pages 89–108 in *Continuity and Discontinuity: Perspectives on the Relationship between the Old and New Testaments*. Edited by John S. Feinberg. Westchester, Ill.: Crossway, 1988.

Robinson, Henry Wheeler. *Corporate Personality in Ancient Israel*. Rev. edn. Philadelphia: Fortress, 1980.

——. *The Cross in the Old Testament*. London: SCM Press, 1955.

Rogers, Cleon L., Jr. 'The Davidic Covenant in Acts–Revelation'. *BSac* 151 (1994): 71–84.

——. 'The Promises to David in Early Judaism'. *BSac* 150 (1993): 285–302.

Roloff, Jürgen. *Die Apostelgeschichte*. Das Neue Testament Deutsche. Göttingen: Vandenhoeck & Ruprecht, 1981.

Routtenberg, Hyman J. *Amos of Tekoa: A Study in Interpretation*. New York: Vantage, 1971.

Rowley, Harold H. *The Servant of the Lord and Other Essays on the Old Testament*. Oxford: Blackwell, 1952.

Rudolph, Wilhelm. *Joel–Amos–Obadia–Jona*. Kommentar zum Alten Testament 13.2. Gütersloh: Gerd Mohn, 1971.

Rusam, Dietrich. *Das Alte Testament bei Lukas*. Beihefte zur Zeitschrift für die neutestamentliche Wissenschaft 112. Berlin: de Gruyter, 2003.

Sanders, Jack T. 'Isaiah in Luke'. Pages 14–25 in *Luke and Scripture: The Function of Sacred Tradition in Luke–Acts*. Edited by Craig A. Evans and Jack T. Sanders. Minneapolis: Augsburg, 1993.

——. 'The Jewish People in Luke–Acts'. Pages 11–20 in *Luke–Acts and the Jewish People*. Edited by Joseph B. Tyson. Minneapolis: Augsburg, 1988.

——. 'The Prophetic Use of the Scriptures in Luke–Acts'. Pages 191–98 in *Early Jewish and Christian Exegesis: Studies in Memory of William Brownlee*. Edited by Craig A. Evans and William F. Stinespring. Atlanta: Scholars Press, 1987.

Schnabel, Eckhard J. *Early Christian Mission*. 2 vols. Downers Grove, Ill.: InterVarsity, 2004.

Schneider, Gerhard. *Die Apostelgeschichte*. 2 vols. Herders Theologischer Kommentar zum Neuen Testament. Freiburg: Herder, 1980–82.

Schubert, Paul. 'The Structure and Significance of Luke 24'. Pages 165–86 in *Neutestamentlichen Studien für Rudolf Bultmann*. Edited by Walther Eltester. Beihefte zur Zeitschrift für die neutestamentliche Wissenschaft und die Künde der älteren Kirche 21. Berlin: Alfred Töpelmann, 1954.

Schwartz, Daniel R. 'The Futility of Preaching Moses (Acts 15,21)'. *Bib* 67 (1982): 276–81.

Schweizer, Eduard. 'The Concept of the Davidic "Son of God" in Acts and Its Old Testament Background'. Pages 186–93 in *Studies in Luke–Acts*. Edited by Leander E. Keck and James Louis Martyn. Nashville: Abingdon, 1966. Reprint, Mifflintown, Pa.: Siglar Press, 1999.

——. 'Concerning the Speeches in Acts'. Pages 208–16 in *Studies in Luke–Acts*. Edited by Leander E. Keck and James Louis Martyn. Nashville: Abingdon, 1966. Reprint, Mifflintown, Pa.: Siglar Press, 1999.

Seccombe, David. 'The New People of God'. Pages 349–72 in *Witness to the Gospel: The Theology of Acts*. Edited by Ian Howard Marshall and David Peterson. Grand Rapids: Eerdmans, 1998.

Sellin, Ernst and Georg Fohrer. *Introduction to the Old Testament*. Nashville: Abingdon, 1968.

Selwyn, Edward Gordon. *The First Epistle of Peter: The Greek Text with Introduction, Notes and Essays*. 2nd edn. London: Macmillan, 1947.

Siker, Jeffrey S. *Disinheriting the Jews: Abraham in Early Christian Controversy*. Louisville: Westminster John Knox, 1991.

Slotki, Israel W. *Isaiah: Hebrew Text and English Translation with an Introduction and Commentary*. Edited by Abraham Cohen. Soncino Books of the Bible. London: Soncino, 1949.

Smith, Billy K. 'Amos'. Pages 23–170 in *Amos, Obadiah, Jonah*. Edited by Billy K. Smith and Frank S. Page. New American Commentary 19B. Nashville: Broadman & Holman, 1995.

Smith, Gary V. *Amos*. Rev. and expanded edn. Fearn, Ross-Shire: Mentor, 1998.

Smith, Mark. 'Berit Am/Berit Olam: A New Proposal for the Crux of Isa 42:6'. *JBL* 100 (1981): 241–43.

Snaith, Norman H. 'Isaiah 40–66: A Study of the Teaching of Second Isaiah and Its Consequences'. Pages 135–264 in *Studies on the Second Part of the Book of Isaiah*. Supplements to Vetus Testamentum 14. Leiden: Brill, 1967.

Soards, Marion L. *The Speeches of Acts: Their Content, Context, and Concerns*. Louisville: Westminster John Knox, 1994.

Squires, John T. *The Plan of God in Luke–Acts*. Edited by Margaret Thrall. Society for New Testament Studies Monograph Series 76. Cambridge: Cambridge University Press, 1993.

Stanley, Christopher D. 'Biblical Quotations as Rhetorical Devices in Paul's Letter to the Galatians'. Pages 700–30 in *Society of Biblical Literature Seminar Papers, 1998. Part Two*. Atlanta: Scholars Press, 1998.

——. '"Pearls Before Swine": Did Paul's Audiences Understand His Biblical Quotations?' *NovT* 41 (1999): 124–44.

——. 'The Rhetoric of Quotations: An Essay on Method'. Pages 44–58 in *Early Christian Interpretation of the Scriptures of Israel*. Edited by Craig A. Evans and James A. Sanders. Journal for the Study of the New Testament Supplement Series 148. Sheffield: Sheffield Academic Press, 1997.

——. 'The Social Environment of "Free" Biblical Quotations in the New Testament'. Pages 18–27 in *Early Christian Interpretation of the Scriptures of Israel*. Edited by Craig A. Evans and James A. Sanders. Journal for the Study of the New Testament Supplement Series 148. Sheffield: Sheffield Academic Press, 1997.

Stein, Robert H. *Luke*. New American Commentary 24. Nashville: Broadman Press, 1992.

Steyn, Gert J. *Septuagint Quotations in the Context of the Petrine and Pauline Speeches of the Acta Apostolorum*. Contributions to Biblical Exegesis and Theology 12. Kampen: Kok Pharos, 1995.

Stott, John R. W. *The Message of Acts: The Spirit, the Church and the World*. Bible Speaks Today. Downers Grove, Ill.: InterVarsity, 1994.

Stowasser, Martin. 'Am 5,25-27; 9,11f. in der Qumranüberlieferung und in der Apostelgeschichte'. *ZNW* 92 (2001): 47–63.

Strauss, Mark L. *The Davidic Messiah in Luke–Acts: The Promise and Its Fulfillment in Lukan Eschatology*. Journal for the Study of the New Testament Supplement Series 110. Sheffield: Sheffield Academic Press, 1995.

Strazicich, John. *Joel's Use of Scripture and Scripture's Use of Joel: Appropriation and Resignification in Second Temple Judaism and Early Christianity*. Leiden: Brill, 2007.

Strong, David K. 'The Jerusalem Council: Some Implications for Contextualization'. Pages 196–208 in *Mission in Acts: Ancient Narratives in Contemporary Context*. Edited by Robert L. Gallagher and Paul Hertig. American Society of Missiology Series 34. Maryknoll, NY: Orbis Books, 2004.

Stuart, Douglas L. *Hosea–Jonah*. Word Biblical Commentary 31. Waco: Word, 1987.

——. 'Malachi'. Pages 1245–396 in *The Minor Prophets*. Edited by Thomas Edward McComiskey. 3 vols. Grand Rapids: Baker, 1998.

Stuhlmueller, Carroll and Donald Senior. *The Biblical Foundations for Mission*. Maryknoll, NY: Orbis, 1983.

Sukenik, E. L. *The Dead Sea Scrolls of the Hebrew University*. Jerusalem: Magnes, 1955.

Swanson, Reuben, ed. *The Acts of the Apostles*, in *New Testament Greek Manuscripts: Variant Readings Arranged in Horizontal Lines Against Codex Vaticanus*. Sheffield: Sheffield Academic Press, 1998.

Talbert, Charles H. 'Promise and Fulfillment in Lucan Theology'. Pages 91–103 in *Luke–Acts: New Perspectives from the Society of Biblical Literature Seminar*. Edited by Charles H. Talbert. New York: Crossroad, 1984.

——. ed. *Luke–Acts: New Perspectives from the Society of Biblical Literature Seminar*. New York: Crossroad, 1984.

Tannehill, Robert C. *The Narrative Unity of Luke–Acts: A Literary Interpretation*. 2 vols. Philadelphia: Fortress, 1986–90.

——. 'Rejection by Jews and Turning to Gentiles: The Pattern of Paul's Mission in Acts'. Pages 83–101 in *Luke–Acts and the Jewish People*. Edited by Joseph B. Tyson. Minneapolis: Augsburg, 1988.

Tasker, Randolph V. G. *The Old Testament in the New Testament*. 2nd rev. edn. London: SCM Press, 1954.

Taylor, Justin. *Les actes des deux apôtres: Commentaire historique*. EBib 41. Paris: J. Gabalda, 2000.

Taylor, Vincent. *The Names of Jesus*. London: Macmillan, 1953.

Thompson, John A. 'The Book of Joel: Introduction and Exegesis'. Pages 727–60 in vol. 6 of *The Interpreter's Bible*. Edited by George A. Buttrick et al. 12 vols. New York: Abingdon, 1956.

Tiede, David L. *Prophecy and History in Luke–Acts*. Philadelphia: Fortress, 1980.

Torrey, Charles Cutler. *The Composition and Date of Acts*. Cambridge, Mass.: Harvard University Press, 1916.

Tov, Emanuel. 'The Septuagint'. Pages 161–88 in *Mikra: Text, Translation, Reading and Interpretation of the Hebrew Bible in Ancient Judaism and Early Christianity*. Edited by Martin Jan Mulder. Compendia rerum Iudaicarum ad Novum Testamentum 2.1. Assen: Van Gorcum, 1988.

Toy, Crawford Howard. *Quotations in the New Testament*. New York: Charles Scribner's Sons, 1884.

Treier, Daniel J. 'The Fulfillment of Joel 2:28-32: A Multiple-Lens Approach'. *JETS* 40 (1997): 13–26.

Turner, Max. *Power from on High: The Spirit in Israel's Restoration and Witness in Luke–Acts*. Sheffield: Sheffield Academic Press, 1996.

Turpie, David McCalman. *The New Testament View of the Old: A Contribution to Biblical Introduction and Exegesis*. London: Hodder & Stoughton, 1872.

Tyson, Joseph B. 'The Gentile Mission and the Authority of Scripture in Luke–Acts'. *NTS* 33 (1987): 619–31.

——. ed. *Luke–Acts and the Jewish People: Eight Critical Perspectives*. Minneapolis: Augsburg, 1988.

Ulrich, Eugene. 'Index of Passages in the Biblical Scrolls'. Pages 649–65 in vol. 2 of *The Dead Sea Scrolls after Fifty Years: A Comprehensive Assessment*. Edited by Peter W. Flint and James C. Vanderkam. 2 vols. Leiden: Brill, 1998–99.

Van den Eynde, Sabine. 'Children of the Promise: On the *ΔIAΘHKH*-Promise to Abraham in Lk 1,72 and Acts 3,25'. Pages 469–82 in *The Unity of Luke–Acts*. Edited by J. Verheyden. Bibliotheca Ephemeridum theologicarum Lovaniensium 142. Leuven: Leuven University Press, 1999.

Van der Merwe, Christo, et al. *A Biblical Hebrew Reference Grammar*. Sheffield: Sheffield Academic Press, 1999.

Van de Sandt, Huub. 'An Explanation of Acts 15:6-21 in the Light of Deuteronomy 4:20-35 (LXX)'. *JSNT* 46 (1992): 73–97.

——. 'The Fate of the Gentiles in Joel and Acts 2: An Intertextual Study'. *ETL* 66 (1990): 55–77.

——. 'The Quotations in Acts 13,32-52 as a Reflection of Luke's LXX Interpretation'. *Bib* 75 (1994): 26–58.

Van Unnik, Willem C. ' "The Book of Acts" – The Confirmation of the Gospel'. Pages 340–73 in *Sparsa Collecta: The Collected Essays of W. C. van Unnik. Part One: Evangelia, Paulina, Acta*. Supplements to Novum Testamentum 29. Leiden: Brill, 1973.

——. 'Der Ausdruck ἕως ἐσχάτου τῆς γῆς (Apostelgeschichte I, 8) und sein alttestamentlicher Hintergrund'. Pages 386–401 in *Sparsa Collecta: The Collected Writings of W. C. van Unnik. Part One: Evangelia, Paulina, Acta*. Supplements to Novum Testamentum 29. Leiden: Brill, 1973.

——. 'Remarks on the Purpose of Luke's Historical Writing (Luke I 1-4)'. Pages 6–15 in *Sparsa Collecta: The Collected Essays of W. C. van Unnik. Part One: Evangelia, Paulina, Acta*. Supplements to Novum Testamentum 29. Leiden: Brill, 1973.

VanGemeren, Willem. *Interpreting the Prophetic Word*. Grand Rapids: Zondervan, 1990.

——. 'The Spirit of Restoration'. *WTJ* 50 (1988): 81–102.

Vawter, Bruce. *On Genesis: A New Reading*. New York: Doubleday, 1977.

Verheyden, Jozef, ed. *The Unity of Luke–Acts*. Bibliotheca Ephemeridum theologicarum Lovaniensium 142. Leuven: Leuven University Press, 1999.

von Rad, Gerhard. *Genesis*. Translated by John H. Marks. Old Testament Library. Philadelphia: Westminster, 1961.

——. *Old Testament Theology*. Translated by D. M. Starker. London: Oliver & Boyd, 1965.

Von Tischendorf, Constantine, ed. *Novum Testamentum Graece*. 2 vols. Editio octava critica maior edn. Leipzig: Giesecke & Devrient, 1872.

Vos, Geerhardus. 'The Eschatological Aspect of the Pauline Conception of the Spirit'. Pages 91–125 in *Redemptive History and Biblical Interpretation: The Shorter Writings of Geerhardus Vos*. Edited by Richard B. Gaffin, Jr. Phillipsburg, NJ: Presbyterian and Reformed, 1980.

Wall, Robert. 'Israel and the Gentile Mission in Acts and Paul: A Canonical Approach'. Pages 437–57 in *Witness to the Gospel: The Theology of Acts*. Edited by Ian Howard Marshall and David Peterson. Grand Rapids: Eerdmans, 1998.

Waltke, Bruce K. and Cathi J. Fredricks. *Genesis: A Commentary*. Grand Rapids: Zondervan, 2001.

Waltke, Bruce K. and Michael P. O'Connor. *An Introduction to Biblical Hebrew Syntax*. Winona Lake, Ind.: Eisenbrauns, 1990.

Watts, John D. W. *Isaiah 34–66*. Word Biblical Commentary. Waco: Word, 1987.

Wehmeier, Gerhard. 'The Theme "Blessing for the Nations" in the Promises to the Patriarchs and in Prophetical Literature'. *Bangalore Theological Forum* 6 (1974): 1–13.

Wellhausen, Julius. *Die kleine Propheten übersetzt und erklärt*. 4th edn. Berlin: Vandenhoeck & Ruprecht, 1963.

Wenham, Gordon J. *Genesis*. 2 vols. Word Biblical Commentary 1–2. Waco: Word, 1987–94.

Wenthe, Dean O. 'Amos 9:11-15: The Blood of Jesus in the Booth of David'. Pages 23–44 in *Hear the Word of Yahweh: Essays on Scripture and Theology in Honor of Horace Hummel*. Edited by Dean O. Wenthe, Paul L. Schrieber and Lee A. Maxwell. St Louis: Concordia, 2002.

Westcott, Brooke Foss and Fenton John Anthony Hort, eds. *The New Testament in the Original Greek*. New York: Macmillan, 1947.

Westermann, Claus. *Genesis 12–36: A Commentary*. Translated by John J. Scullion. Minneapolis: Augsburg, 1985.

——. *Isaiah 40–66*. Translated by David M. G. Stalker. Old Testament Library. Philadelphia: Westminster, 1969.

Wevers, John William. *Genesis*. Septuaginta: Vetus Testamentum Graecum 1. Göttingen: Vandenhoeck & Ruprecht, 1974.

Whybray, Roger N. *Isaiah 40–66*. New Century Bible. London: Oliphants, 1975.

——. *The Second Isaiah*. Old Testament Guides. Sheffield: JSOT Press, 1983.

Wilcox, Max. 'The Old Testament in Acts 1–15'. *ABR* 4 (1956): 1–41.

Williams, Charles S. C. *A Commentary on the Acts of the Apostles*. Harper's New Testament Commentaries. New York: Harper & Brothers, 1957.

Williams, David J. *Acts*. New International Biblical Commentary on the New Testament 5. Peabody, Mass.: Hendrickson, 1990.

Williams, Ronald J. *Hebrew Syntax: An Outline*. 2nd edn. Toronto: University of Toronto Press, 1976.

Williamson, Hugh G. M. *Variations on a Theme: King, Messiah and Servant in the Book of Isaiah*. The Didsbury Lectures 1997. Carlisle: Paternoster, 1998.

Willis, John T. 'Exclusivistic and Inclusivistic Aspects of the Concept of "The People of God" in the Book of Isaiah'. *ResQ* 40 (1998): 3–12.

Wilson, Stephen G. *The Gentiles and the Gentile Mission in Luke–Acts*. Society for New Testament Studies Monograph Series 23. Cambridge: Cambridge University Press, 1973.

Winter, Bruce W. and Andrew D. Clarke, eds. *The Book of Acts in Its Ancient Literary Setting*. Grand Rapids: Eerdmans, 1993.

Witherington, Ben, III. *The Acts of the Apostles: A Socio-Rhetorical Commentary*. Grand Rapids: Eerdmans, 1998.

Wolff, Hans Walter. *Joel and Amos*. Translated by Waldemar Janzen, S. Dean McBride, Jr. and Charles A. Muenchow. Hermeneia. Philadelphia: Fortress, 1977.

Wright, Christopher J. H. *Knowing Jesus through the Old Testament*. London: HarperCollins, 1992.

——. *The Mission of God: Unlocking the Bible's Grand Narrative*. Downers Grove, Ill.: Inter-Varsity, 2006.

Young, Edward J. *The Book of Isaiah*. 3 vols. New International Commentary on the Old Testament. Grand Rapids: Eerdmans, 1965–72.

——. *An Introduction to the Old Testament*. Rev. edn. Grand Rapids: Eerdmans, 1964.

Zehnle, Richard F. *Peter's Pentecost Discourse: Tradition and Lukan Reinterpretation in Peter's Speeches of Acts 2 and 3*. Society of Biblical Literature Monograph Series 15. Nashville: Abingdon, 1971.

Ziegler, Joseph. *Duodecim Prophetae*. Septuaginta: Vetus Testamentum Graecum 13. Göttingen: Vandenhoeck & Ruprecht, 1984.

——. *Isaiah*. Septuaginta: Vetus Testamentum Graecum 14. Göttingen: Vandenhoeck & Ruprecht, 1983.

INDEX OF REFERENCES

BIBLE

OTHER ANCIENT SOURCES

Index of Authors